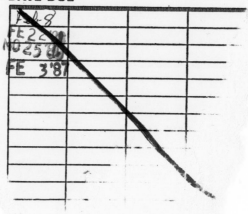

POLITICS, PRESIDENTS

and COATTAILS

POLITICS, PRESIDENTS and COATTAILS

by MALCOLM MOOS

GREENWOOD PRESS, PUBLISHERS
NEW YORK

To My Father

To My Father . . .

PREFACE

On the influence of presidential tickets over congressional elections there is no dearth of opinions. In practice these judgments roam between two extremes. One holds that presidential candidates have a powerful bearing on the outcome of congressional elections, while the other believes that their influence is negligible and that presidential elections and their congressional counterparts are two unconnected events.

The purpose of this volume is to examine that voting behavior in congressional and presidential elections with a view to determining what, if any, are the incipient truths about the relationships between presidential and congressional tickets. A by-product of a larger study on the operation of our two party system in which special emphasis is placed upon the Republican party, a portion of this work has been supported by a grant from the American Philosophical Society. For this encouragement and support I am deeply indebted.

In the preparation of this book more than a few people have given sturdy help and counsel. Foremost were Bertram Koslin and W. Dean Burnham whose association with the author on a related research project tied them in closely with the development of this manuscript from the outset. Mr. Koslin undertook the preparation of the graphs and maps along with several singularly difficult tasks in planning for their reproduction, while Mr. Burnham bore the brunt of the statistical work on the appendix.

For his thorough reading of the manuscript and many helpful suggestions, I am particularly obligated to Professor Julius Turner of Allegheny College. And for his skillful efforts in drafting the graphs for this manuscript a generous word of appreciation to John Spurbeck of The Johns Hopkins University is also in order.

To my colleagues Carl B. Swisher, Thomas I. Cook, and J. Harvey Wheeler, my obligation is large. Besides reading the manuscript, Professor Wheeler contributed several suggestions formally and informally in the course of many inquests on the subject of political behavior. I have also borrowed freely from the discussions I have had with Professor Swisher on American politics, and through Professor Cook I have benefited upon innumerable occasions by his facile technique for presenting systematic analyses. And to my former colleague V. O. Key I am particularly indebted for stimulating an interest in certain aspects of political behavior.

Also helpful in preparing this study have been my students. In particular, Eugene Sekulow, Alvin Deutsch, and I. William Zartman have given their time unstintedly on different occasions and for these efforts they have my sincere thanks.

Elsewhere a number of persons contributed mightily to this study. Prominent among this group are Roy V. Peel, Director of the Bureau of the Census, and A. Ross Eckler, Acting Director of the Census Bureau, both of whom sped several replies in response to inquiries for materials. To Captain Victor Hunt Harding, Executive Secretary of the Democratic Congressional Campaign Committee and his son Kenneth R. Harding go special thanks for their many courtesies in supplying information and for keeping a warm welcome mat out in the old House Office Building. Bernard Lamb and A. B. Hermann of the Republican National Committee were also helpful.

From the Congress of the United States, several Senators and Representatives and their office staffs tendered important assistance. To Hugh Scott Jr., Mike Monroney, Hubert Humphrey, James P. S. Devereux, and August Andresen, my sincere appreciation for their help is hereby recorded.

At the Johns Hopkins University that untiring trio, Margaret Lough, Beatrice Blakslee, and Jane McCubbin Borneman of the Library Staff, cooperated at every turn in facilitating the research for this manuscript. Similarly at the James J. Hill Reference Library, Director Russell F. Barnes, Helen Rugg, and Anna Heilmeier jointly conspired to make periodic visits both profitable and a genuine delight.

A. D. Emmart of the *Baltimore Evening Sun* spared me from many slips in style through his reading of the manuscript, and the study has profited from several discussions that I have had with Newton Aiken and Frank Kent also of the SUNPAPERS, and E. W. Kenworthy of the *New York Times*. Acknowledgment of all the writers I have drawn upon in preparing this study, of course, is out of the question, but I should like to mention three in passing: Arthur Krock, Louis Bean, and Cortez A. M. Ewing.

For coping with the trying task of typing a manuscript with many tables my warm thanks go to Edna L. Fulton. I am also indebted to Gertrude H. Burnham who typed the Appendix in what must have seemed a marathon assignment.

To my Mother who has patiently endured the climate of steady political talk between Father and son for thirty years I should like to express my gratitude for her forbearance. And finally to my wife Tracy who has worked diligently to save me from many errors on the manuscript and to our son Malcolm who arrived the day this book went to press my debt for their sympathetic patience is as great as one can be.

ERRATA

p. 16, par. 3, line 3: *are* instead of *were*

p. 87, last par., line 2: *constituencies* instead of *constituents*

p. 166, line 2: *"Wise men* instead of *"We men*

p. 225: Caption should read *INDEX TO APPENDIX 2*

p. 227: Caption should read *INDEX TO APPENDIX 1*

CONTENTS

FIGURES

MAPS

TABLES

CHAPTER 1

Prophecy and our
Bouncing Ballots

At the approach of an election . . . the eyes of the nation are centered on a single point; all are watching the gradual birth of so important an event. . . . For a long time before the appointed time is at hand the election becomes the most important and all-engrossing topic of discussion. The ardor of faction is redoubled; and all the artificial passions which the imagination can create in the bosom of a happy and peaceful land are agitated and brought to light."[1] So wrote de Tocqueville on his visit to the United States more than a century—or to use a political chronometer—just 26 presidential and 52 congressional elections ago.

National elections are, of course, tumultuous affairs in the United States. To the uninitiated they sometimes threaten to unhinge the Republic. But whatever the carnage of presidential and congres-

---

[1]Alexis De Tocqueville: *Democracy in America* (Rev. ed.; New Colonial Press, New York, 1900), Vol. 1, pp. 124, 134.

sional politics in an election year, once a choice has been made a
calmer season returns. Accustomed as he is to the passing political
parade, the voter becomes inured to the cut and thrust of partisan
strife as well as to the mounting tide of campaign cockahoop.

Much has been said of the vagaries of American voters. Obviously they are of many minds at the approach of a national election.
And with regard to numbers, the voter responds somewhat lamely
at the ballot box on different occasions. Apparently a more spirited
and bitterly contested election has a bearing on his participation.[2]
In the McKinley-Bryan contest he was joined in the polling booth
by 80 to 90 percent of the eligible voters, yet in the Dewey-Truman
tilt of 1948 only 52 percent of the electorate followed him to the
polls.[3] Moreover, for various reasons the voting citizenry that casts
ballots in a midterm election falls far short of the number that pour
out for a presidential race. Even in 1948—a year when the congressional vote compared most favorably with the presidential vote—only
94 people voted for congressional candidates out of every 100 that
voted for President.

Not all the citizenry by any means takes the same delight in
joining the chase to discover the inner mysteries of ballot behavior.
But converts to the field of election analysis—both amateur and professional—are turning up in increasing numbers. Even that distinguished institution of higher learning, Cornell University, acknowledged the presence of a psephologist on its faculty in the summer of
1952—a term coined to describe the study of elections. Pronounced
sef-OL-ogist, it was invented in jest by the Oxford Professor, David
Butler, who, explained that he became so enchanted with his first
exposure to election research on the British general elections of 1945
that he decided to specialize in it. Thus he called himself a psepholo-

---

[2] See V. O. Key: *Politics, Parties, and Pressure Groups* (New York:
Crowell, 1947), pp. 585-86.

[3] Estimates of voting participation in past elections do not always conform,
though they usually depict the same trend. Harold Gosnell sets the figure for
participation in the 1896 election at 89.5 percent. *Why Europe Votes* (University of Chicago Press, 1930), p. 196.

gist—a word taken from the Greek for 'pebble'—and suggesting the Greek practice of holding elections by dropping pebbles in a box.[4]

Quite apart from all conjecture over the voter's vicissitudes by the professional or amateur "psephologists," however, his enthusiasm for turning out at the polls or the reasons behind his like or dislike of a particular candidate, there is one biennial or quadrennial pastime that we can all be for—the prediction of election results. Like the editorial policy of a great Eastern newspaper—"for happiness in a guarded sort of way"—everyone joins hands warmly in the game of determining who the winner will be and why, each sovereign citizen volunteering his judgments according to the lights that he follows.

Of course the undue emphasis that has been accorded political horoscopy in this country, particularly in the past two decades, has not been entirely an unmixed blessing. Thus an occasional thunder-clap that upsets the professionals is to be welcomed, for as H. L. Mencken remarked in perhaps his valedictory election inquest: "The super- or ultra explosion that staved in the firmament of heaven last Tuesday [November 2, 1948] not only blew up all the Gallups of this great free Republic; it also shook the bones of all its other smarties."[5] But though this curiosity over who will win has doubtless been overly-exploited in our national elections, we need not despair that the results are largely negative. Actually the concern of the voter for the secrets of the ballot box serves a constructive purpose. For the person whose curiosity and interest in political behavior lead him to seek the probable answers to what will happen on election day will certainly be exposed to the boisterous currents of debate over the issues. Regard for the issues and curiosity over the results, then, are to some extent interactional. Hence an interest in elections that begins with an analysis of ballot behavior may well encourage a deeper concern for, and understanding of, the compelling issues of

---

[4]See *New York Herald Tribune*, August 8, 1952. This same principle is still applied in certain countries today where low literacy makes such a method of voting a practical expedient. In certain areas of Greece, United Nations supervisory teams observed voting by this method in 1947, the only difference from the ancient practice being the substitution of lead pellets for stones.

[5]*Baltimore Sun*, November 7, 1948.

the day—a result that should help at least in some measure to dispel apathy at the polls. Equally fruitful is the attention such analysis draws to the operation of our party system and this in turn should lead to wholesale re-examinations of both the adequacies and the inadequacies of our political parties. For precisely this reason the investigator of political behavior bears a heavy responsibility for making his statistics sit up and be interesting.

Among the professionals—the journalists, politicians, and scholars—who periodically exhume election statistics from their World Almanacs (or lift them from several reference sources) little need be said in defense of an effort that seeks to analyze the relationship of the presidential and congressional vote. But besides the professionals, untold members of our citizenry—in the words of Mr. Dooley—"await with bated breath th' thrillin' news fr'm th' first precinct iv the foorth ward iv Sheboygan, Wis."[6] Confident in this belief and concurring with Mr. Dooley, this study is intended for all who have a critical interest in political behavior. No violent leaps into the realm of prediction are promised. Such insights revealed in this study that may be germane to speculation about the future, therefore, are to be interpreted by each individual following his own conscience and biases. But since the experts have sometimes been thumpingly wrong, no one would claim—and least of all the professionals—that they be permitted to homestead the field of political behavior. Still in the novitiate stage, the field of political behavior has need for the judgments of scholars, journalists, politicians, critical laymen, and, indeed, the opinions of all who cheerfully admit to a heady enthusiasm while waiting with bated breath for "th' thrillin' news fr'm th' first precinct iv the foorth ward."

The primary concern with this inquiry is with congressional elections. But since the selection of a congressman is often not unaffected by the choice of a President, much of the study deals with the interaction of congressional and presidential elections, and finally with their role in our party system. That we re-examine the party system after looking at the pattern of presidential-congressional vot-

---

[6] Finley Peter Dunne: *Dissertations by Mr. Dooley* (New York: Harper, 1906), p. 201.

ing is indicated by several factors. If, as we shall discover in the following chapter, presidential candidates are running further ahead of their congressional tickets than they did in McKinley's day, the question of whether national tickets have more importance than they used to have is one that should compel our attention. In particular it should command our attention in light of the criticism that the president, though he has risen in prestige and stature as a policy leader, does not possess broad commensurate authority to bring about responsibility in the party he is presumed to lead. Thus our concluding chapter is devoted to a review of the party system—our "principleless politics," as one writer calls it, and an analysis of the modern criticism directed toward it.

In general there are two schools of thought on the matter of a presidential candidate's influence over the success of his party's congressional ticket. One view—the so-called "coattail theory"—holds that the strong momentum generated by the presidential campaign along with the prestige of the presidential candidate helps to sweep into office a sizeable number of congressional candidates.[7] Among the coattail clutchers opinion also divides. One group maintains that the additional interest accelerated by presidential campaigns is a more important element in the operation of the coattail theory than are the political appeal and interpersonal skills of the presidential candidate. At the other pole of coattail opinion we find those who stoutly proclaim that the number of congressmen who can ride into office on the President's coattails is dependent upon the personal charm of the presidential candidate.

Opposed to the coattail theory are the observers who feel that the presidential campaign has little to do with the number of congressmen elected by one party or the other. For example, Professor Cortez A. M. Ewing of the University of Oklahoma in a study of congressional elections covering a fifty-year period concludes that the popularity of the presidential candidate and the presidential campaign

---

[7]See Louis H. Bean: *How to Predict Elections* (New York: A. A. Knopf, 1948), pp. 31-36; and by the same author: *The Midterm Battle* (Washington: American Council on Public Affairs, 1950), pp. 19-22.

have a very limited influence upon congressional elections.[8]   Thus in his judgment the coattail-clutcher theory is vastly exaggerated.

Another theory, though perhaps unlisted and one largely the concern of the practical politician, stresses the importance of minor candidates in helping the head of the ticket. Typical of the reasoning behind this theory is the reply of a Democratic candidate for the House of Representatives in New Jersey. Badly defeated and asked why he bothered to make the race in the first place, he said he had been beseeched to run by the state committee because it would help the presidential candidate, hence he had loyally submitted to the cause and filed his candidacy. And so the question of who helps whom seems to be a matter of endless debate.

Having indicated the battle stands, our task of analysis begins by winnowing from the election tallies of the past, evidence that will aid us in establishing consistent relationships or patterns. So much said, we may now turn to the business at hand—initially an analysis of the presidential-congressional vote during the past fifty-six years.

---

[8]*Congressional Elections 1896-1944* (Norman: University of Oklahoma Press, 1947), p. 26.

CHAPTER 2

Presidential-Congressional Voting

F OR EVEN THE most casual sally into an analysis of ballot box behavior, the demand upon the analyst is to seek meaningful relationships. And in pursuit of this task it is well to begin with the reminder
that nowhere is it easier to stumble in reaching for the evidence than
in the field of politics. For an example let us take one that is fresh
in mind.

Only once since 1888 has a national party won a presidential
election without holding a majority in the House of the preceding
biennium.[1] Thus only once in 62 years—that is to say for one-third

---

[1]In 1888, the Democratic presidential nominee, Cleveland, whose party
won the House in 1886, actually received a greater popular vote than his
Republican opponent Harrison, though he lost the election in the electoral
vote. Cleveland with 5,536,242 popular votes received 168 electoral votes, while
Harrison with a smaller popular vote—5,440,708—won the election with 233
electoral votes.

7

of the life of the Republic—has the party in control of the House
of Representatives lost the following presidential election. Hence
on the face of this record the analyst might be tempted to conclude
that since control of the House in the biennial congressional elections "normally" leads to a presidential victory two years later, a consistent relationship is indicated. But he would be unwise if he
pinned his predictions on this relationship. For the single exception
that blasts any theory about congressional control in the biennium
leading to power two years later occurred in 1948, when Harry
Truman nudged back into the presidency in the closest election
since 1916.

As our illustration suggests, evidence of a voting relationship
is simply one of many elements that must be taken into account in
making a meaningful analysis of political behavior. We must not
be unmindful, therefore, that shifts do occur in relationships that
appear to show a high degree of consistency. And allowances must
be made for such shifts.

Again by way of illustration, we might cite the fact that it is
normal for a successful presidential candidate to run ahead of the
total vote of his congressional ticket. Yet Harry Truman was elected
though he ran behind his congressional ticket—a circumstance which
probably made him the only president ever to win the presidency
who did not lead his congressional ticket. Or to take another example, it might be noted that before World War I it was customary
for presidential candidates and their congressional tickets to receive
approximately the same number of votes. But since 1918, all but
one of the winning presidential candidates of both major parties
have run well ahead of their congressional tickets. Here also we are
reminded that allowances need to be made for such shifts, and that
past relationships "must be supplemented by current indications and
measures of the factors dealt with."[2]

---

[2] Louis H. Bean: *Ballot Behavior* (Washington: American Council on
Public Affairs, 1940), p. 88.

PRESIDENTIAL AND CONGRESSIONAL TICKETS: A REVIEW OF VOTING RELATIONSHIPS

The task, then, of this second chapter, is to present a comparison between presidential candidates and their congressional tickets as regards their voting strength. Or stated otherwise, our purpose here is to examine the relationship of the presidential candidates and their congressional tickets in terms of their respective ability to bring out the vote and their relative success in influencing a party victory. Having indicated the voting strength of presidential candidates in relation to their congressional tickets, the next problem is to determine whether such relationships as are established are consistent over the period under analysis, 1896-1950. Thus the voting relationships that are found must be demonstrated to be the rule rather than the exception. This done, we may then direct our inquiry to an evaluation of the significance of these relationships.

Compacting first the results of national elections since 1896, several factors need to be noted in analyzing the relationship between the presidential and the congressional vote. Since 1896 there have been fourteen presidential and twenty-eight congressional elections. In the presidential sweepstakes the Republicans have won seven and the Democrats have won seven, while in the congressional field the GOP has won fifteen elections and the Democrats thirteen.

With one exception, as we have noted, the winning presidential candidate has always garnered a larger vote than the total for his party's congressional ticket. In an earlier period, however, the presidential and total congressional vote of his party were much closer together than they are today, the reasons for which we shall presently examine.

Looking elsewhere, the party out of power—as every student of politics knows—usually makes from moderate to heavy gains in the mid-term congressional elections (except for 1934). Moreover, it is likewise common knowledge that the total congressional vote in mid-term as well as presidential election years lags behind the presidential vote.

Yet the real question—the actual influence of the presidential candidate, campaign, or both, on congressional elections—has thus far been largely a matter of conjecture. "The unanswered question of the Middle Ages," notes political horoscopist Louis Bean, "of 'How many angels can dance on the point of a needle?' has its counterpart in political discussion today: 'How many congressmen can ride into office on the president's coattails?' "

Measuring Presidential Popularity. At the outset of our inquiry that seeks to compare the relative voting strength of presidential candidates and their congressional tickets certain assumptions are indicated, the validity of which may be tested as we go along. First, the great bulk of the voting citizenry will be voting a straight party ticket at the presidential-congressional level, that is to say most voters who cast ballots for a Democratic presidential candidate will also vote for a Democratic congressional candidate. Second, if we find the presidential candidate running well ahead of his party's congressional ticket, we may assume that he helps the congressional candidates who trailed behind him. Conversely, if the congressional ticket runs ahead of the presidential candidate an assumption is warranted that the presidential candidate was a hindrance to the party ticket generally. In examining the evidence, therefore, the things we will be looking at, are how far presidential candidates run ahead of their tickets, how consistently they run ahead, and in how many districts the presidential or congressional candidate runs ahead. And if we find that the differences in presidential-congressional voting behavior are relatively slight or that the relationships are inconsistent, then we may conclude that the coattail influence is not very significant.

One measure of the popularity of the presidential nominee to the congressional candidates of his party may be had by dividing each presidential candidate's vote by the total vote for his party's congressional candidates in each election year.[3] Thus if the vote for the presidential candidate is much greater than the vote for the party's congressional candidates we might infer that the presidential nominee has helped to pull at least a few congressmen into office.

---

[3]The actual calculation is as follows:

$$\frac{\text{Presidential Candidates' Vote}}{\text{Total Congressional Candidates' Vote}} \times 100 = \%$$

Looking at the 28 major party candidates for the last 14 presidential elections we find that the highest popularity registered for a presidential candidate in relation to his party's congressional vote was 114.9 percent. Theodore Roosevelt hit this mark in 1904, and Charles Evans Hughes repeated in 1916. The lowest showing was the 76.5 percent in 1924 of John W. Davis, whose true voting strength was badly undermined by the Progressive party candidacy of Robert M. La Follette who polled five million votes. The average popularity ratio between the presidential and congressional candidates is 104.4 percent. In other words, of the 28 presidential candidates from 1896 through 1948, the lead of the presidential candidate over his congressional ticket has averaged 4.4 percent.[4] This average, it will be noted, is for both successful and unsuccessful presidential candidates. (See Table I.)

TABLE I[5]

PRESIDENTIAL CANDIDATES FROM 1896-1948

Ranked according to the percentage:	$\dfrac{\text{Presidential Vote}}{\text{Total Congressional Ticket's Vote}} \times 100 == \%$		
1. Theodore Roosevelt*	Republican	1904	114.9%
2. Charles Evans Hughes	Republican	1916	114.9%
3. Franklin D. Roosevelt*	Democrat	1936	112.6%
4. Franklin D. Roosevelt*	Democrat	1944	112.3%
5. Franklin D. Roosevelt*	Democrat	1932	112.2%
6. Herbert C. Hoover*	Republican	1928	111.9%
7. Franklin D. Roosevelt*	Democrat	1940	111.8%
8. Warren G. Harding*	Republican	1920	110.4%
9. Woodrow Wilson*	Democrat	1916	110.1%
10. William H. Taft*	Republican	1908	106.0%
11. Calvin Coolidge*	Republican	1924	105.6%
12. Wendell Willkie	Republican	1940	105.1%
13. William J. Bryan	Democrat	1900	105.1%
14. Thomas E. Dewey	Republican	1948	105.0%
15. William B. McKinley*	Republican	1900 ·	103.7%
16. Alfred E. Smith	Democrat	1928	103.6%

[4] Professor Cortez A. M. Ewing has pioneered in this type of comparison between presidential and congressional voting. His rankings are not the same as those listed in the above Table. See. Congressional Elections: 1896-1944, p. 36.

[5] The asterisk notes the successful candidates.

TABLE I⁵– (Continued)

Ranked according to the percentage:	Presidential Vote		
	Total Congressional Ticket's Vote		× 100 = %
17. Thomas E. Dewey	Republican	1944	103.3%
18. William B. McKinley*	Republican	1896	102.7%
19. William J. Bryan	Democrat	1896	102.4%
20. William H. Taft	Republican	1912	101.3%
21. Herbert C. Hoover	Republican	1932	100.9%
22. Woodrow Wilson*	Democrat	1912	100.3%
23. James S. Cox	Democrat	1920	100.3%
24. Harry S. Truman*	Democrat	1948	99.9%
25. Alton B. Parker	Democrat	1904	98.0%
26. William J. Bryan	Democrat	1908	97.8%
27. Alfred M. Landon	Republican	1936	97.3%
28. John W. Davis	Democrat	1924	76.5%

The record of successful presidential candidates ranges from Theodore Roosevelt's high of 114.9 percent in 1904, down to the 99.9 percent that marked the performance of Harry Truman in 1948. Interestingly enough, Truman is the only successful candidate since 1896 who managed to win a presidential election even though he trailed his congressional ticket. In fact, it is highly probable that President Truman was the only candidate since the beginning of popular elections for President to win without leading his congressional ticket. Except for Truman's, the poorest record of comparative presidential popularity was that of Woodrow Wilson, who ran only three-tenths of one percent (100.3%) ahead of his own congressional ticket in the three-party contest of 1912. Summarizing the experience of the fourteen presidential elections since 1896, we find that the fourteen successful presidential candidates have led their congressional tickets by an average margin of 7.5 percent.⁶

Looking at the range of the unsuccessful candidates, the record varies from the low of 76.5 percent, established by John W. Davis in 1924, to the 114.9 percent recorded for Charles Evans Hughes in 1916. Since Hughes ran so far ahead of the average—100.8 percent—

---

⁶The task of determining the relationship of presidential to congressional voting prior to 1896 is of dubious value, since the available data grows more incomplete and chaotic the farther back that research is pursued.

for unsuccessful candidates, and since Davis' low of 76.5 percent may be attributed to the third-party candidacy of La Follette in 1924, the true range of the unsuccessful candidates may be more accurately depicted by deleting the two extremes. This done, the range then runs from 97.3 percent—the record of Alfred Landon in 1936—to 105.1 percent, established by Wendell Willkie in 1940.

By way of an important explanatory postscript to the remarkable showing of Hughes, it will be recalled that the 1916 election in which Hughes and Wilson were pitted against each other was the closest presidential election since the Cleveland-Harrison contest of 1888. The final electoral vote in 1916 gave the Democrats 277, and the Republicans 255. If 1,904 people in the State of California had changed their minds and voted for Hughes instead of Wilson, Hughes would have been President in 1916. The presidential race of 1916 was also extraordinarily close in the State of New Hampshire, where Wilson won by the slim margin of 76 votes out of a total state vote of approximately 87,000. In New Mexico, Wilson won by 2,530 votes out of the 65,000 cast, and in North Dakota he won by but 1,725 votes out of the state-wide total of 108,000 cast. Certainly these examples add emphasis to the fact that Hughes' percentage of 114.9 in the exceptional campaign of 1916 was an unusual figure. Significant for the Republican partisans as well as the student of American politics generally, is the fact that except for Hughes, Wendell Willkie established the best record of any of the unsuccessful presidential candidates.

The 1948 Upset. Since 1948 was the first election in 64 years when the party losing the mid-term congressional election held on to the presidency two years later, a brief analysis of the last presidential election is in order. In 1948 Harry S. Truman received 24,105,695 votes, or 49.4 percent of the total presidential vote. For the same election the Democratic congressional candidates garnered 24,113,282 votes, or 52.5 percent of the total congressional vote. Thus Truman, though running .04 percent behind the total Democratic and allied congressional vote (see Map 1)*, still managed to win the presidency.

---

*One interesting facet of political behavior suggested by Map 1 is that presidential candidates seem to run better than their tickets in the strongholds of the opposition party.

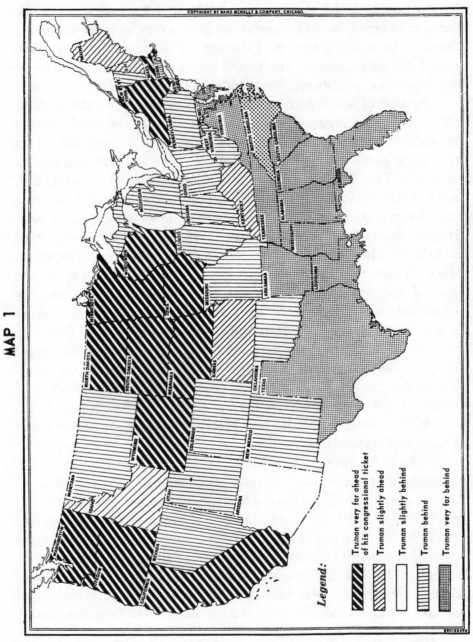

MAP 1

Truman's Vote and the Democratic Congressional Ticket Vote, 1948

Legend:

Truman very far ahead
of his congressional ticket

Truman slightly ahead

Truman slightly behind

Truman behind

Truman very far behind

COPYRIGHT BY RAND MCNALLY & COMPANY, CHICAGO.

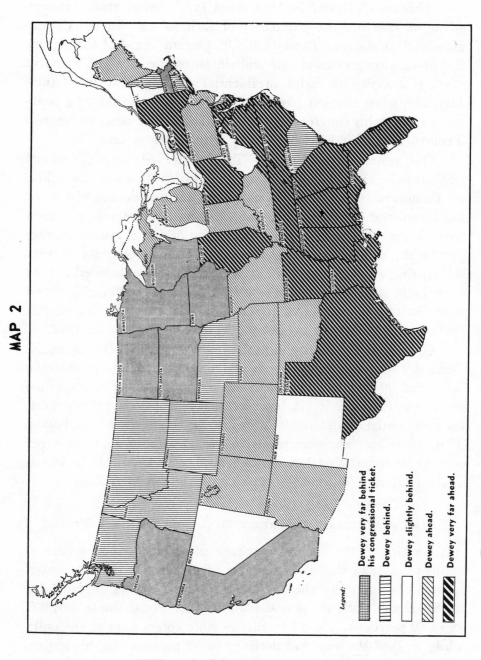

MAP 2

Dewey's Vote and the Republican Congressional Ticket Vote, 1948

Legend:

Dewey very far behind
his congressional ticket.

Dewey behind.

Dewey slightly behind.

Dewey ahead.

Dewey very far ahead.

Thomas E. Dewey in 1948 fared much better than Truman, when we compare the popularity of each to his own party's congressional candidates. Dewey ran 5.02 percent ahead of the average Republican congressional vote and almost reached the 107.5 percent mark that eight successful presidential candidates achieved since McKinley's first election (see Map 2). Thus Dewey attained a popularity ratio to his congressional candidates of 105.2 percent, whereas Truman ran behind his own party with 99.96 percent.

One reason, of course, why Truman trailed his congressional ticket may be accounted for by the Democratic voters who cast ballots for Democratic Congressional candidates, but presidential-wise voted for Thurmond or Wallace. Probably two million votes slipped away from Truman because of the latter candidacies. Perhaps another part of the explanation for the unusual electoral behavior in 1948 was apathy. Approximately the same number of people voted in 1944 as in 1948, although there were several million more eligible voters in the latter year. In fact, on the basis of a general rise in the eligible electorate. one observer predicted a 60 million turnout for 1949.

One additional postscript to the 1948 election needs to be noted. Generally speaking, out of every 100 votes cast for the presidential nominees, 90 were cast for congressional candidates. The surprising fact of the 1948 election is, however, that out of every 100 votes cast for presidential candidates, 94 were cast for congressional candidates. Thus there was an increase above the average of four votes per centum for congressional over presidential candidates in 1948, whereas the total vote fell short of expectations by twelve million.

CHANGING PATTERNS IN PRESIDENTIAL-CONGRESSIONAL VOTING

Looking at the entire experience of presidential-congressional voting since 1896, the following salient factors emerge. At the outset it should be noted that there was a much higher voting interest prior to 1920 than during the period 1920 to 1948. For example, in 1896, 75 to 80 percent of the potentially eligible voters went to the polls, while in 1948 the vote had declined to 52 percent. In this setting, 1920 seems to have been the turning point—the year, it might be remarked, that women first had the vote.

dential years, the fact remains that in the elections before the first
World War, with an average turnout of between 70 and 80 percent,
almost as many p ·sons voted for congressmen as President. Yet
since World War I, a voting turnout that has ranged between 50
and 60 percent has resulted in an average of only 90 people voting
for congressmen out of every 100 who cast ballots for a presidential
candidate. Turnout as the explanation for a larger presidential than
congressional vote, therefore, does not seem to be a controlling
argument.

The Growth of the Presidential Office. Laying aside the more
probable causes for the larger disparity between the presidential and
congressional vote after 1920, one is compelled to delve deeper into
the tapestry of American constitutional life since the start of the
present century.

Beginning with Theodore Roosevelt, the presidency took a new
turn. It assumed a new life, observed Professor Swisher "under the
direction of a man who, by contrast with most of his predecessors,
exercised its powers to the utmost."[7] As Theodore Roosevelt himself
conceptualized the office, the chief executive should be:

> . . . a steward of the people bound actively and affirmatively to do
> all he could for the people. . . . I decline to adopt the view that what was
> imperatively necessary for the nation could not be done by the President
> unless he could find some specific authorization to do it. . . .[8]

Not caring "a rap for the criticism of people who spoke of my
'usurpation of power,'" TR gave the presidency an "organic connection with Congress." In terms of number and importance of
legislative accomplishments, comments political historian Wilfred E.
Binkley, "Roosevelt's seven years' stand unsurpassed by any previous
administration."[9]

Vitalizing the leadership of the presidency by his concept of the
office as one where the executive ought to be "peculiarly represent-

---

[7]Carl B. Swisher, *American Constitutional Development* (Boston: Hough-
ton-Mifflin, 1943), p. 527.

[8] *An Autobiography* (New York:The Outlook Company, 1913), p. 389.

[9]*President and Congress* (New York: A. A. Knopf, 1947), p. 194..

ative of the people as a whole," Roosevelt's stint of service left a permanent imprint—one soon to be reaffirmed vigorously by two of his successors, Woodrow Wilson and Franklin Roosevelt. And the failure of Republican rajahs to comprehend this changed concept of presidential responsibility for public policy guidance and legislative leadership was shortsightedness that became increasingly harmful to the stature of GOP prestige. In fact what the party directorate of the GOP failed to recognize in the absence of any sense of history, was "that in emasculating the great office they were seriously damaging if not dooming their party." Elsewhere in a stimulating commentary, another careful student of American politics reaches a similar conclusion in his current assessment of Republican prospects. "The most basic of all Republican contradictions," reports Sam Lubell, is "the GOP's fondness for a weak president." Between the "traditional Republican affection for weak presidents," and the compelling urgency for the exercise of broad leadership at home as well as abroad, Lubell sees an inconsistency in Republican doctrine that is a real handicap. And in this view no doubt he is right.[10]

Additional factors, of course, that have promoted the ascendency of the presidency in our political system are many. Among them are the power of special interest groups whose rapacious raids upon the Congress make the role of the President as a reconciler of competing forces in favor of the national welfare increasingly important. Prominent also among the contributory elements to increased stature for the presidential office is the enlarged scope of American action in foreign affairs—"the need for speed, the need for technical knowledge (often confidential and secret material), and the need for clear and even concentrated leadership."[11] Astride the complexities of modern society, Congress has been too often over-flogged by its critics, as a slough of indecision and ineffectual temporization. But however unfair much of the criticism—some of the reasons for which we shall explore later—the national legislature has yielded ground in public esteem to both the President and the bureaucracy. And one of the

---

[10] *The Future of American Politics* (New York: Harper, 1952), p. 242.

[11] See Ernest Griffith: *Congress: Its Contemporary Role* (New York: New York University Press, 1951), p. 1.

effects of this loss in prestige, no doubt, has been the tendency of
the voter to be more casual in congressional than in presidential
balloting.

Technological and Sociological Factors. Quite apart from
changes that have tended to elevate the presidential office at the expense of congressional prestige, are two factors that have contributed
to the further disadvantage of the congressional candidate. One,
we might say, is technological, the other sociological.

Amidst the raucous preachments of a presidential campaign it
has become more difficult for congressional candidates to get an easy
hearing. The development of mass media, both audio and visual,
that bring the presidential candidates into homes sometimes daily
as campaigns increase in tempo, tends almost to supersaturate the
voter with election appeals. In consequence the voter finds it a strain
to follow the progress of congressional candidacies with the alertness
and intensity that we might desire. Congressional candidates also are
handicapped financially by the steadily mounting costs of radio, tele-
vision, and other means of communicating with the voters. Although
managers of presidential campaigns often plead that they are inade-
quately financed to win an election, the fact remains that the resources are usually sufficient to communicate the case of the presidential candidate to the voter more effectively than that of the average congressional candidate.

On the sociological side it may be said that changes, particularly
in metropolitan areas, over the past fifty years have made it very
difficult for congressional candidates to get audiences during presidential campaigns. Even in rural areas and small towns one would
not expect to find a turnout of the citizenry today such as the one
that greeted the debates of Lincoln and Douglas. But a growing
urbanism has meant that except in the poorer areas of cities, large
political clubs no longer have active memberships and many partisan
clubs that do manage to hold modestly attended meetings are forced
to rely upon city-wide recruiting policies. Not surprising, therefore,
is the fact that congressmen seem to be conducting more nomadic
campaigns—devoting their time to quick handshaking visits to mill
and factory entrances, or using the famed filling station technique
that Mike Monroney employed when he went to the Senate in 1950.

Common was the congressional complaint after the 1948 campaign of poorly attended meetings, and in consequence many congressmen, rather than risk serious loss of time forsook such appearances in favor of street-corner barnstorming. Thus, looking at the situational advantages of the presidential and congressional candidates during a national election, the latter very definitely seem to be in the less fortunate position in the matter of getting a hearing—again a circumstance that may have a bearing on the reduced size of the congressional vote.

Portents of an Upsurge in Congressional Voting? Certainly the broad evidence of the past thirty years has failed to disclose any immediate upsurge in congressional voting—an increase that would heave the congressional vote up to the level it reached in the election of 1896. Nonetheless, one possible lead ought to be suggested that may hold a clue for an enlarged congressional vote in the elections that lie ahead.

In the 1948 election, it will be recalled, the congressional tickets did comparatively well in relation to the vote of the presidential candidates. Actually, 94 out of every 100 who voted for President cast ballots for congressmen, an increase of 4 percent for congressional candidates over presidential candidates in that year. Since the CIO's Political Action Committee and the AFL's corresponding organization—Labor's League for Political Action—have been devoting increasing energy to congressional elections in recent years, this activity may account for an upswing trend in congressional voting. Voting scorecards are being kept on individual congressmen and more vigorous efforts are being made to educate union members on the respective merits of congressional candidates. In 1948, particularly, the concentrated attack on the 80th Congress may have helped to increase participation in congressional elections. In any case it is reasonable to suppose that if greater attention continues to be focused on the records of congressmen by unions it will lead to similar activity by other interest groups, with the consequence that the renewed emphasis on Congress may lead voters to the pattern of earlier days in which the turnout for congressional elections approximated the vote for President.

PRESIDENTIAL PASSING MARK?

Whatever the portents for a return to an election pattern where the vote of the congressional tickets approximates that of the presidential nominees, it must be repeated in summary that in the fourteen presidential elections since 1896, the fourteen winning candidates have led their congressional tickets by an average margin of 7.5 percent. And with 107.5 percent as an approximate guidemark for the successful presidential aspirant, the experience of all twenty-eight candidates divides as follows:

Of nine candidates who exceeded the 107.5 percentage marker between 1896 and 1948, eight were elected (see Table I). But of the nineteen who failed to reach this mark—who failed to run at least 7.5 percent ahead of the congressional ticket average—only six were elected to the presidency. That the candidate who reaches the White House usually runs comfortably ahead of his ticket is, therefore, hardly a debatable matter. But this pattern is subject to sudden change, as we all remember. And because this comparison is based on national totals rather than on a district by district basis, its significance should not be overemphasized, the reasons for which we shall see more clearly as we train our sights elsewhere.

Keeping in mind the general relation of presidential-congressional voting, it serves our purpose at this point to localize our analysis to certain specific cases. Since it seems reasonable to assume that if presidential candidates and their campaigns influence congressional elections the outcome is more likely to be affected in'the closely contested districts, we may begin by looking at the marginal constituencies. By our own definition, marginal districts are the constituencies that have oscillated between the two parties by a 45-55 percent vote.

CHAPTER **3**

The Marginal Congressional Districts

W ITHIN THE RIMS of at least one hundred congressional districts election hassles are so closely contested that they are actually decided —to use Pindar's apophthegm—"by the shade of a shadow." It is in these districts that we often find recounts and sometimes formally contested election cases that are ultimately decided by the House of Representatives. Here, again, we find the decisions being made at the ballot box that will entrust the legislative control of the Republic to one party or the other. For want of a better term, we may define these districts as marginal.

The determinant selected for the marginal districts is the range running from 45 to 55 percent of the Republican slice of the two-party vote covering the elections over the period beginning in 1942 through 1950. On the basis of this index there are 60 Republican and 45 Democratic marginal seats. (See location of these districts in Map 3.) To facilitate analysis, these 105 marginal districts have in turn been reduced in number to what may be termed the *critical* marginal districts—of which there are 42. Not included in our regular political travelogue are eight states that contain marginal congressional districts, but do not have any constituencies that fall into the critical marginal category. The location of the marginal districts in these states is given in Maps 25 and 26. The *critical* marginal districts embrace the congressional constituencies where the Republican popular vote ranges from 48.5 to 51.5 percent. Of the *critical* marginal districts, 25 are Republican and 17 Democratic.[1] All the marginal districts are listed for the House in Table II. Table III gives the same information for the Senate. Complete tabulations giving the Republican percentage of the major party vote by district for every congressional election from 1938 through 1950 are listed in the Appendix.

TABLE II

CONGRESSIONAL MARGINAL DISTRICTS BY STATES

AL—At Large

State	Republican marginal-districts	Total	Democratic marginal districts	Total	Statewide Total
California	1,9,10,11.16	5	18,23	2	7
Colorado	3	1	1,4	2	3
Connecticut	2,AL	2	1,3	2	4
Delaware	AL	1	—	0	1
Idaho	1	1	—	0	1
Illinois	2,3,4,12,13,26	6	9,21	2	8
Indiana	3,4,5,6,7,11	6	8	1	7
Kansas	2	1	—	0	1
Kentucky	3	1	—	0	1
Maine	1	1	—	0	1
Maryland	2	1	—	0	1
Massachusetts	8	1	2	1	2
Michigan	6,17	2	14	1	3
Minnesota	—	0	3,6	2	2
Missouri	6,11,12	3	1,2,3,5,8	5	8
Montana	2	1	—	0	1
Nebraska	1,2	2	—	0	2

(Continued on following page)

---

[1] In the designation of all the marginal districts a few borderline cases were included even though their conformance to the arbitrary range seemed not to warrant such inclusion.

TABLE II (Continued)

CONGRESSIONAL MARGINAL DISTRICTS BY STATES

AL—At Large

State	Republican marginal-districts	Total	Democratic marginal districts	Total	Statewide Total
Nevada	—	0	AL	1	1
New Jersey	2,12	2	4,10,11,13	4	6
New York	17,27,35,43,44	5	1,4,5,16*	4	9
Ohio	2,11,14,16,AL	5	3,6,9,18*	4	9
Oklahoma	1,8	2	—	0	2
Oregon	3	1	—	0	1
Pennsylvania	3,6,23,25,26,29	6	1,2,5,10,11,13,21	7	13
Utah	—	0	1,2	2	2
Washington	3	1	1	1	2
West Virginia	—	0	1,2,3,4	4	4
Wisconsin	4,5	2	—	0	2
Wyoming	AL	1	—	0	1
TOTALS		60		45	105

*New York's 5th and Ohio's 3rd districts are now Republican marginal districts as a result of special elections.

TABLE III

THE MARGINAL SENATORIAL SEATS BY STATE (EXCLUSIVE OF THE SOUTH)

State	Number of Republican Marginal Seats	Number of Democratic Marginal Seats
California	1	—
Connecticut	—	1
Delaware	1	—
Indiana	1	—
Maryland	1	—
Missouri	1	—
Montana	1	—
Nevada	1	—
New Mexico	—	1
New York	1	—
Utah	1	—
Washington	1	—
West Virginia	—	1
Wyoming	—	1
TOTALS	10	4

MAP 3   27

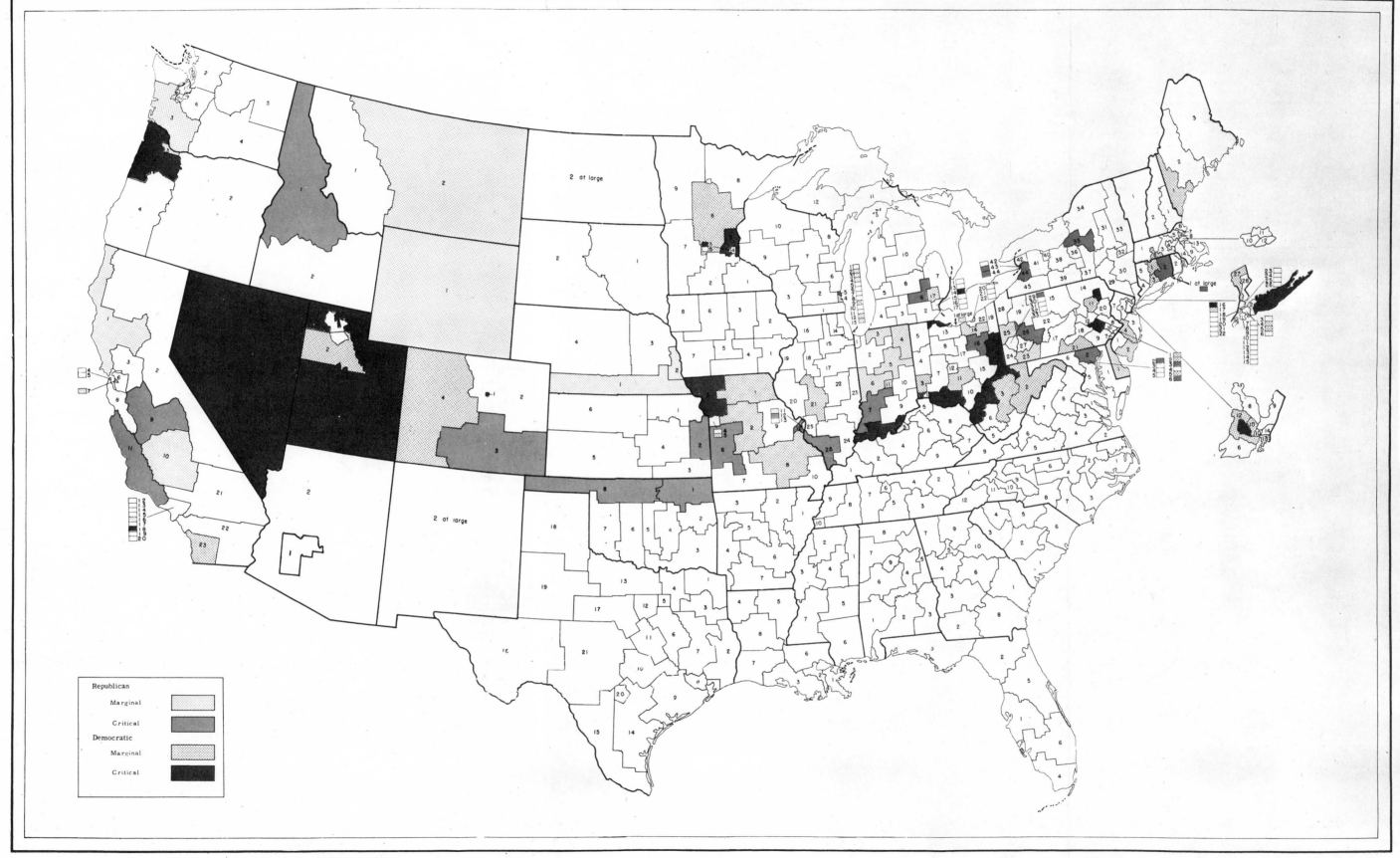

Republican
    Marginal
    Critical
Democratic
    Marginal
    Critical

NATION-WIDE DISTRIBUTION OF MARGINAL AND CRITICAL MARGINAL
CONGRESSIONAL DISTRICTS BY PARTY

As we begin our tour of the marginal districts, a few comments are in order. For obvious reasons, thirteen Southern states, where Democratic congressional candidates are "shoo ins" at the general election, have been omitted.[2] And since the Census of 1940 led to a reapportionment of congressional seats in several states, our point of departure for determining the marginal districts is the 1942 midterm election. Certain exceptions, however, are to be noted. Pennsylvania, for example, reapportioned by a Democratic legislature in 1941-42, was redistricted again for good measure when the Republicans resumed control of the Keystone State in 1943. New York, on the other hand, did not get around to redistricting until 1943-44, while Illinois and Arizona, though not required to redistrict, both did so in 1947-48. With these exceptions the identification of all marginal districts has been determined upon the basis of their behavior in the past five congressional elections.

MARGINAL DISTRICTS AND REGIONALISM

When identifying the marginal districts it is also helpful to know something of the broad political behavior of the regions or states within which they are situated. It is true, of course, that most communities throughout the nation move with the tide in their voting behavior, that is to say they tend to follow or go along with the political trend that has set in generally across the country. Such conformity, it might be added, is not always widely recognized. Astride the heavy Republican pluralities of the 1920's, for example, the uniformly sharp decline of GOP strength among ten of our largest cities was a portent of major change as Professor Eldersveld has pointed out, yet the circumstance was certainly not widely reported.[3] (See Table IV.)

---

[2] Arkansas Louisiana South Carolina
Alabama Mississippi Tennessee
Florida North Carolina Texas
Georgia Oklahoma* Virginia
Kentucky

  *Two marginal districts are included for Oklahoma.

[3]Samuel J. Eldersveld: "The Influence of Metropolitan Party Pluralities in Presidential Elections since 1920," *American Political Science Review*, 43 (1949), p. 1196.

TABLE IV
METROPOLITAN PLURALITIES IN PRESIDENTIAL ELECTIONS 1920-32*

City	1920	1924	1928	1932
New York City	R 441	R 137	D 454	D 871
Chicago	R 367	R 360	R 21	D 249
Philadelphia	R 218	R 360	R 143	R 71
Pittsburgh	R 54	R 23	R 7	D 25
Detroit	R 167	R 219	R 88	D 86
Cleveland	R 51	Prog. 7	D 13	D 42
Baltimore	R 39	R 10	R 9	D 81
St. Louis	R 57	R 43	D 14	D 103
Boston	R 32	R 18	D 99	D 102
Milwaukee	R 27	Prog. 30	D 29	D 97
San Francisco	R 63	R 5	D 1	D 74
Los Angeles	R 122	R 181	R 304	D 180

*In thousands.

TABLE V
METROPOLITAN PLURALITIES IN PRESIDENTIAL ELECTIONS 1936-48

City	1936	1940	1944	1948
New York City	D 1367	D 718	D 774	D 488
Republican %	24.6	38.8	38.4	41.0
Chicago	D 555	D 313	D 418	D 315
Republican %	33.1	41.5	38.6	41.4
Philadelphia	D 210	D 178	D 150	D 7
Republican %	37.9	40.0	41.1	49.6
Pittsburgh	D 101	D 70	D 57	D 58
Republican %	29.3	38.4	39.2	38.9
Detroit	D 183	D 149	D 209	D 152
Republican %	31.1	37.0	35.0	38.1
Cleveland	D 163	D 153	D 129	D 86
Republican %	23.5	30.1	32.1	36.7
Republican %	30.1	36.7	37.7	29.5
Milwaukee	D 138	D 73	D 61	D 54
Republican %	17.9	35.1	38.3	39.0

(Continued on following page)

TABLE V   (Continued)

METROPOLITAN PLURALITIES IN PRESIDENTIAL ELECTIONS 1936-48

City	1936	1940	1944	1948
San Francisco	D 130	D 63	D 74	D 7
Republican %	25.0	39.7	39.1	48.8
Los Angeles	D 400	D 251	D 220	D 8
Republican %	28.7	38.9	40.4	46.8
Baltimore	D 113	D 87	D 51	D 24
Republican %	31.7	36.0	40.8	45.2
St. Louis	D 132	D 65	D 70	D 100
Republican %	33.0	41.9	39.6	35.4
Boston	D 114	D 90	D 82	D 141

Similarly, since 1936 the ascent of the Republican presidential vote in a majority of our largest cities has been little publicized. (See Table V.)[4] In both cases the trends move together. But finding this relationship in urban voting among cities scattered throughout the nation does not negate the possibility of influences on voting that are distinctly regional.

Despite local conformance with national political tides, as the above similarities in metropolitan voting trends suggest, contradictions of such movements do occur as a result of regional and local influence. For a crackling example we need hark back no further than 1948 when Harry Truman was saved by what Louis Bean called a "green uprising" against Republican farm policy in five midwestern states. Some indication of the non-conformance of these states with the general tide of that election year is suggested by the chart below showing the extraordinarily heavy shift toward the Democratic party during the 1949 presidential election in 92 of the top 100 hog-producing counties in the country. (See Figure 1.)

---

[4]Figures for urban-metropolitan areas are taken from a variety of sources, but primarily from E. E. Robinson's *They Voted for Roosevelt* (Stanford University Press, 1947) for the period 1932-44, and from official sources and the *World Almanac* for the 1948 election.

FIGURE 1

PERCENTAGE OF DEMOCRATIC SHIFT 1944-48 IN 92 OF FIRST 100 HOG
PRODUCING COUNTIES

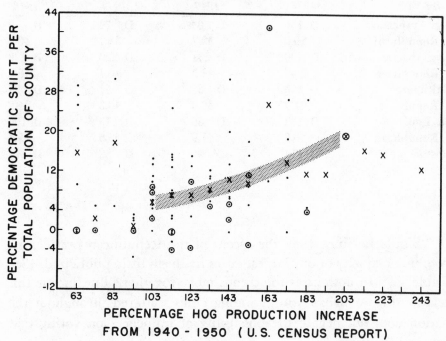

On the horizontal, or x axis, Figure 1 shows the percentage increase in hog production in 92 leading counties from 1940 to 1950.
The vertical, or y axis, shows the percentage shift per total county
population from the Republican to the Democratic party between
the 1944 and 1948 presidential elections. Looking at the J curve indicated on the scatter diagram of Figure 1, we see that as the percentage
increase in hog production over 1940 rises, the Democratic shift also
rises.[5] Stated bluntly, the evidence seems to suggest that as prosperity
from hog production increased, the Democratic vote also increased.
It should be remembered, of course, that other factors closely related
to hog production, such as the corn crop, also figured importantly in
this Democratic shift.

-----

[5]No attempt has been made to correlate the Democratic shift with the
increase in hog production since the number of counties involved were too
few to warrant a correlation study.

Interestingly, most of the 70 rural counties among the 92 leading hog producing counties showed the greatest shift to the Democratic party. Among the 22 counties having a significant urban vote,
only five lie above the mean for the average shift of the entire group
(92) while 16 lie below and one county lies directly on it. The urban
counties are encircled on the chart. This distinction between the
suburban and urban leading hog-producing counties seems to confirm the Republican experience generally in 1948, namely that the
GOP fared better in the cities and towns than in the countryside.

Iowa, preeminently the land of the corn-fed hog—with 54 of
the leading hog-producing counties and 42 of her counties among
the top 200 wealthiest agricultural counties in the nation—gave
Dewey a victory of 47,000 votes over Franklin Roosevelt in 1944, yet
went for Truman by 28,000 votes in 1948—a Democratic net shift of
75,000 votes.[6]   On only three previous occasions since 1872—the tripartite split in 1912, in 1932 when corn was selling for ten cents a
bushel, and in 1936—had Iowa gone Democratic. Why? Because of
price declines for pork and corn, the lack of grain storage facilities,
and the unalloyed fear that a Republican administration would
dilute price supports for farm products.

Regionalism, then, though many of the dissident influences it
exerted in the heyday of "King Cotton," "Free Silver," and the "Corn
Belt" have been soaked out, has by no means faded to a significance
of pure literary enchantment. The political pigmentation of the
nation, together with its cultural and economic variations, still holds
many surprises and jolts for the student of political behavior. As a
clinching postscript, Sam Lubell's case study of isolationism adds an
additional mite of authority. Thus in 1940, Lubell notes that Roosevelt's proportion of the major party vote dropped off roughly 1 percent throughout the country. But of the twenty counties in the
United States where his loss was in excess of 35 percent—"five times
the national average"—nineteen "are predominantly German speaking in background."[7]

---

[6]A detailed explication of this shift will be presented in a forthcoming
volume on the Republican party.

[7] *The Future of American Politics* (New York: Harper, 1952), p. 132.

Again, whether we look .at Hungry Horse, Montana; Painted
Post, New Mexico; or Woonsocket, Rhode Island, there are compelling reasons for seeking clues to political behavior in the politics
of the region. It is in the region that we are able to discern slow tran-
sitional upturns or declines in party strength. Not to be forgotten,
moreover, in assessing the imprint of regionalism is the fact that not
once during the twentieth century has the Democratic party received
less than 87 electoral votes or held less than 131 seats in the House.
But no comparable regional loyalty has cushioned the GOP. The
Republican electoral score fell on one occasion to 8, and its membership in the House has dipped to a scant 89. Even in eras of change
and rapid transition in American politics, regionalism is not to be
discounted, as becomes steadily apparent when we examine presidential-congressional voting relationships.

Agreement on the configurations that bound regions is often a
matter of contention. The sections chosen for this analysis, however,
have broad acceptance. They have been selected primarily on a political, rather than an economic or geographic basis, and are identified in Table VI.

TABLE VI
1948 PRESIDENTIAL VOTING BY STATES AND SECTIONS; NEW REAPPORTIONMENT, 1952

State and Section	Popular Vote, 1948			Electoral Vote					
				1948			1944	1952	
	R	D	Other	R	D	Ot.	R	D	
NEW ENGLAND	1,830,370	2,029,289	126,427	20	20	0	8	32	40
Connecticut	437,754	423,297	22,197	8	....	....	....	8	8
Maine	150,234	111,916	2,637	5	....	....	5	....	5
Massachusetts	909,370	1,151,788	94,189	....	16	....	....	16	16
New Hampshire	121,299	107,995	2,146	4	....	....	....	4	4
Rhode Island	135,787	188,736	3,179	....	4	....	....	4	4
Vermont	75,926	45,557	1,899	3	....	....	3	....	3
MIDDLE ATLAN.	6,405,137	6,211,607	827,044	109	8	....	....	117	113
Delaware	69,588	67,813	1,672	3	....	....	....	3	3
Maryland	294,814	286,521	15,400	8	....	....	....	8	9
New Jersey	981,124	895,455	72,976	16	....	....	....	16	16
New York	2,841,163	2,780,204	653,160	47	....	....	....	47	45

(Continued on following page)

TABLE VI— (Continued)
1948 PRESIDENTIAL VOTING BY STATES AND SECTIONS; NEW REAPPORTIONMENT, 1952

State and Section	Popular Vote, 1948			Electoral Vote 1948			1944		1952
	R	D	Other	R	D	Ot.	R	D	
Pennsylvania	1,902,197	1,752,426	80,525	35	....	....	....	35	32
West Virginia	316,251	429,188	3,311	....	8	....	....	8	8
E. N. CENTRAL	5,266,461	5,258,787	160,602	32	53	....	38	47	85
Illinois	1,961,103	1,994,715	28,228	....	28	....	....	28	27
Indiana	821,079	807,833	27,302	13	....	....	13	....	13
Michigan	1,038,595	1,003,448	67,566	19	....	....	....	19	20
Ohio	1,445,684	1,452,791	37,596	....	25	....	25	....	25
W. N. CENTRAL	3,156,236	3,569,503	128,758	22	48	....	44	26	68
Iowa	494,018	522,380	21,866	....	10	....	10	....	10
Kansas	423,039	351,902	13,878	8	....	....	8	....	8
Minnesota	483,617	692,966	35,643	....	11	....	....	11	11
Missouri	655,039	917,315	6,274	....	15	....	....	15	13
Nebraska	264,774	224,165	....	6	....	....	6	....	6
North Dakota	115,139	95,812	9,765	4	....	....	4	....	4
South Dakota	129,651	117,653	2,801	4	....	....	4	....	4
Wisconsin	590,959	647,310	38,351	....	12	....	12	....	12
SOUTH	1,971,769	3,476,940	1,207,056	....	109	39	....	148	146
Alabama	40,930	....	174,050	....	....	11	....	11	11
Arkansas	50,959	149,659	41,857	....	9	....	....	9	8
Florida	194,280	281,988	101,375	....	8	....	....	8	10
Georgia	76,691	254,646	87,423	....	12	....	....	12	12
Kentucky	341,210	466,756	13,262	....	11	....	....	11	10
Louisiana	72,657	136,344	207,325	....	....	10	....	10	10
Mississippi	5,043	19,384	167,763	....	....	9	....	9	9
North Carolina	258,572	459,070	73,567	....	14	....	....	14	14
Oklahoma	268,817	452,782	....	....	10	....	....	10	8
South Carolina	5,386	34,423	102,762	....	....	8	....	8	8
Tennessee	202,914	270,402	76,967	....	11	1	....	12	11
Texas	282,240	750,700	114,305	....	23	....	....	23	24
Virginia	172,070	200,786	46,400	....	11	....	....	11	12
MOUNTAIN	797,604	927,240	33,462	....	32	....	9	23	32
Arizona	77,597	95,521	4,217	....	4	....	....	4	4
Colorado	239,714	267,288	8,235	....	6	....	6	....	6

TABLE VI—(Continued)
1948 PRESIDENTIAL VOTING BY STATES AND SECTIONS;
NEW REAPPORTIONMENT, 1952

State and Section	Popular Vote, 1948			Electoral Vote					
				1948			1944		1952
	R	D	Other	R	D	Ot.	R	D	
Idaho	101,514	107,370	5,932	....	4	....	....	4	4
Montana	96,770	119,071	8,437	....	4	....	....	4	4
Nevada	29,357	31,291	1,469	....	3	....	....	3	3
New Mexico	80,303	105,464	1,296	....	4	....	....	4	4
Utah	124,402	149,151	2,752	....	4	....	....	4	4
Wyoming	47,947	52,354	1,124	....	3	....	....	3	3
PACIFIC	2,542,488	2,632,446	275,743	6	33	....	....	39	47
California	1,895,269	1,913,134	213,135	....	25	....	....	25	32
Oregon	260,904	243,147	20,029	6	....	....	....	6	6
Washington	386,315	476,165	42,579	....	8	....	....	8	9
UNITED STATES	21,970,065	24,105,812	2,759,002	189	303	39	99	432	531

NEW ENGLAND

Starting our travelogue through the marginal districts with the New England region, we find that, more than any other, this group of states has shown a consistent Democratic gain in strength since 1924. For the first time since the advent of the Republican party (except in 1912) the section was carried by the Democrats in 1932. Recent political tendencies in this area, moreover, have been even more Democratic than in the zenith of Franklin Roosevelt's landslides, particularly in such industrial states as Massachusetts and Rhode Island. The behavior of the Bay State and "Little Rhody" is particularly noteworthy when we recall that for the nation as a whole the Democratic tide has been receding since the epochal election of 1936.

Beginning alphabetically with Connecticut, we find that this state has divided its loyalty between the two major parties in a crisply impartial fashion. Three times it sided with the Republican presidential nominee—1928, 1932, and 1948—by close margins, and three times with the Democratic candidate—1936, 1940, and 1944, again by thin margins.

Gubernatorial races have been closer, if anything, in recent years than the presidential races, frequently being decided by a relative handful of Socialist votes. Back in 1946 the Republican candidate won a United States Senate seat handily, but following his resignation in 1949 to accept a state judgeship, the Republican party took quite a hammering at the next midterm election. In the 1950 election to select six congressmen, *two* senators, a governor, and most of the legislature, the Democratic party had its best off-year success since 1938. Both the Democratic candidates, Senators McMahon and Benton, were elected—the latter by a tight squeeze. While the Democratic governor, Chester Bowles, lost his fight for re-election in a photo finish, his party managed to regain control of the state Senate. Capping this good fortune, the Democrats held two of the six congressional seats—an unusual feat for a midterm election—and actually increased their percentage of the congressional vote from 50.0 percent in 1948 to 50.6 in 1950! Certainly, by comparison with recent off-year contests, the election year of 1950 represented a sturdy Democratic victory, whatever augury this may have for the future.

MAP 4

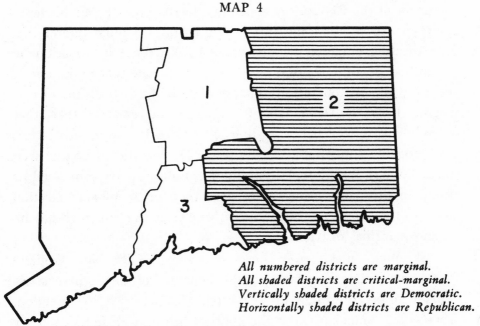

All numbered districts are marginal.
All shaded districts are critical-marginal.
Vertically shaded districts are Democratic.
Horizontally shaded districts are Republican.

Connecticut: 2 critical marginal districts
2nd dist. R—New London
At Large R—The entire state

In the second district, Republican H. Seeley-Brown defeated the Democratic incumbent in 1950. This area has oscillated between the two parties a great deal in the past eight years. The Republicans have carried it three times and the Democrats twice—both times in presidential years. Covering the eastern third of the state, this constituency is more rural in its characteristics than most, if not all, of the other districts in the state and includes a sizeable number of people of Portuguese, French-Canadian, and Italian descent.

The Connecticut Congressman-at-Large is A. N. Sadlak, a Republican. Since 1942 the Republicans have carried the state four times as a district at large and the Democrats once. In the 1948 election Dewey's 50.8 percent of the major party vote in Connecticut quite possibly helped to lift Sadlak back into office, since the latter won with only 50.2 percent.

In Massachusetts the Republicans polled the lowest wedge of the major party presidential vote in 1948 that the GOP has ever received in the Bay State. One factor in this rout of the Great Emancipator's party can probably be credited to the bad political judgment of the Republican-controlled legislature. It was this legislature that sponsored a measure providing for a popular referendum on a measure empowering physicians to distribute information on the subject of contraception. The result in a state that ranks among the top three in Roman Catholic population, was a landslide of first magnitude for the Democrats. It might also be remarked that other amendments on the ballot dealing with labor law were also factors that probably contributed to the heavy Democratic turnout. Even in the midterm election of 1950, the Republican party continued its slump in this state, losing more decisively for an off-year election than it ever had heretofore. Massachusetts at this juncture has no critical marginal districts.

Skipping quickly over the northern tier of the New England group, one interesting facet in the behavior of these three states bears mention. Throughout New England generally Alfred Landon, whose 1936 campaign leaves the political historian little to say other than that he had the initials of Abraham Lincoln, actually fared better than Willkie in 1940 and Dewey in 1944. Particularly is this phenomenon noticeable in Maine, where the Republicans almost lost in 1940; New Hampshire, where the GOP presidential nominee lost by a larger margin than in 1936; and in Vermont, where the Republican ticket was weaker in 1940 than in 1936. There are no critical marginal congressional districts in the latter three states.

Perhaps the reason for Landon's better showing than either Willkie or Dewey made in New England lies partly in the growing internationalist tendencies of the region and partly in the class composition of the parties. Traditionally GOP territory, New England as an area is relatively speaking internationalist, strongly industrialized, and relatively Catholic. Since 1928, the Democratic party has become more and more identified with internationalism, pro-labor policies, and pro-Catholic in its sentiments. Thus the lengthy Republican tradition has given way before new political forces, particularly in the Southern part of New England.

Rhode Island is a land of disappointing defection for the GOP. Not since 1938 have the Republicans captured the state. Furthermore, the Democratic percentage has been constantly climbing, while the Republican share of the vote has been steadily declining, though twisting and turning with small ups and downs. While the Republicans were able to capture both congressional seats and the governorship in 1938, they have not been able to buck the strong Democratic tide since that year. The GOP loss in the senatorial race of 1950 was the heaviest in the history of the Republican party.

THE MIDDLE ATLANTIC

The Middle Atlantic region is the industrial backbone of the nation. For the first time since 1932 a state was actually carried by the Republicans in this section in 1948—not one state, to be sure, but five out of the six. Only West Virginia remained in the Democratic column. The Republican margin of victory, however, was very slight. Yet by contrast to earlier years, the GOP upturn was substantial, even though it must be qualified by keeping in mind that two of the states—New York and Maryland—were probably kept out of the Democratic presidential column by the Wallace Progressive

party candidacy. The GOP has made modest gains in the off-year
elections throughout the entire region, though in New York the
political picture is blurred. Certainly New York presented a mixed
result in 1950, with Dewey retaining the governorship by a large
majority, Lehman winning the Senate seat by a handsome margin,
though not as large as Dewey's, and the House elections resulting in
victories for 23 Democrats and 22 Republicans.

MAP 5

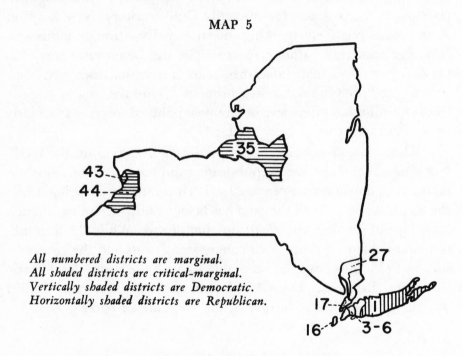

All numbered districts are marginal.
All shaded districts are critical-marginal.
Vertically shaded districts are Democratic.
Horizontally shaded districts are Republican.

New York: 4 critical marginal districts
        1st dist. D—Long Island from Nassau County eastward
        35th dist. R—Utica area
        43rd dist. R—Buffalo
        44th dist. R—Buffalo

In the first district, the Democratic Congressman E. Greenwood
defeated the Republican incumbent, W. Kingsland Macy, in 1950
by about 300 votes—a mighty slim majority when approximately
150,000 votes were cast. Since Macy received 77.3 percent of the

votes in 1946, and 67.6 percent in 1948, his defeat in 1950 was undoubtedly attributable to his involvement in the Hanley affair and his row with Dewey. For allegedly making public a copy of a letter written by Lieutenant Governor Hanley which referred to certain pledges that the latter claimed to have received from Governor Dewey, Macy suffered heavy ballot losses. Following his defeat he charged the Dewey forces with "cutting" him in the election. In presidential years this district is usually Republican by about 70 percent. This would indicate that Greenwood, the Democratic incumbent, will probably lose his seat in 1952. Since 1944 the district has been Republican three times, and Democratic once. The district is a suburban residential and farming area adjacent to New York City.

The Republican congressman from the 35th district, W. R. Williams, defeated the Democratic incumbent in 1950. Since 1944 (New York was redistricted in 1943) the Republicans have captured the congressional seat three times, and the Democrats have carried it once. This district contains industrial developments including knitting mills and other textile factories. It has a poor slum area extensively spread throughout the city of Utica.

The Democratic incumbent of the 43rd district was defeated by E. T. Radwan, Republican, in 1950. Since 1944 this district has gone Republican three times and Democratic once. The heavy Truman victory in Buffalo in 1948 was undoubtedly a major factor in delivering this congressional seat, as well as the 44th district, to the Democratic party. The former is located in the heavily urbanized area of Buffalo, and the latter includes part of Buffalo and most of the rest of Erie County.

In the 44th district, Republican J. C. Butler defeated the Democratic incumbent in 1950. Since 1942 this district has been Democratic once and Republican three times. The Democratic victory in 1948 in this congressional district was undoubtedly helped along by Truman's thumping 1948 majority in both Buffalo and Erie County. The 44th district is primarily urban, though it has some rural sections.

New Jersey yielded its first Republican presidential victory in twenty years in 1948 by a modest margin. The GOP also won the governorship in 1949—a result aided and abetted, no doubt, by the defection of many Democrats, particularly in Jersey City, from the Hague-backed candidate. In two congressional districts in the industrial-residential northeastern corner of the State, however,

Democratic currents stepped up. Here for the first time in 1948 the
Democrats picked up two seats and held on to them in 1950.

MAP 6

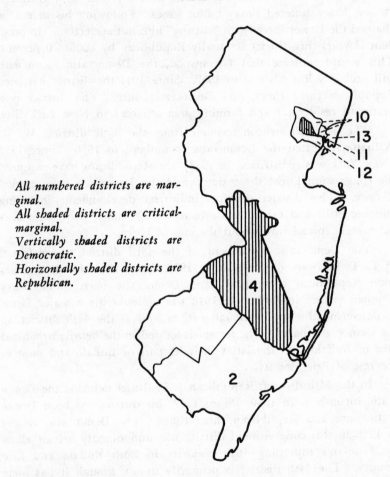

All numbered districts are mar-
ginal.
All shaded districts are critical-
marginal.
Vertically shaded districts are
Democratic.
Horizontally shaded districts are
Republican.

New Jersey: 2 critical marginal districts
     4th dist. D—Trenton, Burlington area
     11th dist. D—Newark

In the 4th district C. R. Howell defeated the Republican
incumbent in 1948. Since 1942 this district has been Democratic
twice and Republican three times. Congressman Howell won by a
landslide in 1948, in an area which during presidential election

years is strongly Democratic. This district encompasses a truck-farming area and considerable industrial development in and about Trenton.

H. J. Addonizio, Democrat, defeated the 11th district Republican candidate in 1948 by a very narrow majority and upped his margin of victory in 1950 to 52.1 percent of the two-party vote. Since 1942 this district has gone Democratic twice and Republican three times. Mr. Truman carried it in 1948 by a handsome majority, though it should be remembered that Newark normally gives a two-to-one Democratic majority in presidential elections. The constituency is highly industrial in nature.

Pennsylvania seems to be astride two mounts, politically speaking. Still Republican in 1932, it shifted in 1936 to the Democrats for the first time since the birth of the Republican party, and stayed Democratic in 1940 and 1944. In 1948 the Keystone State reverted to its traditional Republican allegiance, but Dewey's majority, let it be recorded, was proportionately no larger than Hoover's in 1932. Moreover, in 1950 a Democratic gain trimmed down the margin of Republican victory in gubernatorial and senatorial races below the percentage mark set by Dewey two years earlier. Broadly stated, the Eastern part of the state shifted more determinedly into the Democratic column in 1950, while Western Pennsylvania generally rallied to the Republican ticket in larger numbers than in 1948.

The closeness of the election manifested itself also in the selection of a State Legislature. Though the Republicans managed to win a majority in both houses, it is not as large as might normally be anticipated for an off year. That the Democratic trend in Eastern Pennsylvania has not been reversed since the 1950 general election is suggested by the Democratic upset in the Philadelphia mayoralty race of 1951. Disclosures of corruption have inspired victories for the Democrats in Philadelphia in two municipal elections and, as the GOP's Senator Duff remarked, the recruitment of Democratic workers in the City Hall for the first time in many years gives the Democrats a new and important vantage point in Pennsylvania politics. Quite appropriately then does this Commonwealth bear the name—the "Keystone State."

MAP 7

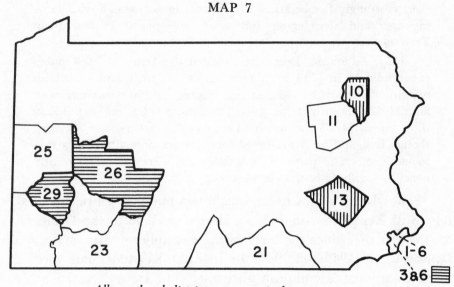

All numbered districts are marginal.
All shaded districts are critical-marginal.
Vertically shaded districts are Democratic.
Horizontally shaded districts are Republican.

Pennsylvania: 6 critical marginal districts
    3rd dist. R—Philadelphia City
    6th dist. R—Philadelphia City
  10th dist. D—Scranton area
  13th dist. D—Reading area
  26th dist. R—Johnstown area
  29th dist. R—Northern suburb of Pittsburgh and North-
                      ern Allegheny County

      Hardie Scott, Republican, defeated the Democratic incumbent
in 1946, and has been re-elected in successive third district congressional campaigns with ever-decreasing majorities. When he was first
elected to Congress in 1946 he received 62.1 percent of the vote. His
voting advantage has diminished steadily until, in 1950, he was
elected by only 50.3 percent of the vote. Encased by the city of
Philadelphia, the third district is a highly urbanized constituency.

      In the 6th district the Democratic incumbent was defeated in
1946 by Hugh D. Scott, Jr., Republican. Representative Scott has
been re-elected since that year with ever-decreasing majorities, winning a nip-and-tuck battle in 1950 by a bare 500 votes. Since 1944

(the state was redistricted in 1943), the Republicans have carried the district three times, and the Democrats once. This district is in North Philadelphia, and is predominantly residential.

H. P. O'Neil, Democrat, of the 10th district, defeated the Republican incumbent in 1948. Truman's strong 1948 showing in this district and the Democratic congressional victory of O'Neil reflect again that a national candidate aids his party's congressional ticket. Since 1944 this district has yielded three Democratic victories and one Republican. The population of this district has steadily been declining since 1930. Its main sources of revenue are derived from coal mines and steel.

In the 13th district G. M. Rhodes defeated the Republican incumbent in 1948 and was re-elected in 1950. Since 1944 this district has gone Republican once and Democratic in the other three congressional races. The dominant resources of the constituency, located in and about Reading, are coal and industry together with some agricultural production.

J. P. Saylor, Republican, won a special election in 1948, which was held as a result of the death of the Democratic incumbent in an airplane tragedy. Since 1944, however, the district has gone Republican three times and Democratic once. Interestingly enough, the Democratic presidential candidate has won in every election year since 1936. The district is almost equally divided between a Democratic industrialized area about Johnstown with many steel mills and coal mines, and an agricultural section to the West which is generally Republican.

In the 29th district, H. D. Denny, Jr., Republican, defeated the Democratic incumbent in 1950. Yet two years earlier—1948—by receiving 57.1 percent of the vote—approximately the same percentage of the vote that Truman harvested in the district—the Democratic congressional candidate jumped his party's showing a full 9 percent over the 1946 mark of the Republicans. Since 1944 this district has gone Democratic once and Republican three times. A prosperous residential area suburban to Pittsburgh, it is generally Republican.

Republican from 1896 to 1936, Delaware since the latter year has had the unmistakable tendencies of a GOP truant. Like its neighbor Pennsylvania, Delaware went Republican in 1932 (largely because of the GOP majority in industrialized New Castle County, Wilmington), only to be captured by Roosevelt in each of his successive campaigns thereafter. But in 1948 Dewey took Delaware's elec-

toral vote in stride, running far ahead of the Republican presidential
vote in four previous elections in Wilmington as well as other industrial areas of the state. Elsewhere in the political spectrum of Delaware, however, the GOP comeback in the presidential election was
dimmed by the defeat of the Republican candidates for governor
and senator.*

In Maryland the Republican presidential vote climbed from 39
percent of the major party vote in 1932 to win the state from Truman
by a whisker (8,293) in 1948.[8] Two years later—1950—the GOP
won the governorship and a Senate seat. The gubernatorial nominee
not only won by the largest majority ever given a chief executive,
but fared considerably better than the GOP candidate for governor
in the heavily Republican state of Kansas.

MAP 8

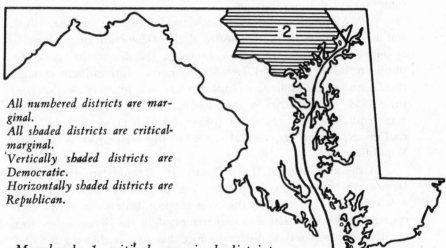

All numbered districts are mar-
ginal.
All shaded districts are critical-
marginal.
'Vertically shaded districts are
Democratic.
Horizontally shaded districts are
Republican.

Maryland: 1 critical marginal ·district
          2nd dist. R—Baltimore County and part of Baltimore City

In the 2nd district, Republican J. P. S. Devereux defeated the
Democratic incumbent by the narrow margin of 50.8 percent of
the vote, not an inconsiderable feat for this traditional Democratic
stronghold. Since 1942 this district has been Democratic four times

---

*There are no critical-marginal districts in Delaware.

[8]Wallace received 9,983 votes in this election, and Thurmond, the States'
Rights candidate, 2,476.

and Republican once. In 1950 General Devereux was helped into
office by the solid majority of the Republican gubernatorial candidate. The chances for Republican retention of this seat may well
have been reduced through the 1951 reapportionment which chopped
off precisely the areas in Baltimore City where Devereux polled
sufficient strength to offset heavy local majorities of Baltimore County.

Maryland's 1950 election, of course, was undeniably an exceptional one. The Democratic gubernatorial nominee was defeated in
the primary by popular votes, but won renomination through a unit-
rule system similar to the one employed in Georgia. In consequence,
many followers of the defeated Democratic primary candidate supported the Republican nominee, Theodore R. McKeldin, who was
making his third try for the governorship. McKeldin's landslide
vote was undoubtedly a factor in bringing about the defeat of
Senator Millard Tydings, along with Senator McCarthy's charges
against Owen Lattimore. Tydings, who began running for the Senate
in 1926, had never before received less than 60 percent of the vote.

Unique among the states of the Middle Atlantic region in 1948
was West Virginia. Last carried by the GOP in 1928, and strongly
Democratic ever since, the state with the motto "Mountaineers
Always Free" gave Dewey a smaller vote in 1948 than in 1944—the
only state in the section where the GOP presidential vote showed
a decrease. Only once since 1928 have the Republicans captured
a Senate seat in this State (1942), and the GOP has won a majority
of the major party vote in House elections on just two occasions—
1942 and 1946. In 1948 the heavy Democratic majorities spread
through presidential, as well as gubernatorial, senatorial, congressional, and legislative contests.

Well known for its mining industries, one element that may
have loomed large in West Virginia's atypical ballot behavior of 1948
was the mine worker's hostility to the Taft-Hartley Act, enacted a
year earlier. Fortifying this observation is the fact that the only four
counties out of 88 that Senator Taft failed to carry in his spectacular
Ohio win in 1950 were coal mining counties or counties with a
heavy admixture of income derived from coal mining.[9] All four

[9]Belmont, Clinton, Jefferson, and Lawrence Counties.

counties, incidentally, lie just a leap across the Ohio River from West Virginia.

While improving somewhat in the 1950 midterm election, the GOP showing again was less significant than usual for an off-year contest. In some instances the congressional vote was close, but at the final tally the Democrats held onto all six House seats.

MAP 9

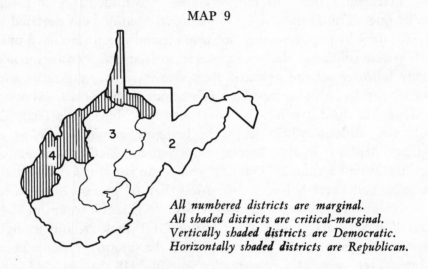

All numbered districts are marginal.
All shaded districts are critical-marginal.
Vertically shaded districts are Democratic.
Horizontally shaded districts are Republican.

West Virginia: 2 critical marginal districts
1st dist. D—Wheeling, Morgantown area
4th dist. D—Parkersburg, Huntington aera

R. L. Ramsey, Democrat, of the 1st district, defeated the Republican incumbent in 1948. Here again the presidential majority of 57.9 appears to have been a factor in helping the Democratic congressional candidate gain 57.3 percent of the vote. Democratic three times since 1942 and Republican twice, this district is located in the West Virginia panhandle, noted for its steel mills and coal mines, together with a substantial amount of agriculture.

In the 4th district the Republican incumbent was defeated by Democrat M. G. Burnside in 1948. Since 1942 the constituency has gone Republican three times, and Democratic twice. In congressional races, at least, this area is the most Republican part of West Virginia. It includes the middle-sized city of Huntington and the prosperous farmlands along the Ohio and Kanawha Rivers. Though predominantly an agricultural district, the area has some industry in and about Huntington.

A quick recap of political behavior in the Middle Atlantic region tells us the following: barring the three-party contest of 1912 and the loss of a handful of electoral votes (6 and 4 respectively) when Maryland split her electoral vote in 1904 and 1908, the Republicans have carried this section in every election from 1896 through 1928. Beginning its defection from the GOP voting habit in 1932, the area yielded not one GOP electoral vote in three presidential elections—1936, 1940, and 1944, a period during which the total Republican electoral vote never once topped 99. Since Dewey picked up 109 electoral votes from the Middle Atlantic states alone in 1948, the return to the GOP fold of this area in one election is a strong reminder of its importance to a Republican national victory.

EAST-NORTH CENTRAL

The configuration of the East-North Central section embraces all of the Old Northwest with the exception of Wisconsin, that is to say, Illinois, Indiana, Michigan, and Ohio. Only once—1916—in two-party contests from 1896 to 1932 did the Democrats capture a single state within this region. Even in the GOP midwestern debacle of 1948 the Republicans won a slim plurality of the popular vote in this region. In 1932 and 1936 the Democrats captured all four states in this region while the Republicans have taken a pair of these states in the last three presidential elections: Michigan and Indiana in 1940 and 1948; and Ohio and Indiana in 1944. While Indiana since 1940 has been marginally Republican and Illinois similarly Democratic, both Ohio and Michigan rest squarely on the fence. Indeed, it has been said that the number of invalid votes in the Ohio 1948 election exceeded the Democratic plurality by quite a margin, and it is certain that in Michigan the 1948 Progressive vote alone was larger than the Republican edge over the Democratic vote.

Certainly the recent zigs and zags of the East-North Central states at election time have made spectrum analysis of this region a real challenge. For example, the GOP made strong gains in this area in 1946. But while the Republicans held the governorship of all four states in 1946, the general elections of 1948 and 1950 replaced the GOP governors with a quartet of Democratic chief executives. Retrospectively perhaps it is easy to say that straws in the wind suggesting a Republican reversal in 1948 were not wanting. The violent quake in the 1947 Indiana municipal elections that turned over a major share of Hoosier local government to the Democrats may have been a more meaningful portent than the pre-election polls of 1948.[10] Similarly, of course, Republican successes in the 1951 municipal elections of Indiana might have some bearing on the political decisions of 1952, though it should be remarked that the Republican swing was not as pronounced as the Democratic one of 1947.

In 1950 the GOP experienced important victories among the East-North Central group, notably the re-election of Taft by the whopping majority of 437,000 votes and the defeat of Democratic Majority Leader, Scott Lucas, by Everett Dirksen. The same elections also gave the GOP a tighter rein on control of the legislatures among these states, and resulted in the recapture of several congressional seats. By and large, however, the 1950 midterm election was not the GOP upsurge of 1946. In Ohio 19 of 23 congressmen who won election in 1946 were Republican; but in 1950 only 15 out of 23 in the Buckeye congressional delegation were Republicans. Taft, though decisively successful, ran behind GOP House candidates in five congressional districts, and there were numerous hints that in Ohio, as in Michigan, Indiana, and Illinois, the balloting was not entirely satisfactory from the GOP standpoint. There were eight Negro wards in Cincinnati, Toledo, and Cleveland where Taft ran behind the vote chalked up by Governor Dewey in 1948. Continuance of such a trend in this region could be very serious for the Republican party. By 1950 there were 50 percent more Negroes living in this section (2,134,000) than in 1940. Negroes doubled in Michigan in this period, raised their population 60 percent in Illinois, and 38 percent in Ohio. Moreover, if Roper's study of Negro voting participation in the North gives us an accurate estimate of turnout the Negro vote may determine the outcome of elections in several

[10] See J. Harvey Wheeler: *The Indiana Municipal Elections:1947* (Bureau of Politics, Indiana University, Bloomington, 1948).

states. For example, he finds that nearly 70 percent of the Northern Negroes go to the polls generally as against a 50 percent average turnout for all voters in the country. They also are strongly inclined to base their vote on one issue, he finds—civil rights for minorities.[11] Clearly in the struggles ahead for control of the four East-North Central states the political priests of the GOP are going to have to weigh seriously the significance of Negro editor Robert L. Vann's words when he urged his people of Pennsylvania to bolt the Republican party in 1932: "My friends, go turn Lincoln's picture to the wall. That debt has been paid in full."

THE CRITICAL MARGINAL DISTRICTS OF THE EAST-NORTH
. CENTRAL REGION

Not surprising in view of the evenly matched performances of the major parties in this section, is the fact that it contains several critical marginal districts. Nor is it a curious circumstance that Ohio leads all the rest—even Illinois—in the number of such districts.

MAP 10

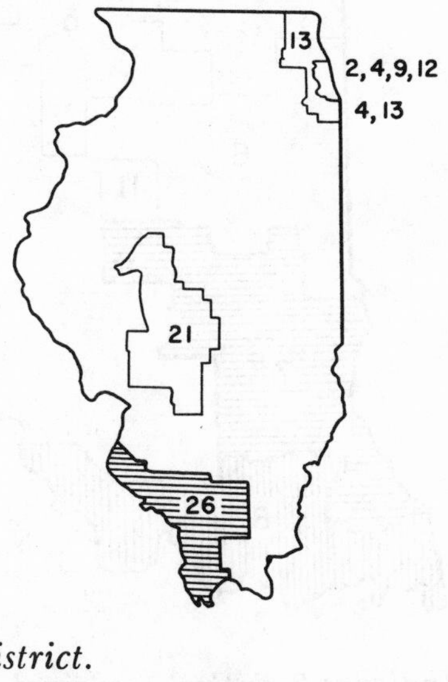

All numbered districts are marginal.
All shaded districts are critical-marginal.
Vertically shaded districts are Democratic.
Horizontally shaded districts are Republican.

Illinois: 1 critical marginal district.
26th dist. R—Includes Cairo, in Southern Illinois, known as "Egypt."

---

[11]See *New York Herald Tribune*, July 28, 1952.

Republican C. W. Bishop defeated the Democratic incumbent in 1946. Percentagewise, however, the Republican congressional vote of 1950 was less than that of 1948, despite the fact that the GOP proportion of the vote in 1950 was generally higher than in 1948. Since 1948 (this state was redistricted in 1947) the Democrats have not won this district, and the Republicans have taken it twice. Situated near the junction of the Ohio and Mississippi Rivers, this district contains coal mining areas (particularly Franklin, Perry, and Williamson Counties) and also raises grain and corn. More Republican in the Northern corn growing area the Southern part of this district which is Democratically inclined, was Copperhead territory during the Civil War. The constituency went Republican in 1948 by the thin margin of 50.3 percent.

MAP 11

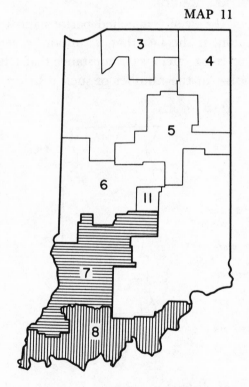

All numbered districts are marginal.
All shaded districts are critical-marginal.
Vertically shaded districts are Democratic.
Horizontally shaded districts are Republican.

Indiana: 2 critical marginal districts
   7th dist. R—Southwestern part of the state
   8th dist. D—Southern border of the state, running along the Ohio River from Wabash to Louisville

Republican W. G. Bray of the 7th district defeated the Democratic incumbent in 1950 by a vote of 50.3 percent. Beginning in 1942 the Republicans have won the district four times and the Democrats have carried it once. Although the Republican presidential candidate carried the district by 50.8 percent of the vote in 1948, it was not by a large enough margin to carry along the Republican congressional candidate.

In the 8th district, W. K. Denton, Democrat, defeated the Republican incumbent in 1948. Since 1942 the Democrats have won the district twice and the Republicans three times. Very likely Truman's heavy 1948 vote defeated the Republican incumbent and permitted a Democrat to take the seat. Traces of the Confederacy are still in evidence in this district, and the Democrats usually have the upper edge in presidential elections. Composition of the district is characterized by a large metropolitan population which has been built up by an expansion of Evansville and the suburbs of Louisville and Cincinnati. Its urban nature, however, is partially disguised by the fact that the district spreads over such a wide area. More recently—1948—the retirement of the progressive Republican Charles La Follette, may account for an improvement in Democratic fortunes in this constituency.

MAP 12

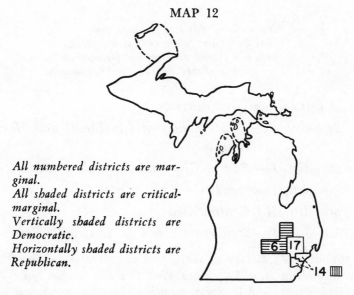

All numbered districts are marginal.
All shaded districts are critical-marginal.
Vertically shaded districts are Democratic.
Horizontally shaded districts are Republican.

Michigan: 1 critical marginal district
14th dist. D—Located in Detroit

Democrat L. C. Rabaut defeated the Republican incumbent in
1948 and was narrowly re-elected in 1950. Since 1942 the Democrats
have held the seat four times and the Republicans once.

MAP 13

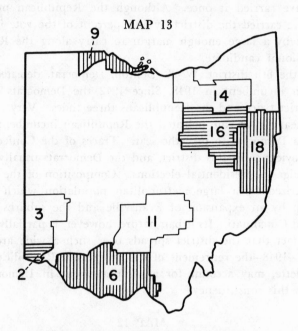

All numbered districts are marginal.
All shaded districts are critical-marginal.
Vertically shaded districts are Democratic.
Horizontally shaded districts are Republican.

Ohio: 5 critical marginal districts
> *2nd dist. R—Western half of Cincinnati and Hamilton*
> *County*
> *6th dist. D—East of Cincinnati and along Ohio River*
> *9th dist. Independent—Toledo area*
> *16th dist. R—Canton area*
> *18th dist. D—Steubenville and St. Clairsville area.*

Republican W. E. Hess of the second district defeated the Democratic incumbent in 1950. Since 1942 this district has gone Republican four times and Democratic once. The lone Democratic win
occurred in 1948. Of Cincinnati's two congressional districts the
second is uniformly more Democratic than the first.

In the 6th district J. G. Polk, Democrat, defeated the Republican incumbent in 1948, and in 1950 he was re-elected by 50.8 percent of the major party vote. Since 1942 this district sided with the Republicans three times and with the Democrats twice. It is traditionally Democratic in presidential and congressional elections, rural in nature, and has less fertile soil than many areas of Ohio.

An Independent candidate, Frazier Reams, who once affiliated himself with the Democratic party, defeated the Democratic incumbent in the 9th district election. Two years earlier the Democrat who was unhorsed by Independent Reams in 1950 unseated a Republican Congressman. Since 1942 the 9th district has gone Republican three times, Democratic once, and Independent once. It embraces all of Toledo, and is a predominantly urban and industrialized district, though it has some rural sections.

Republican F. T. Bow of the 16th district defeated the Democratic incumbent in 1950. This district holds the city of Canton. In presidential election years it has been favorably disposed toward Democratic congressional candidates. Even with the Republican party making substantial gains in the presidential vote in recent elections (Dewey carried the district in 1948 by a slim margin of 51.4 percent), the Democratic congressional candidate was elected. The constituency combines both a large rural area and a heavy industrial population. Since 1942 it has gone to the Republicans three times and to the Democrats twice.

In the 18th district W. L. Hays, Democrat, defeated the Republican incumbent in 1948. Since Truman led Democratic congressional candidate Hays by 2.4 percent of the vote, "the Missouri Wonder," as Mencken knighted the Chief Executive in 1948, probably rode Hays in on his coattail. Since 1942 the 18th district has been Republican three times and Democratic once.

WEST NORTH CENTRAL

No section in America has been as variable in its recent political behavior as the West North Central. Home of such political bedouins as "Sockless" Jerry Simpson, Robert La Follette, George Norris, and a galaxy of other stellar mavericks, this region has been at once a bastion of Republican loyalty and the scene of thunderous upheavals.[12] From 1860 through 1928 this section has been carried as

[12]For a stimulating account of these experiences, see Russell B. Nye: *Midwestern Progressive Politics* (Michigan State Press, East Lansing, 1951).

a unit by the Republican ticket in every election but 1912 and 1916.
It was carried by the Democrats in 1932 and 1936, and in 1940 and
1944 it was the lone area in the country to be captured by the GOP.
But after the Republicans had won a majority of these states and a
plurality of their popular vote in 1940 and 1944, the revolt of the
corn belt in 1948 swung the region back into the Democratic column.
Broadly stated, the West North Central section has been far more
variable in its party support and electoral behavior in recent years
than New England, the Middle Atlantic, or the East North Central
sections. For example, in North Dakota we find a variation in party
support ranging from 18.9 percent Democratic (1920) to 71.3 percent
Democratic (1936) of the two-party vote.

The greatest Democratic upsurge and the worst Republican decline in the country between 1944 and 1948 was reflected in this
region—the wheat belt, the corn belt, the farm belt in general—the
"green uprising" as Louis Bean so artfully phrases it. In 1944 the
Republicans carried Iowa, Kansas, Nebraska, North Dakota, South
Dakota and Wisconsin—six out of the eight states in the section—
while the Democrats won two—Minnesota and Missouri. In 1948 the
Republican ticket lost Iowa, Wisconsin, Minnesota and Missouri by
an overwhelming vote. Elsewhere the GOP dipped below its 1944
percentage in every other state of the section. For the most part the
impressive Democratic gains were confined to the rural areas, and
where the Democratic slice of the vote did increase in large cities of
a particular state, it was invariably a smaller gain than the percentage
increase for the state at large. This was true for every state in the
West North Central section with sizable cities.

In 1946 the Republicans scored a near-landslide in this region.
They carried every state, including traditionally Democratic Missouri. In 1950, however, the picture was considerably brighter for
the Democrats than it had been four years earlier. Although the Republicans made gains in Iowa, Minnesota, and Wisconsin, they were
unable to touch Missouri, where the GOP lost a Senator who had
been elected in the presidential year of 1944, and the Democrats
retained 9 of the 13 congressional seats—a remarkable off-year showing. In Minnesota, the Democrats held all of the congressional seats
they won in 1948, including the 6th district, which had been repre-

sented by the GOP Congressman Harold Knutson from 1916 to 1948. Strong also for a non-presidential election was the Democratic showing in Kansas and Nebraska. Interestingly enough, the GOP fared better in Maryland in 1950 than in Nebraska.

THE CRITICAL MARGINAL DISTRICTS OF THE WEST NORTH CENTRAL STATES

MAP 14

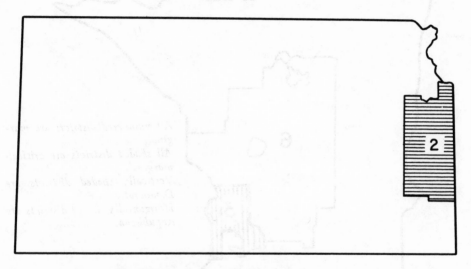

All numbered districts are marginal.
All shaded districts are critical-marginal.
Vertically shaded districts are Democratic.
Horizontally shaded districts are Republican.

Kansas: 1 critical marginal district
    2nd dist. R—Extends from Kansas City South along the Eastern border

Republican E. P. Scrivner is the incumbent in this 2nd district. The GOP has held onto this district ever since 1942, but by ever-decreasing majorities. Scrivner won in 1950 by just 52 percent of the vote, while in the early 1940's the GOP margin was as high as 59 percent. The spreading strength of the Democratic vote in Kansas City seems to be spilling over into this district and jeopardizing GOP control. The 2nd was the only district in Kansas that Truman carried

in 1948. It has a larger industrial area than any other part of the
state, with the possible exception of the 4th district.

MAP 15

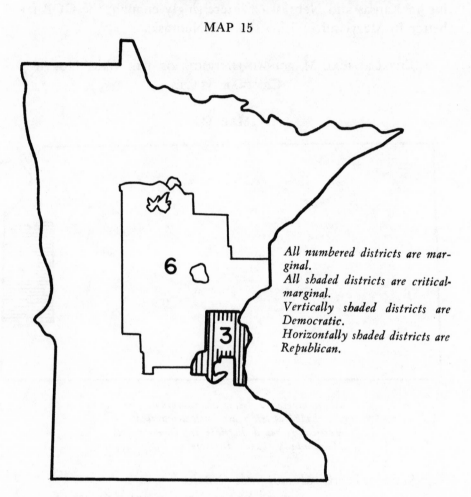

All numbered districts are mar-
ginal.
All shaded districts are critical-
marginal.
Vertically shaded districts are
Democratic.
Horizontally shaded districts are
Republican.

Minnesota: 1 critical marginal district
  3rd dist. D—A district extending from Minneapolis into
    surrounding suburban areas

In the 3rd district R. W. Weir, Democrat-Farmer Labor, defeated the Republican incumbent in 1948 and was re-elected in 1950,
by 51.8 percent of the vote. Since 1942 the Democrats have held
the district four times and the Republicans once. Generally speaking it is an urban constituency adjoined by a large rural appendage.

MAP 16

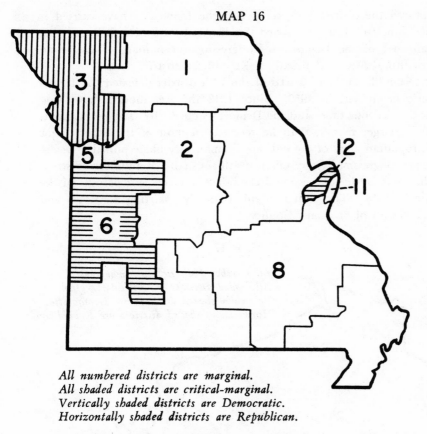

All numbered districts are marginal.
All shaded districts are critical-marginal.
Vertically shaded districts are Democratic.
Horizontally shaded districts are Republican.

Missouri: 3 critical marginal districts
   3rd dist. D—St. Joseph
   6th dist. R—An area lying South of Kansas City along
      the Kansas State border.
   12th dist. R—Located in St. Louis City and St. Louis
      County

Democrat P. J. Welch defeated the Republican incumbent in
the 3rd district in 1948 and was re-elected in 1950. Truman carried
the district with 59 percent of the vote in 1948, and Congressman
Welch received 58.8 percent. Since 1942 the Democrats won the
district twice and the Republicans three times. The district encases
a rich agricultural area and the northern suburbs of Kansas City,
together with St. Joseph.

In the 6th district Republican O. K. Armstrong defeated the
Democratic incumbent in 1950. Since 1942 the Republicans have

captured the district four times and the Democrats have carried it
once. In 1948 Truman carried the district by a 3 percent larger vote
than that of the Democratic congressional candidate. This is an
agricultural area and usually a Republican district.

Republican T. B. Curtis of the 12th district defeated the Democratic incumbent in 1950. Since 1942 the Republicans have won
the district four times and the Democrats once. By carrying St. Louis
with a larger margin than he received in most of the other major
metropolitan areas of the nation, Truman very likely pulled a Democratic congressman into office in this usually Republican district.
The Democratic congressional candidate received 55.2 percent of the
vote in 1948. The 12th is a suburban area skirting St. Louis and
includes all of St. Louis County.

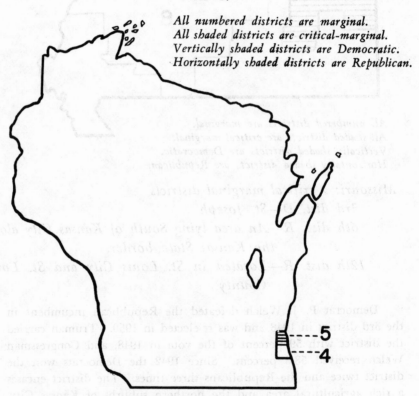

MAP 17

All numbered districts are marginal.
All shaded districts are critical-marginal.
Vertically shaded districts are Democratic.
Horizontally shaded districts are Republican.

Wisconsin: 1 critical marginal district
5th dist R—The Northern part of Milwaukee City and
Milwaukee County

In the 5th district Republican C. J. Kersten defeated the Democratic incumbent in 1950. This constituency presents a striking example of an intimate relation between the presidential and congressional vote. In 1944 both the congressional Republican and presidential candidates received 41 percent of the vote, while in 1948 they obtained 43 percent. But in the off-presidential year—1946—the Republican candidates harvested 55 percent of the vote. Two years later, however, the heavy Milwaukee vote for Truman leads one to conclude that the President was responsible for bringing in two Democratic congressmen in the Milwaukee Area. Since 1942 Republicans have won the 5th congressional seat twice, and the Democrats three times.

THE SOUTH

The "unity of the region the South" writes V. O. Key, "has been greatly exaggerated in the national mind."[13] Yet despite its "variety, its nuances," and its subtleties that "range across the political spectrum," the South for all of its internal modulations has favored a one-party system since the 1870's and 1880's more than any other part of the country.

Since Reconstruction the area slipped into the GOP presidential column just once—1928. In that debacle—an election that even some Dixiecrats would like to festoon with crepe—Herbert Hoover won a popular and electoral majority in the section, carrying Florida, Kentucky, North Carolina, Oklahoma, Tennessee, Texas, and Virginia. Even in the Harding lunge toward "normalcy" in 1920 when the GOP ticket polled more than 60 percent of the popular vote, only two of these thirteen states—Oklahoma and Tennessee—wound up in the Republican ledger.

Throughout the depression decade and on through 1944 Democratic support in the region was continuous and overwhelming. At the moment GOP representatives hold seats in but three of these states—Kentucky (two out of nine); Oklahoma (two out of eight); and Tennessee (two out of ten). Moreover, except for three other

---

[13]V. O. Key; *Southern Politics* (New York: A. A. Knopf, 1949), p. ix.

states—North Carolina, Texas, and Virginia—where the Republicans have held seats not presently occupied, the GOP has never since the days of Reconstruction made a successful trespass in congressional elections.

Post World War II developments that probably began in 1938 make it unsafe to assume that the traditional solidity of the South in national elections will continue. Certainly the 1948 loss of 39 electoral votes by the Democratic party in this section, accompanied by a brisk Republican vote in Virginia and Florida, suggests that some splintering forces are at work that may bring about gradual change in the political behavior of this region.[14]

Taking a deep look at Dixie in his brilliantly conceived study, *A Two Party South?*, Alexander Heard, of the University of North Carolina, assesses the prospects and concludes that "there can be little doubt that much of the South is moving closer to competitive party politics." In the long run, he writes,

> . . . Southern conservatives will find in neither a separatist group nor in the Democratic party an adequate vehicle of political expression. If this is true they must turn to the Republican party . . .
>
> The development in the South of an urban middle class—in accord with the Holcombe thesis for the nation—susceptible to the blandishments of both a liberal and conservative party, would give the Republican party a potential source of votes in those states where it could achieve some kind of competitive equality.[15]

Not unnaturally it is on the fringes of the South—at its northern-most and southern extremities—that faster political changes may be in the making. In Florida, Pinellas County has increased its Republican vote to the point where some observers believe the election of a GOP congressman for the congressional district is possible in 1952. And at the northern extremity—Oklahoma—the GOP near-

---

[14]Dewey won 37.0 percent of the vote in Houston in 1948, while Truman received 47.1 percent. Since Dewey's 1944 percentage was 14.7 his 1948 vote represents a gain of 22.3 percent in four years.

[15]University of North Carolina Press, Chapel Hill, 1951, Pp. 247-48.

miss for the governorship in 1950 and the recapture of two congressional districts in a vote that was extraordinarily large for an off-year, may be indicative of peripheral political changes for the South. Whatever its course, however, the South is a region in transition, and amidst the flotsam of social and economic readjustments the politics of the region are hardly likely to remain unaffected.

The Critical Marginal Districts of the South

Only at the extreme midwestern perimeter of this section are there districts of a marginal character. Elsewhere, the districts held by both Democrats and Republicans are predominantly under the control of one party or the other.

MAP 18

All numbered districts are marginal.
All shaded districts are critical-marginal.
Vertically shaded districts are Democratic.
Horizontally shaded districts are Republican.

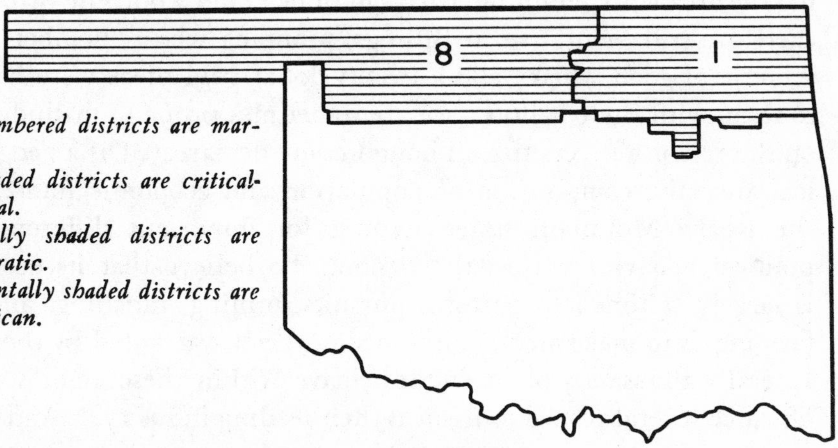

Oklahoma: 2 critical marginal districts
        1st dist. R—Tulsa
        8th dist. R—Enid, panhandle district

In Oklahoma's 1st, Republican G. B. Schwabe (died in 1952) defeated the Democratic incumbent. Since 1942 the district has gone Republican three times and Democratic twice. Agriculture and industry play an almost equal role in the economy of this district, with one of the major sources of revenue being oil. Tulsa also has a large Negro population. As an interesting aside it might be remarked that this constituency contains Indian Reservations. Since Truman's victory here in 1948 marked the first time a Democratic presidential

nominee carried the district since 1936, one can assert with a fair
degree of authority that the congressional candidate was boosted into
office by the presidential vote.

In the 8th district Republican Page Belcher defeated the Democratic incumbent in 1950. This constituency has gone Republican
four times since 1942, and Democratic once. In 1948 it was the only
district in Oklahoma that Truman failed to carry. Though Mr.
Truman lost in this district in 1948, however, a Democratic congressman was elected by a comfortable majority. Primarily a wheat-
producing district, the 18th district is the most consistently Republican constituency in Oklahoma.

THE MOUNTAIN REGION

The Mountain states often conjure a mixture of recklessly conceived notions about their politics. Accustomed as we are to associat-
ing the area with gambling, barroom brawls, and wholesale bribery—
there are still men alive in Billings, Montana who remember when
a bottle of good whisky and a twenty-dollar gold piece were handed
to them with their ballots—we are sometimes prone to misjudgment
on the region's diversities. Though easily demarcated as a geographical area, the composition of population and economic interests in
the Rocky Mountain states account for important differences in
political behavior within the region. To believe that its economy
is largely confined to pastoral pursuits, mining, ranching, and dry
farming, is to make an assumption simply not warranted by the facts.
Literally thousands of businesses thrive within these eight states—
of which several regard tourism as their leading industry.[16] And while
the area's economy tends toward greater diversity, it should also be
noted that certain cultural carryovers of the past contribute to differences in attitude within the region. New Mexico, for example, is the
only state in the Union where ballots are printed in both English
and Spanish to accommodate a sizeable Spanish-speaking population.

Spreading out the full picture of ballot behavior in the Mountain
states we find that these states show perhaps the most extreme variations of any in the nation. In 1896, when the Populists and Demo-

---

[16]Thomas C. Donnelly: *Rocky Mountain Politics* (University of New
Mexico Press, Albuquerque, 1940), p. 7.

crats united behind the North Platte Orator, the result was the largest majority any party ever received, nor has this record ever been touched subsequently. Yet the dimensions of the landslides of 1904 and 1920, when the Mountain states spun back abruptly into the Republican column, afford impressive evidence of the variability of this region. In 1916, for example, the Democrats won 60 percent of the two-party vote in the Mountain states, while in 1920 this percentage skidded down to 38 percent.

Since the New Deal sweeps in the depths of the depression some of the Mountain states have nudged back toward the Republican line. Thus, in 1940 Willkie carried Colorado, while in 1944 the total popular vote of the Republican and Democratic presidential nominees in this section came close to being a draw. Yet notwithstanding the close overall vote, Dewey carried just two Mountain States—Colorado and Wyoming—both, by the way, the meeting place of the true West and the prairies of the Middlewest. Conforming with their major 1948 upset in the adjacent West North Central States, the Republicans also lost Colorado and Wyoming in the latter year.

Some improvement in GOP fortunes in the Mountain states is indicated as we look further West in the region. In New Mexico, Colorado, Eastern Montana, and Wyoming, Republican losses were very heavy in 1944, while in Idaho and Western Montana, the GOP vote showed a slight gain. But in the westernmost bracket of Mountain states—Nevada, Utah, and Arizona—the upturn in the GOP vote reflected substantial gains, not the least of which was the election of the first Republican governor in the region in ten years.

Republicans fared well in 1946 in the Mountain states, and probably even better in 1950—a circumstance not generally true for any other section of the country. GOP Senate seats were wrested from Democrats in Idaho, Montana, Nevada, and Utah, and sweeping gains were made in terms of congressional seats. Republican Senate seats were won in Idaho and Utah in 1950, and GOP governorships were battened down for the first time since 1928 in Arizona and New Mexico; Nevada for the first time since 1930; Wyoming for the first time since 1938; and Colorado for the first time since 1944. Thus while the Republicans held two of the eight governorships in this region in 1946—Idaho and Montana—in 1950 they occupied seven of eight gubernatorial chairs. Only in Montana where a GOP chief executive had been lost in the Democratic tide of 1948, were the Republicans without a governor in the Mountain states.

THE CRITICAL MARGINAL DISTRICTS OF THE MOUNTAIN REGION

As we might anticipate from the very wide swings in party support, there are a number of critical marginal districts among the Mountain states. Fully half of them—Colorado, Idaho, Nevada, and Utah—contain critical marginal districts.

MAP 19

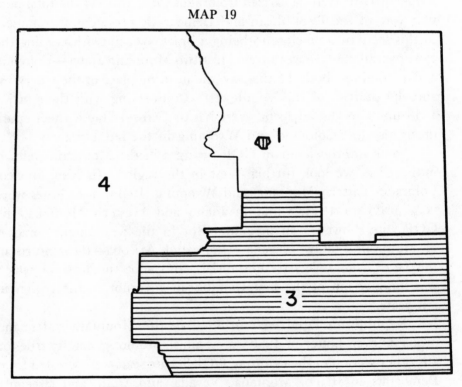

All numbered districts are marginal.
All shaded districts are critical-marginal.
Vertically shaded districts are Democratic.
Horizontally shaded districts are Republican.

Colorado: 2 critical marginal districts
1st dist. D—Denver municipal area
3rd dist. R—Pueblo

Democrat B. C. Rogers of Colorado's 1st district succeeded Democrat J. A. Carroll in 1950. This has been a closely contested district, and it was carried by Truman in 1948. Since 1942 the Democrats have carried the district four times, while the Republicans have held it only once.

Republican J. E. Chenoweth of the 3rd district defeated the Democratic incumbent in 1950. This constituency has gone Democratic once, and Republican four times, since 1942. It covers the southeastern corner of Colorado, includes a large Mexican population, and is an agricultural area. There seems no reason to doubt that in 1948 Truman carried in the Democratic congressional candidate.

MAP 20

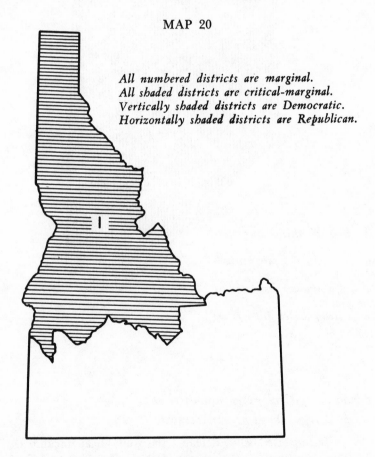

All numbered districts are marginal.
All shaded districts are critical-marginal.
Vertically shaded districts are Democratic.
Horizontally shaded districts are Republican.

Idaho: 1 critical marginal district
1st dist. R—Northern half of the state, or panhandle region

Since 1942 this district has been Democratic three times and Republican twice. Subsequent to 1932 the Democrats have always carried the district in presidential years, the only Republican victories coming in the midterm elections of 1946 and 1950 when the GOP candidate skimmed through with narrow margins.

MAP 21

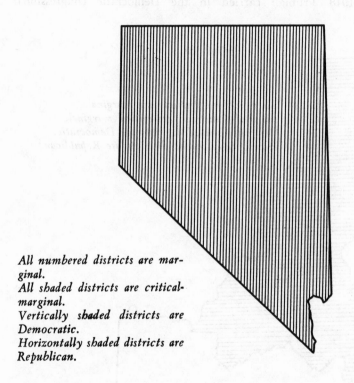

All numbered districts are marginal.
All shaded districts are critical-marginal.
Vertically shaded districts are Democratic.
Horizontally shaded districts are Republican.

Nevada: 1 critical marginal district
At Large D—The entire state

W. S. Baring, Democrat, defeated the Republican incumbent in 1948. The Democratic congressional candidate received 50.6 percent of the vote, while Mr. Truman carried the state by 51.6 percent of the vote. In 1950 Baring made a better showing than he did in 1948.

MAP 22

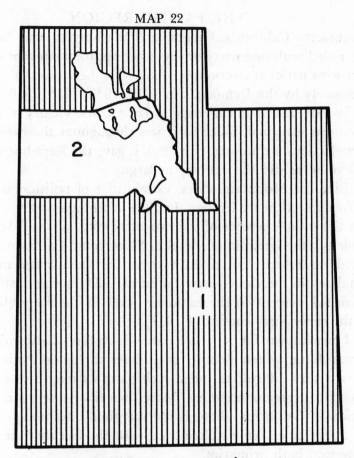

All numbered districts are marginal.
All shaded districts are critical-marginal.
Vertically shaded districts are Democratic.
Horizontally shaded districts are Republican.

Utah: 1 critical marginal district
    1st dist. D—The entire area of Utah outside of Salt Lake
        City and surrounding area

W. K. Granger, Democrat, incumbent for the last ten years, has averaged about 51 percent of the vote in the off-presidential election years, whereas in presidential years he has won an average that ranges from 56 to 59 percent. Presumably that is another significant instance where a strong national party candidacy has a positive influence on the fortunes of the local congressional candidates. Since 1942 the district has never been carried by the Republican party.

THE PACIFIC REGION

Embracing California, Oregon, and Washington, the Pacific states have rolled with one party or the other approximately as one or the other wins national elections. Along with the nation, it was carried handsomely by the Democrats in 1912, 1932, 1936, 1940, and 1944. But in 1916 and 1948 the scope of Democratic victory in the Pacific region was marginal, much as it was throughout the nation. In all other elections, beginning with 1896, it gave the Republicans its electoral votes, as did the country at large.

Like the Mountain states, variabilities of political behavior in the Pacific section are legion. In 1904 Washington gave the Republican ticket 78.3 percent of the two-party vote, yet in 1936 the GOP vote fell to the ignominious level of 31 percent. California has given as little as 8.4 percent of its vote to the Democratic presidential candidate (in the three-party contest of 1924, and an insulting decimal of 0.7 percent to the national ticket of the Republican Party (in the three-party contest of 1912).

Long known for its loose party discipline, California's system of cross filing which permits candidates to file in both primaries makes it very difficult to judge each party's strength in any district with a fair degree of accuracy. More than likely there are additional districts in California (besides the marginal ones noted) where the vote might be extremely close except for the fact that the same candidate won both primaries.

The Republicans found the years 1946 and 1950 to their liking in the Pacific states, with 1946 perhaps the better of the two. At this midterm election the GOP retained a Senate seat in California while taking one from the Democrats in normally Democratic Washington. Republican efforts to unhorse Senator Magnuson (Democrat) of Washington in 1950, however, were of no avail. California's Governor Warren, while not winning both Republican and Democratic nominations in 1950 as he did in 1946, nonetheless won re-election by a blockbuster majority of one million votes. But equally impressive, if not more so, was Senator Morse's (Republican) 1950 re-election bid in Oregon where he snaffled more than three-quarters of the two-party vote, a figure far outstripping recent Republican records in Oregon.

THE CRITICAL MARGINAL DISTRICTS OF THE PACIFIC STATES

MAP 23

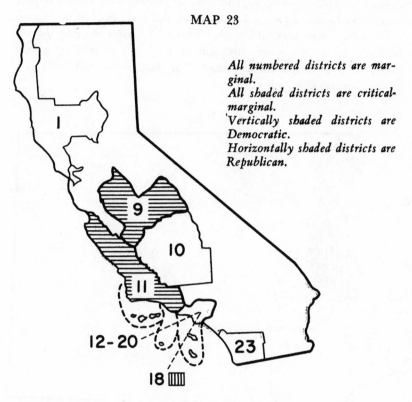

All numbered districts are mar-
ginal.
All shaded districts are critical-
marginal.
Vertically shaded districts are
Democratic.
Horizontally shaded districts are
Republican.

California: 3 critical marginal districts
    9th dist. R—Fresno, Central Valley
    11th dist. R—The Coastal area north of Los Angeles
    18th dist. D—The Los Angeles suburban district

Republican A. O. Hunter of the 9th district defeated Democratic incumbent C. F. White in 1950 by a margin of 2 percent.
Broadly speaking, this district is usually carried by the Democratic
presidential nominee in presidential elections. Since 1940 the 9th has
been Republican five times and Democratic once. Truman's 57 percent of the popular vote in 1948 undoubtedly was a material factor
in electing a Democratic congressman by a vote of 52 percent. Agriculture is a major industry in the economy of this district.

In the 11th California district, E. K. Bramblett, Republican,
defeated the Democratic incumbent in 1946. Dewey carried the district by 2 percent in 1948. Since 1942 the Republicans have won the

district three times, and the Democrats twice. This constituency
combines several wealthy agricultural districts with certain important coastal towns between Los Angeles and San Francisco.

C. Doyle, Democrat, of the 18th district defeated the Republican
incumbent in 1948. Since 1942 the district has gone Republican
twice, and Democratic three times. The 18th is located in a Los
Angeles suburban area.

MAP 24

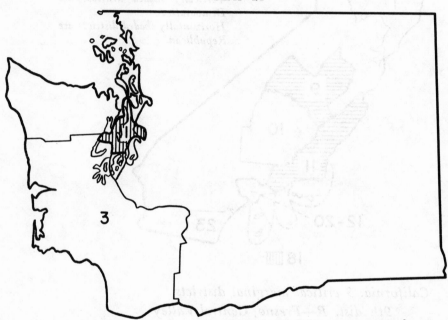

All numbered districts are marginal.
All shaded districts are critical-marginal.
Vertically shaded districts are Democratic.
Horizontally shaded districts are Republican.

Washington: 1 critical marginal district
1st dist. D—Seattle, Bremerton area

Democrat H. D. Mitchell of the 1st district defeated the Republican incumbent in 1948. In districts 1, 2, and 6, the general
Bremerton, Seattle, Tacoma area, the Republican vote declined approximately 10 percent between the midterm election of 1946 and
the presidential election in 1948. Truman won 55 percent of the
major party vote in this district in 1948, a sufficiently powerful vote,
apparently, to pull the Democratic congressional candidate into port

MAP 25:

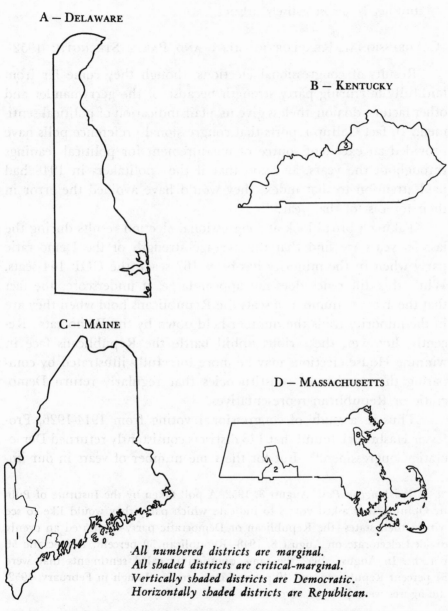

A – DELAWARE

B – KENTUCKY

C – MAINE

D – MASSACHUSETTS

All numbered districts are marginal.
All shaded districts are critical-marginal.
Vertically shaded districts are Democratic.
Horizontally shaded districts are Republican.

Not included in our regional political travelogue are 8 states that contain marginal congressional districts, but have no constituencies that fall into the critical marginal category. The marginal districts in these states are located in maps 25 and 26 pictured on pages 73 and 75.

by a margin of 52.7. Since 1942 the Republicans have captured the district once, while the Democrats have won it four times. This constituency is almost entirely urban.

CONGRESSIONAL REAPPORTIONMENT AND PARTY STRENGTH: 1952

Results of congressional elections, though they come far from faithfully mirroring party strength because of the gerrymander and other factors, do nonetheless give us a fair indication of political sentiment. In fact Gallup reports that congressional preference polls have provided an excellent source of measurement for political leanings throughout the years, and says that if the "polltakers in 1948 had paid attention to that index, they would have avoided the error in their forecast of that year."[17]

Taking a broad look at congressional election results during the last 56 years we find that the average strength of the Democratic party when in the minority has been 167 seats; the GOP 164 seats. While this difference does not appear large, it underscores the fact that the average number of seats the Republicans hold when they are in the minority trails the number held down by the Democrats. Recently, however, the serious uphill battle the Republicans face in winning House elections may be more forcefully illustrated by comparing the number of constituencies that regularly return Democratic or Republican representatives.

Thus in a study of congressional voting from 1914-1926, Professor Hasbrouck found that 148 districts consistently returned Democratic Congressmen.[18] But for the same number of years in our im-

---

[17]*Washington Post*, August 8, 1952. A poll taken by the Institute of Public Opinion that asked voters to indicate which party they would like to see win in their states—the Republican or Democratic party—indicated an evenly divided electorate on August 8, 1948—Republican 50 percent, Democratic 50 percent. In August, 1952 the same question revealed sentiments that were 51 percent Republican and 49 percent Democratic, though in February, 1952, the figures were just the reverse.

[18]P. D. Hasbrouck: *Party Government in the House of Representatives* (New York: Macmillan, 1927), p. 172. Congressional redistricting in the latter period covering 1938-1950 makes it impossible to give a precise answer on the number of consistently Democratic or Republican constituencies. The

MAP 26:

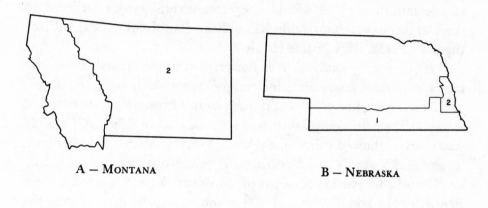

A – Montana   B – Nebraska

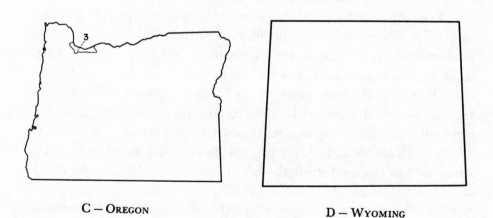

C – Oregon   D – Wyoming

All numbered districts are marginal.
All shaded districts are critical-marginal.
Vertically shaded districts are Democratic.
Horizontally shaded districts are Republican.

mediate study (twelve—1938-1950) we find that approximately 122 districts are consistently Republican and 169 Democratic (see Appendix). What these latter figures indicate, of course, is that the Democrats have a relatively large number of districts on which they can count in times of adversity, while the Republicans can depend on a much smaller number of seats at such times. For example, the Republican congressional contingent was reduced to a mere 89 seats in the landslide of 1936, but the most severe setback suffered by the Democrats in comparable Republican landslides (1920) still left them with 132 seats in the House.

Redistricting and Political Power. An unascertainable and certainly important factor affecting congressional elections, is the degree of change wrought by the reapportionment of congressional seats and electoral votes in compliance with the Census of 1950. Of the 48 states, seven showed gains (California, Florida, Maryland, Michigan, Texas, and Virginia and Washington), while nine lost seats (Arkansas, Illinois, Kentucky, Mississippi, Missouri, New York, Oklahoma, Pennsylvania, and Tennessee). Foremost among the gainers were the sun-kissed competitors—California with seven and Florida with two—while the chief losers were Pennsylvania, losing three, and Missouri, New York, and Oklahoma, each of which lost two.

Looking initially at the direction of long term trends in internal migration before weighing the immediate political effects of reapportionment, three important observations may be made. First, since 1912 the coastal areas of the country show an appreciable gain —35—in electoral votes, particularly in the Southern and Western regions, while simultaneously there has been a dramatic reduction of electoral votes in the agricultural heart of the nation—the Middle West. In all the Middle West has lost 26 electoral votes since 1912. Also down in electoral strength—by 10 votes—since 1912, is the older

---

figures cited, however, are reasonably accurate. Hasbrouck's task in determining the number of consistently Democratic and Republican districts in an earlier period was made easier by the fact that there was no redistricting during the years on which he based his study. For 1952, Republican experts were claiming 178 seats as safely Republican, and conceding 160 as safely Democratic. See *Baltimore Sun*, Aug. 19, 1952.

industrialized area of the Northeast and New England (partly offset by New Jersey's gain of two since 1912).

A second unmistakable directional trend of internal migration has been the decisive movement toward urbanization—a movement which is slowly being reflected by an increase in congressional apportionment for urban centers, and particularly in the suburban areas surrounding our cities. Missouri, for example, shows this trend very clearly in her latest redistricting (still being contested). Losing two seats under the 1950 Census, Missouri wiped out two rural districts and reapportioned them as mixed urban-rural districts, while preserving intact the established congressional representation of her two great metropolitan areas, St. Louis and Kansas City. Thus with one quarter of the population of the nation now concentrated in twelve centers that the Census Bureau designates as "urbanized areas," the impact of this shift is gradually being reflected in an increased urban congressional representation. Table VII below, which has been taken from the Gallup Political Almanac, reflects this change in the number of urban and mixed urban-rural districts.

TABLE VII[19]

DISTRIBUTION OF SEATS BY PARTY BY TYPE OF AREA
HOUSE OF REPRESENTATIVES

Districts	1950	1948	1946	1944
Northern Big City Districts Seats held by:				
Democrats	64	74	41	70
Republicans	30	20	52	23
Others	1	1	1	1
	95	95	94	94
Northern Rural Districts Seats held by:				
Democrats	25	29	15	23
Republicans	59	55	71	62
Others	....	....	....	1
	84	84	86	86

TABLE VII[19] (Continued)

DISTRIBUTION OF SEATS BY PARTY BY TYPE OF AREA
HOUSE OF REPRESENTATIVES

Districts	1950	1948	1946	1944
Northern Mixed Districts				
Seats held by:				
Democrats	30	42	17	33
Republicans	104	92	116	100
Others	....	....	....	....
	134	134	133	133
South				
Seats held by:				
Democrats	116	118	115	117
Republicans	6	4	7	5
Others	....	....	....	....
	122	122	122	122

A third and final observation to be made on internal migration as it affects the balance of political power in the nation, is the shift in electoral votes away from the so-called "safe" states whether of Democratic or Republican faith, to the new "doubtful" states and sections—regions where the rivalry between parties is so close that neither party can claim them as safe territory. As Professors Hinderaker and Farrelly demonstrate, this movement has led to an increase of fourteen electoral votes in the new doubtful states and has accounted for a corresponding decline in the number of states that can be counted upon to be consistently in one party column or the other.[20] Pre-eminent as an example of a doubtful state is California. Since the Civil War, presidential elections have been decided by 250 votes or less three times in California, and by less than 7,000, four times. And its Democratic average of the two-party vote of 49.1 percent in this century makes it very likely the most doubtful

---

[19]*The Gallup Political Almanac* (Garden City, 1952), p. 66.

[20]"Congressional Reapportionment and Political Power," *Law and Contemporary Problems*, 17 (1952), pp. 349-351.

state in the nation—a mighty important prize, one might hasten to add, with its current bag of 32 electoral votes.

Summating the factors of internal migration for the past half-century, then, it may be said that they point to the growth of the doubtful political areas at the expense of the more solidly partisan regions as people drift from the traditional politics of their birth-places to urban centers and mixed urban-rural, industrial and residential districts. Thus, in response to the large influx of people of divergent backgrounds, the political spectrum of America has become represented in some of these areas and politically they have tended to become fluid and "doubtful" in their behavior. Not at all surprising, therefore, is the fact that 30 of the 46 critical-marginal congressional districts we have identified are located in urban or mixed urban-rural areas.

Reapportionment and the Immediate Prospects. In the long run the growing urbanization, accompanied by an increased congressional representation, would appear to favor the Democratic party if metropolitan voting behavior continues to follow the pattern of the past thirty years. Factors that may affect this tendency will be discussed in a later chapter, but at this point it may be in order to look at the more immediate consequences of the recent reapportionment.

Looking at the short-term view, some slight advantage may have accrued to the Republican party as a result of the reapportionment of 1951. States with Democratic governors and legislatures controlled the redrawing of 75 congressional district boundaries, while 103 congressional districts have been recarved in states where Republicans are in full command. Fifty-three districts are in states where neither party is in complete control.[21]

---

[21]Looking at five elections under the reapportionment after the 1940 Census (1942, 1944, 1946, 1948, and 1950) one writer reports that only 114 of 435 House seats "ever switched from one party to another." In other words before any general election vote was cast in the last decade the fate of 321 seats had already been decided by tradition and by state legislatures. Chalmers Roberts: "The Donkey, the Elephant, and the Gerrymander." *The Reporter,* 7 (September 16, 1952), p. 33.

It would be uncharitable, of course, to assume that partisan bias necessarily leads to use of the gerrymander with reckless abandon. Yet as realists we know that legislatures are not indifferent to partisan advantage when the task of reapportionment lies before them. In Pennsylvania, for example, which lost three seats, the GOP legislature has labored to make Democratic areas absorb as much of the loss as possible. And in New York City where two seats were lost, a Republican legislature saw to it that the two seats which the state lost as a whole were actually squeezed out of the overwhelmingly Democratic borough of Brooklyn.

Looking elsewhere, the Democratic legislature in Tennessee did not saw up the Republican section of this state, but absorbed the loss of one congressional seat by doing away with the old fourth district—a Democratic district. And in Oklahoma where the Republicans have probably lost a seat, the Democrats appear likely to lose one also, so no real change will result here. In the Democratic bailiwicks of Arkansas and Mississippi the loss of seats obviously is to the disadvantage of the Democrats, and in the new districts of Maryland and Virginia, though carved by Democratic legislatures, GOP congressional candidates seem to have a modest chance. Finally in assessing the spectacular gain of California with seven new seats, the prospects would seem to indicate a Republican edge in at least two of the seven new districts, and possibly four, and in the judgment of one observer who had the research direction of the redistricting, "the rearrangement of boundary lines in two existing districts might make it more possible for Republicans to defeat Democratic incumbents.[22] All in all, for the very short run, the 1951 reapportionment might give the Republicans an additional six seats, though as in all things political this gain is far from a certainty. But in the long pull with a growing urbanization and increase in urban congressional seats, unless the GOP can win new converts in the cities a further loss of Republican seats is probable.

Leaving aside the conjectural and returning to our major purpose—a study of the interaction of presidential-congressional voting,

---

[22]David G. Farrelly and Ivan Hinderaker: "Congressional Reapportionment and Political Power," *loc. cit.,* p. 354.

our next task is to select representative examples of the three types of congressional districts which we shall designate and to examine the voting behavior of each in detail. We may begin by looking first at the strictly one-party districts.

CHAPTER 4

Coattail Chasing

T HE TRUE MEASURE of the presidential nominee's coattail influence on congressional elections is befogged by several factors. Among them are divergencies in policy between the presidential and congressional candidates, personality differences, factional structures peculiar to given locales that induce the voter to cut one candidate or the other on the same ticket, differences in the size of the vote cast for the respective candidates, the total turnout, and a variety of other elements.

Notwithstanding the forces that combine to produce variations in presidential-congressional voting within the same party and to make difficult any judgment on the effect of the presidential on the congressional vote, we do find a definite parallelism in the presidential and congressional vote. This gross parallelism, moreover, is more strikingly evident when strong political tides surge across the nation. For this reason the presidential and congressional vote should be considered as a unit. Broadly conceptualized the dual, or parallel, movement of the presidential-congressional vote might be likened to a double-decked roller coaster ascending and descending the inclines, slopes, or sharp drops and climbs of its course.

Aware of the interlocking character of voting preferences, not a few congressional candidates yearn to hitch on to the coattails of a presidential nominee who appears to be equipped with an over-drive and bids fair to outdistance the field in popular appeal. Quite aside from sectionalism, for example (See Table VIII) it is no mere coincidence that the preponderant majority of Republican congress-men from the 60 marginal districts supported General Eisenhower in the pre-convention capers of 1952 (See Table IX). Table IX indicates that of the GOP congressmen from the marginal dis-tricts, 50 percent were publicly committed to presidential candidates, and 58 percent if the probable commitments are counted. If Eisen-hower is credited with all of the congressional supporters presumed to have favored his candidacy but not publicly committed, his total backing among the Republican marginal districts was approximately 63-69 percent, while Taft's was 17-20 percent. When the doubtful congressmen are put in Taft's column, Eisenhower still had 54-63 percent of the GOP congressmen from the marginal districts in his

TABLE VIII

REGIONAL AND CANDIDATE BREAKDOWN IN CONGRESSIONAL POLL—1952

Region	Eisenhower	Taft	Warren	Total Committed	Total Marginal
New England	3	—	—	3	4
Mid. Atlantic	8 [9]	1		9 [10]	15
E. N. Central	3 [4]	1	—	4. [5]	21
W. N. Central	3 [4]	2	—	5 [6]	6
Mountain	[2]	2		2 [4]	4
South	1	—	—	1	3
Pacific	1	—	5	6	7
TOTALS	*19 [24]*	*6*	*5*	*30 [35]*	*60*

Legend: The brackets indicate probable commitments. If the figures 8 [9] appear, this means 8 and probably 9 were committed to the presiden-tial candidate at the head of the column.

camp, and Taft had only 20-31 percent. Quite obviously, then Republican congressmen from marginal districts tended to favor General Eisenhower as the party nominee for President in 1952, firm in the belief that Ike's coattails would provide a surer ride to victory than the coattails of other Republican hopefuls.

Clearly, then, the possible effect of the presidential candidate's

TABLE IX

REPUBLICAN MARGINAL CONGRESSIONAL DISTRICTS COMMITTED BY CANDIDATES, 1952

State	Eisenhower	Taft	Warren	Total Marginal Districts
California	—	—	5 (10,16,1,9,11)	5
Colorado	—	—	1 (3)	1
Connecticut	1 (2)	—	—	2
Delaware	1 (A.L.)	—	—	1
Idaho	—	1 (1)	—	1
Illinois	not committed			6
Indiana	3 (6,7,11) 10	—	—	6
Kansas	1 (2)	—	—	1
Kentucky	1 (3)	—	—	1
Maine	1 (1)	—	—	1
Maryland	not committed			1
Massachusetts	1 (8)	—	—	1
Michigan	—	1 (17)	—	2
Missouri	2 (6,11)	1 (12)	—	3
Montana	2	—	—	1
Nebraska	1	1 (2)	—	2
New Jersey	1 (12)	—	—	2
New York	1 (35) 44	1 (27)	1	5
Ohio	—	—	—	5
Oklahoma	not committed			2
Oregon	1 (3)	—	—	1
Pennsylvania	5 (3,6,23,26,29)	—	—	6
Washington	not committed			1
Wisconsin	not committed			2
Wyoming (A.L.)	—	—	—	1
TOTALS	19 (24)	5	7	60

Legend: The parentheses indicate the identity of the marginal districts; the brackets indicate probable commitments. A.L. means At Large. This information was compiled on the basis of 2 private congressional polls conducted by Representative Hugh Scott, Jr., of Pennsylvania and Representative Walter Norblad of Oregon in April, 1952.

popularity looms large for the congressmen from the tight districts. But conceding the compelling nature of the motivations that may guide the marginal district congressman's ideas on presidential nominees, the possible effect of the presidential candidate's popularity on the congressional vote in the non-marginal districts must not be minimized. The reason is that the presidential candidate symbolizes the hopes and aspirations not only of his party's followers, but, additionally, the desires and expectations of several million independent voters. Potentially at least he may create in the popular mind the image of Theodore Roosevelt's ideal and be "peculiarly representative of the people as a whole." No single congressional candidate has such an opportunity of symbolizing the hopes and aspirations of the entire party's electorate along with the necessary complement of independent voters to make a winning combination.

It would be doing disservice to the facts, however, to overcapitalize the potential influence of the presidential nominee's coattail. In many instances, some of which we will presently examine, the congressional candidate leads the presidential nominee, and there are, of course, a liberal number of constituencies known as "safe" districts where congressional candidates have little to fear regardless of the power of the appeal of the presidential nominee.

Conversely, therefore, it is quite possible for the presidential candidate to have an adverse rather than uplifting effect upon the political fortunes of congressional candidates. In Iowa's sixth congressional district, for example, Representative Dolliver seems to run at least ten percent behind his normal voting percentage for midterm elections when he is teamed with a presidential candidate. Conceivably, then, there are situations where the presidential rather than the congressional candidate might be the coattail clutcher. In any case we do find constituencies where the presidential candidate definitely pulls down the vote of the congressional candidate. Yet in either setting—whether the presidential or congressional candidate leads at the ballot box—the votes of both move in parallel trends, that is to say, both move up or down together from election to election.

The parallel trends in presidential-congressional elections so characteristic of our national political behavior may be forcefully illustrated by grouping congressional districts into the following categories: the strictly one-party districts, the predominantly one-party districts, and, finally, the marginal districts. Such a tripartite grouping, of course, does not imply that all congressional districts fall into one of three categories. It is merely a convenient arrangement for analysis. Actually the congressional districts fall into a range that stretches from the one-party districts to the critical marginal districts. Moreover, there is a generous measure of overlapping between the three categories. The fact remains, however, that the three major groupings do exist, a circumstance that enables us to select examples from each to illustrate the parallelism of presidential-congressional voting behavior.

THE ONE-PARTY DISTRICT

The one-party districts may be roughly identified as those districts where one or the other of our major parties has no opposition in the biennial congressional elections. Strictly speaking, there are no Republican one-party districts. But the Democrats hold about twenty percent of the total 435 House seats as one-party districts. Democratic congressional candidates had no Republican opponents in 87 districts (almost exclusively in the South) in 1950 and no opposition in 63 districts during the 1948 presidential election—the Republicans normally fielding more House candidates in a presidential year.

The First District of Arkansas. To illustrate a strong Democratic one-party congressional district, the first district of Arkansas is suitable. Here in the northeast corner of the Wonder State not a single Republican has run for Congress since 1928. The same congressman—E. C. Gathings—has represented this district since 1938, a typical uninterrupted service stint that underscores the fact that party splits in the one-party congressional districts of the South are rare. Routinely, incumbents tend to remain in power over long periods of time, usually receiving their party's renomination at each successive congressional race. It is only in the primaries, it must be recalled, that incumbents are actually subject to an upset.

In summary, one-party congressional districts may be said to have the following characteristics: First, one of the two major parties in the United States is totally absent from congressional campaigns, and two-party competition is limited to presidential candidates during national campaigns. Second, one person normally homesteads these seats for many terms. Third, if there are intra-party struggles the real battles have already been resolved in the primary election. The factions in a one-party state, as V. O. Key reports in his *Southern Politics,* can be as partisan as the two-party electoral system throughout the rest of the United States. Nevertheless, the primary usually resolves factional fights, at least to the extent that while some hurts and stings linger on, independent candidacies are not often undertaken. Fourth, when splits that lead to the candidacy of an independent do occur within the party in power, it is rarely possible even under such circumstances for the minority party to file a candidate and win in a three-way contest. One of the rare exceptions occurred in the eighteenth district of Texas in 1950 when a Democratic subfactional scrap led to an independent candidacy in a special election and the third Republican congressman since the Civil War was elected.

In leaving this discussion of the strictly one-party congressional districts, the factors to be borne in mind as we proceed to trace the presidential-congressional parallelism in voting behavior are twofold: First, the presidential and congressional vote in the strictly one-party constituencies are closely related. Uniformly the congressional vote runs ahead of the presidential vote for the obvious reason that there is normally no opposition at the congressional level, whereas in the presidential contest we do find opposition though it is inconsequential. Second, the relationship of the congressional-presidential vote remains unimpaired no matter who the nominees may be at either level. Thus the relationship is consistent and can be shown to be essentially the same over time.

THE PREDOMINANTLY ONE-PARTY DISTRICTS

Standing midway between the strictly one-party districts and marginal districts are the constituents that are predominantly controlled by one of the two major parties. These districts differ from the strictly one-party areas in that the minority party almost always files a candidate and rarely permits an election to go by default. Typical of this group is the first district of Tennessee, the Kentucky ninth, Illinois thirteenth, Kansas first and fifth, Massachusetts fifth and sixth, Michigan seventh, Nebraska third and fourth, New York forty-fifth, Ohio tenth, Pennsylvania ninth, and the North Dakota and Vermont at Large districts.

The First District of Tennessee. Somewhat different from other predominantly one-party GOP districts because of the prevalence of independent candidacies, the first district of Tennessee nonetheless affords an interesting example of this type of constituency.

In 1942, 1944, 1946, and 1948, no Democratic congressional candidates entered the election lists, though more than 20,000 votes were cast for the Democratic presidential candidates in 1944 and 1948. Incumbent Congressman B. Carroll Reece, with two interruptions, has occupied this seat since March 4, 1921. Both breaks in his service were for two-year periods when the seat was held by other Republicans. In presidential election years such as 1944 and 1948, when no Democratic congressional candidate was entered, of course, the Republican percentage of the two-party presidential vote in Tennessee's first district is below the 100 percent mark of the congressional candidates. Though GOP presidential candidates sometimes receive 90 percent of the vote in the first district, their average normally ranges from 75 to 85 percent.

A split in the Republican ranks in this heavily Republican district, however, drops the frequent voting percentage mark of 100 abruptly. A case in point is the party fracture in this constituency in 1950. Following the schism each Republican faction launched candidates, one running on the GOP ticket, the other campaigning as an independent. Obviously in this case the Democrats were prompted to enter a candidate only because of a Republican family quarrel—enlivened by the fact that the Republican congressman who represented the district in the preceding Congress and who failed to win the nomination over Mr. Reece was the independent candidate. Thus the Democratic 1950 congressional vote rose from zero, where it had remained for ten years, to 18,260. And in this instance the Republican candidate polled less than half of the total vote with an independent and Democratic candidate pitted against him. Yet, even in this tri-cornered contest the GOP congressional nominee carried the election. Independent candidacies in most of the predominantly one party districts are not frequent occurrences, however, as they appear to be in the Tennessee first district.

A frequent characteristic of the predominantly one-party district is a wide disparity between the vote of the congressional candidate and his party's presidential nominee. Representative Dolliver's district—the sixth of Iowa—affords an excellent illustration of this type of bailiwick.

FIGURE 2

THE SIXTH CONGRESSIONAL DISTRICT OF IOWA

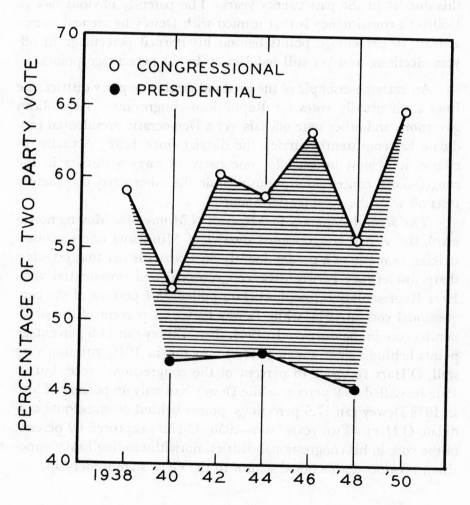

The Sixth Congressional District of Iowa. Looking closely at the graph in Figure 2 showing the congressional and presidential voting behavior of Iowa's sixth district, we shall observe that in 1944 Dolliver won 58.8 percent of the vote and in 1946 he scored 63.4 percent. But in 1948 Dolliver dropped back to 55.8 percent of the congressional vote, while presidential nominee Dewey trailed him lamely in this congressional district with only 45.5 percent of the presidential vote. Thus, Dewey's vote in this district was 10.4 less than Dolliver's in 1948, and 11 percent behind Dolliver's 1944 vote. Moreover, in 1950 Dolliver bounced back with a vote of 64.9 percent—the highest vote that any Republican congressional candidate has received in this district in the past twenty years. The patently obvious fact in Dolliver's constituency is that teamed with Dewey he seemed to run at least 10 percentage points behind his normal percentage in off-year elections, and yet still led Dewey by 10 percentage points.

An extreme example of the predominantly one-party district, the Iowa sixth usually votes for Republican congressmen, Republican governors, and other state officials, yet a Democratic presidential candidate has consistently carried the district since 1932. Actually, of course, it is most unusual for one party to carry a district in the congressional contest continuously while the other party consistently trots off with the presidential honors.

The Second Congressional District of Minnesota. Moving northward, the second congressional district of Minnesota offers another striking example of a predominantly one-party district that reveals a sharp discrepancy between the congressional and presidential vote. Here Representative Joseph O'Hara polled 75.7 percent of the congressional vote in 1944, while Dewey took 61.1 percent of the presidential vote in the district. In 1944, then, Dewey ran 14.6 percentage points behind Congressman O'Hara. Again, in 1946, running very well, O'Hara received 76 percent of the congressional vote, but in 1948 he polled 63.9 percent while Dewey had only 46 percent. Thus, in 1948 Dewey ran 17.9 percentage points behind congressional candidate O'Hara. Two years later—1950—O'Hara captured 60 percent of the vote in his congressional district, notwithstanding heavy opposition because of a factional schism in the GOP state leadership.

The First District of Indiana. Also a predominantly one-party district is the first of the Hoosier State where we find an exceptionally close relationship between the presidential-congressional vote even when one party consistently loses both the House and presidential vote in this bailiwick. The Democratic party has carried both its congressional and presidential nominees for the full period under

FIGURE 3

THE FIRST CONGRESSIONAL DISTRICT OF INDIANA

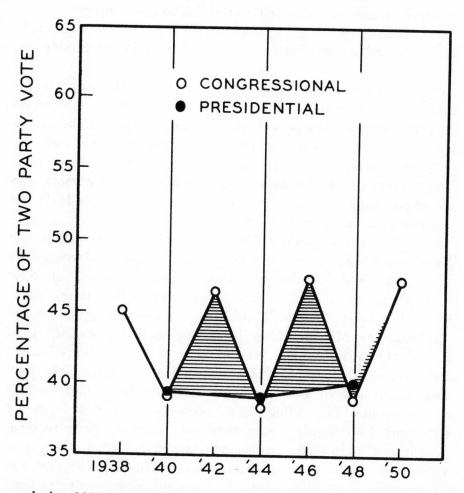

analysis—1938-50. Self-evident, as the graph for this district reveals, is the tight relationship between the presidential-congressional vote.

In presidential years, the Democratic congressional nominee improves his percentage of the two-party vote, running slightly behind the victorious Democratic presidential nominee. Convoyed, then, by his party's presidential nominee, the Democratic congressional candidate makes a better showing in this district. On the other hand, GOP congressional candidates lose popular support when accompanied by their presidential nominees, and rally at the midterm election stands.

Rounding out our sketch of the predominantly one-party districts, the following salient characteristics seem to emerge:

1. Broadly speaking, the majority party is much stronger in its state-wide and congressional contests than it is in the presidential race.

2. To a lesser extent than is true of the strictly one-party districts, congressmen in predominantly one-party districts tend to remain in office over long periods of time. In contrast with the strictly one-party districts, congressmen from these areas are occasionally interrupted in their long periods of service. For example, Republican Congressman Harold Knutson of the sixth district in Minnesota, who served continuously from March 4, 1917 until January 3, 1949, was defeated by a Democrat in 1948.

3. Most predominantly one-party districts are located in the North, notably in Maine, New Hampshire, Vermont, Massachusetts (Democratic and Republican), Rhode Island (Democratic), New York (Democratic and Republican), Pennsylvania, New Jersey, Maryland, Ohio, West Virginia, Illinois, Indiana, and Michigan; Wisconsin, Minnesota, Missouri, Iowa, North and South Dakota, Nebraska, Kansas, Montana, Colorado, New Mexico, Arizona, Idaho, Washington, Oregon, and a few in California, though it is difficult to draw strict conclusions on one-party districts in the latter state because of the system of cross filing: In Clarence Lea's old first district of California, for example, Lea, a Democrat, won both party nominations from 1938 to 1946. But when he retired in 1948, different individuals won the major party nominations, and the district reverted to its Republican normalcy, about 54.5 percent of the two-party vote.

THE MARGINAL DISTRICTS

It is largely in the marginal districts that elections are won or lost. Moreover, with few exceptions it is here—in these hundred-odd constituencies that trundle back and forth across the 50 percentage point line—that we find the closest parallelism between the presidential and congressional vote. Because of the critical part these districts play in determining which party will control the House, six representative examples have been selected for analysis. The six

FIGURE 4

THE FOURTH CONGRESSIONAL DISTRICT OF MINNESOTA

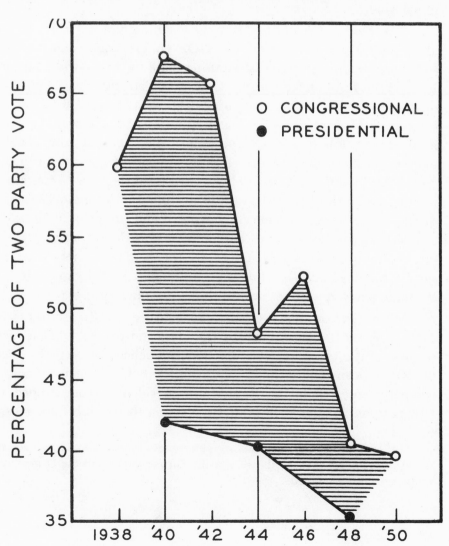

districts, in turn, have been subdivided into two groups on the basis of the discrepancy they show between the presidential and congressional vote.

The first group—the fourth district of Minnesota, the third of Colorado, the eighteenth district of Ohio and the first of Idaho—is arranged in sequential order beginning with the constituency that illustrates the greatest divergence between the presidential and congressional vote. The second group—Connecticut's second district, the second of Colorado, the twenty-third of Pennsylvania, and the eighth of Missouri—is representative of districts that show an extraordinarily close relationship between the presidential and congressional vote.

The Fourth District of Minnesota. Our graph for this district (St. Paul) demonstrates that the GOP congressional nominee has sometimes led his presidential running mate by a very wide margin. In 1938 the Republican congressional candidate received 60 percent of the vote, and in the presidential election year of 1940 he upped his vote to 68 percent, while the Republican presidential nominee finished far below with just 42 percent of the two-party vote. At the midterm election of 1942 the GOP congressional nominee won decisively again with approximately 66 percent of the vote.* Certainly on the basis of this brief interval the electorate of Minnesota's fourth district seems to think of the congressional and presidential elections as two distinct events. In this respect the fourth district of Minnesota is almost unique. Few indeed are the examples where even for such a single election presidential and congressional candidates of the same party appear to have no influence on each other.

From 1944 on, however, the gap between the Republican percentage of the two-party vote for Congress and the Republican percentage of the two-party vote for the presidency narrows. In 1944 the Republican congressional candidate fell below 50 percent of the two-party vote, while the Republican presidential vote slipped to 40.3 percent. At the 1946 midterm election the Republicans recap-

---

*In computing the Republican percentage of the two-party vote in Minnesota's Fourth district, the vote of the Farmer-Labor and the Democratic candidates are combined.

tured the congressional seat with 52 percent of the vote only to lose
it when Mr. Dewey ran for the presidency in 1948. In the 1948
election the GOP congressional nominee polled only 40.6 percent
of the vote, while Mr. Dewey stumbled along with 35.2 percent. Thus
certainly in 1944 and 1948 there seems to be a relationship between
the presidential and the congressional vote—quite a departure from
the experience of 1940. So in 1944 and 1948 the GOP presidential
candidate apparently had a negative influence on the vote of the
Republican congressional nominee.

One further postscript on the maverick tendencies of Minnesota's fourth district needs to be mentioned in passing. In 1950, instead of picking up strength, the GOP congressional nominee ran
behind the 1948 vote. In 1948 the Republican percentage of the two-
party vote for Congress was 40.6, whereas in 1950 it dropped to 39.6
—a full percentage point. This type of voting behavior, of course,
is extraordinarily rare. Normally the party out of power gains in
off-presidential election years. Thus the fourth district of Minnesota, though it illustrates a discernible parallelism between the congressional and presidential vote for a given party, is in many respects
an atypical example. It has been included to demonstrate the unusual, but it should be borne in mind that the exceptions are rare
and that most of the marginal districts in the United States do not
follow this pattern.

For this illustration, as well as all subsequent ones, a convenient
way to follow the relationship of presidential-congressional voting in
the Democratic party is simply to invert the graph. This done, we
merely have to think of the scale in reverse. The subtraction of the
Republican percentage of the vote from 100, then, leaves us with
the Democratic percentage of the two-party vote. Thus, if the Republicans have obtained 60 percent of the two-party vote, the Democrats have obviously won 40 percent. Adopting this procedure we
find that what was true of the Republican party in Minnesota's
fourth district presidential-congressional voting relationship holds
true for the Democratic party as well. Hence when there is a huge
disparity in percentage points between the Republican presidential
and congressional vote, a corresponding disparity will turn up between the Democratic presidential and congressional ballot count.

Conversely, when the two candidates run close together in the Republican party, they will also run close together in the Democratic party. It is for this reason that it is not necessary to present detailed analyses for both parties—a project that would only serve to crowd and confuse our pages.

Third District of Colorado. Colorado's third district, like. Minnesota's fourth, is a constituency where we find a sizable distance between the percentage vote received by congressional and presidential candidates. A glance at the graph shows that, like the fourth district of Minnesota, the Republican congressional candidates consistently

FIGURE 5

THE THIRD CONGRESSIONAL DISTRICT OF COLORADO

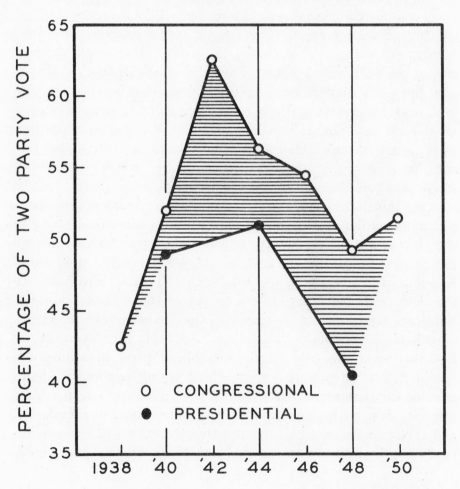

run ahead of their party's presidential nominee. In 1938 the Republican percentage of the two-party vote for Congress was low: roughly 43 percent—rising to 52 percent in 1940, and to 63 percent in 1942, the peak for this congressional district. Readily apparent in comparing the presidential years with biennial elections is the close parallel between the presidential and congressional nominees when they run together. When the congressional candidates run in the biennial elections without the presidential candidate of their party, they obtain a far higher percentage of the two-party vote. The cross-hatched area indicates the disparity between the presidential and congressional nominees for the Republican party, at the same time, of course, that it shows the disparity between the Democratic presidential and congressional candidates.

Up to 1942 the percentage difference between the congressional and presidential vote in Colorado's third district was very small. Since then, however, this difference has widened, and in recent years the Republican candidate for Congress has run far ahead of the Republican nominee for President. Since the GOP presidential nominee carried the district by the shadow of a 51 percent margin in 1944, it seems probable that it was the congressional coattail here that helped pull the Republican presidential candidate over the wire. In 1948, though the Republican candidates for both congress and the presidency lost the district, the same relationship holds true. The Republican candidate for Congress is still running far ahead of the Republican nominee for President. The difference between Mr. Dewey's figure and the defeated Republican congressional candidate's in 1948 was 8.8 percent. Here one might venture the judgment that the GOP presidential nominee pulled the congressional nominee beneath the 50 percent marker. Conversely, in 1944 the Democratic presidential nominee, Roosevelt, running ahead of his party's candidate for Congress, almost carried the district. Undoubtedly he was instrumental in lifting the percentage mark of the Democratic congressional candidate from 38 percent in 1942 to 44 percent in 1944. Situationally the relative positions of the Democratic presidential and congressional nominees held constant in 1948. Truman received almost 60 percent of the two-party vote—a winning margin that certainly boosted the fortunes of the Democratic candidate for Congress, who received 51 percent of the vote in 1948, though in 1946 the party's congressional candidate mustered only 45 percent of the two-party vote.

Again the close relationship between presidential and congressional voting in Colorado's third district holds true for both parties. Presidential and congressional candidates sometimes show quite a disparity between their voting percentages. But in no instance do their percentage differences result in an election where the congressional candidate wins and the presidential candidate loses the district, or vice versa. Both win or lose together. Thus the crucial point for evaluating the parallelism and interaction of presidential-congressional voting is that a relationship between the two can be established and that it is possible to demonstrate that presidential and congressional candidates go through the same troughs and peaks together.

Eighteenth District of Ohio. Ohio's eighteenth district represents yet another category into which marginal districts occasionally fall. As the graph depicts for 1944, the Republican congressional nominee won, but the GOP presidential nominee failed to carry the district. Although this result is unusual, it sometimes occurs. In other respects, however, the voting behavior of this district is quite typical. The congressional vote uniformly runs ahead of the presidential vote. Using the Republican ticket for illustration, we find the Republican congressional nominee winning the biennial elections of 1938 and 1942. Running with a losing presidential nominee in 1940, however, he lost the district. Apparently the GOP presidential nominee in this district has a deterrent effect upon Republican congressional candidacies—an effect suggested not only by the 1940 election but by the two following presidential contests as well. While the Republican presidential candidate received 45 percent of the vote in 1944, the GOP nominee for Congress received 51 percent—a three percent poorer showing than he made in the 1942 biennial election. Without the presidential nominee in 1946, the Republican congressional candidate hit 60 percent—the highest percentage of any GOP House nominee since 1938. Yet two years later—in 1948—the Republican nominee for Congress dropped to the low level of 46 percent, and the GOP presidential nominee received 43 percent of the vote.

FIGURE 6

The Eighteenth Congressional District of Ohio

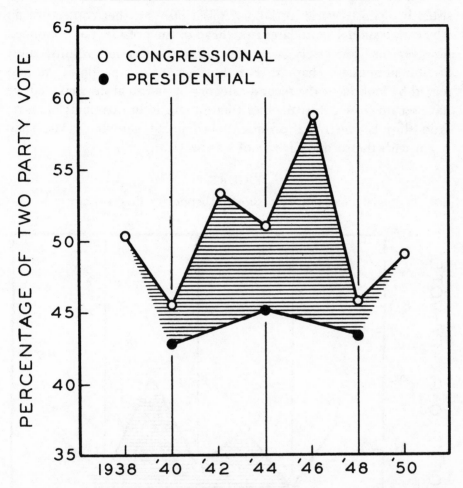

Compacting our analysis of Ohio's eighteenth district, the significant findings again are the close relationship in the votes of the presidential and congressional candidates when they run together, and the fact that they march through the same troughs and peaks together. It may be noted in passing that in Ohio's eighteenth district, as in some of our other examples, such as the Minnesota second, district the GOP congressional candidate successfully distinguished himself from the presidential nominee by standing as a candidate peculiarly representative of the pulse of the constituency. In this case the congressional candidate had a voting record somewhat typical of

several Ohio congressmen—conservative and anti-internationalist,
though in this particular district the congressman voted rather consistently against restrictive labor legislation. Further conjecture on
why congressional candidates run ahead of the presidential nominees,
however, or, conversely, why the opposite situation results, must
await a subsequent chapter. For the moment our purposes are best
served by looking at the second category of marginal districts that we
have set up—the constituencies where there is an extremely close relationship between the presidential-congressional vote. We shall
begin with the second district of Connecticut.

FIGURE 7

THE SECOND CONGRESSIONAL DISTRICT OF CONNECTICUT

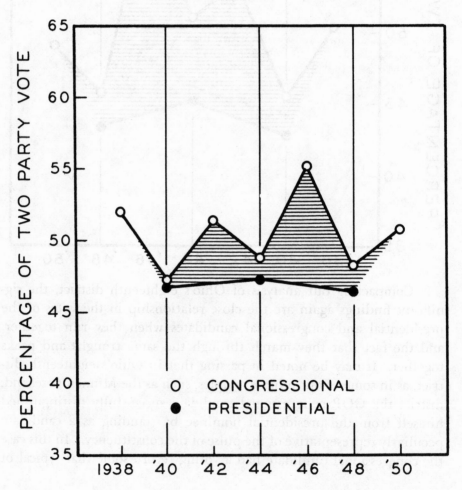

The Second District of Connecticut. This district shows a tight relationship between the presidential-congressional vote. Following the graph we note that in 1938 the GOP congressional candidate's vote was well above the 50 percent line, dropping below the marker in 1940 when he ran with the presidential nominee of the party. In the biennial election of 1942 the GOP congressional candidate nudged back into the winning column, only to lose again in 1944 when he was teamed with the Republican presidential nominee. However, in 1944 he did not lose by as great a margin as he did in 1940, and it would seem that the Republican nominee for President had less of an influence upon the Republican aspirant for Congress in 1944 than he did in 1940. Picking up the cycle again in the midterm election of 1946 we find the Republican candidate for Congress climbing into the winning column with approximately 55 percent of the vote. But the see-saw teeters downward again in 1948. Joined with the Republican presidential candidate, the congressional nominee lost the district in 1948 and then bounded back to win in 1950 —again a biennial election.

For the Democratic party it is the presidential candidate who seems to tow along the congressional nominees in this district. Without the nominee for President as a team mate, the Democratic congressional candidate is retired in midterm election years.

Essentially, then, the bouncing behavior of Connecticut's second district seems to yield Republican congressional victories when the House nominee is not running with a presidential candidate, Democratic congressional triumphs when the House candidate is flanked by a winning presidential candidate.

The Second District of Colorado. Colorado's second is a marginal district of fitful fluctuation. It defies predictability, any way or at any time. It is an illustration of what we have already called the "critical" marginal districts. In 1938 the Republican nominee for Congress lost. In 1940 he won, quite likely because he was towed in by the fine showing of presidential nominee Willkie. But in 1942 he broke all records for the Republican party in this district, by nailing down almost 69 percent of the vote. From this lofty perch he slid considerably in 1944, climbing back again in 1946 almost to the pinnacle he hit in 1942. Yet the backslide of 1944 was re-

peated in 1948—another presidential election year—when the GOP
nominee barely won re-election. His presidential running mate in
the latter year appears to have been slightly influential in preventing
his defeat. In 1950 the table tilts once more, and the GOP congressional nominee coasts in with a "safe" margin of victory.

Again the pattern repeats. In Colorado's second district, as elsewhere, despite unpredictable bolts toward one party and then the
other, a close relationship between presidential-congressional voting
within the same party is maintained, candidates winning or losing
together.

FIGURE 8

THE SECOND CONGRESSIONAL DISTRICT OF COLORADO

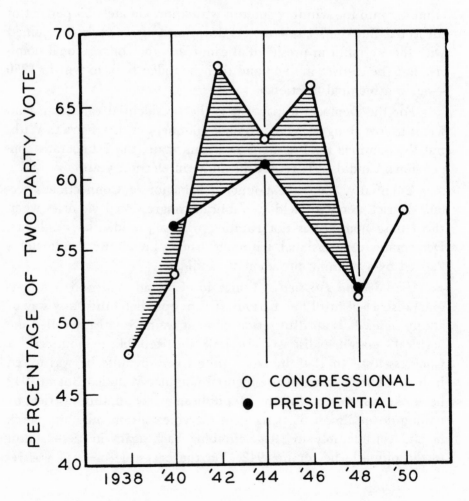

The Twenty-Third District of Pennsylvania. Located in the eastern part of the Keystone State, this district, the twenty-fourth, shows an extremely close parallelism prior to 1941-43. Moreover, there is little tendency to split tickets here in presidential years. Uniformly since 1944 Democrats have won a majority in presidential years—an advantage they have yielded to Republicans in off-year elections. In 1940 Roosevelt carried the district, receiving 56.7 percent of the vote, and the Democratic candidate for Congress won by 57.6 percent—a differential of a mere 1.9 percentage points. Again

FIGURE 9

THE TWENTY-THIRD CONGRESSIONAL DISTRICT OF PENNSYLVANIA

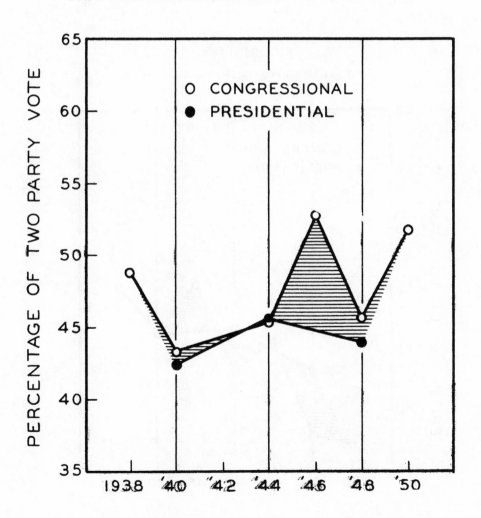

in 1944 the district turned in Democratic majorities for both offices,
Roosevelt receiving 54.5 percent of the vote, and his congressional
running mate 54.6 percent. Obviously the differential between these
two races is negligible. Although the Republicans recaptured the
district in 1946, they lost it again in 1948 only to re-win it in 1950.
Truman received 56.0 percent of the vote in the 1948 election, while
his congressional ticket polled 54.3 percent of it. Once more we find
that the differential is very small between the two races. Indisputably, then, presidential and congressional candidates run closely
parallel to each other; since the district is a critical-marginal district,
it divides its favors between the two parties frequently. Since 1944
the turnover in congressmen has been very great. Four elections
have been held, and four different men have held the office
since 1944.

FIGURE 10

THE FIRST CONGRESSIONAL DISTRICT OF IDAHO

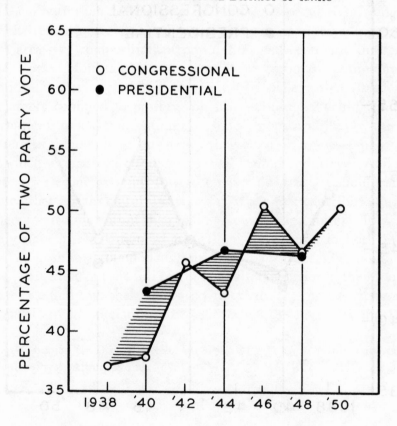

First District of Idaho. This district covers the northern half
of Idaho. Though overwhelmingly Democratic before 1938, since
that time it has shown a generally consistent Republican gain, the
Republican congressional vote climbing from 37.2 percent to 50.5
percent. Twice in the last four elections the Republicans have won
this House seat, but only in the midterm years and by scanty margins. In the presidential years the Democratic presidential candidate
has been uniformly successful, and, since the congressional vote
moves reasonably parallel to the Democratic presidential vote, the
Republicans have been prevented from winning the seat in these
years. Back in 1940 the presidential and congressional candidates
were separated by 5.5 percentage points, but this difference has
worn off to 3.6 percent in 1944 and a scant 0.4 percent in 1948.
Thus the parallelism between presidential and congressional candidates has become increasingly close and its political behavior suggests that the party winning the presidential vote is the strong
favorite to pick up the congressional seat.

Eighth District of Missouri. Few if any are the districts where
we will discover the percentage vote of presidential and congressional
candidates as nearly identical as in Missouri's eighth district. Since
1938 the Republicans have captured this seat twice—in 1942 and
1946—while the Democratic candidates have won five times (twice
by tiny pluralities). Of particular interest in this diversified constituency is the fact that at no time since 1940 have the presidential
and congressional votes differed by as much as one percentage point.
In 1940 the Republican presidential nominee won 49.7 percent of
the two-party vote in the district, and the GOP congressional nominee polled 48.9—a skimpy difference of 0.8 percent. At the 1942
midterm battle the Republicans had their first success in this district
since the beginning of the New Deal tide in the early 1930's. It was
victory by an uneasy margin, however, and in 1944, when Dewey
received 49.7 percent of the vote, the Republican candidate for
Congress polled 49.5 percent. Curiously, the presidential and congressional nominees were again separated by a mere 0.2 percent. In
1946 the GOP congressional candidate carried the district, but narrowly, and in the wake of the Truman landslide two years later the
Republican vote plunged to its lowest level since 1936. Once more,

however, the relation of presidential and congressional candidates
was inordinately close. With Dewey winning 41.9 percent of the
vote, the Republican congressional candidate received 42.8 percent.
Thus, even in a year of violent political transition for this district,
the difference between presidential and congressional candidates was
only 0.9 percent. The election of 1950 showed the usual party-out-
of-power gains, but only to a point slightly above the percentage
figure recorded in 1938.

Stretched before us the political behavior of this constituency
shows not only that the votes of presidential and congressional can-

FIGURE 11

THE EIGHTH CONGRESSIONAL DISTRICT OF MISSOURI

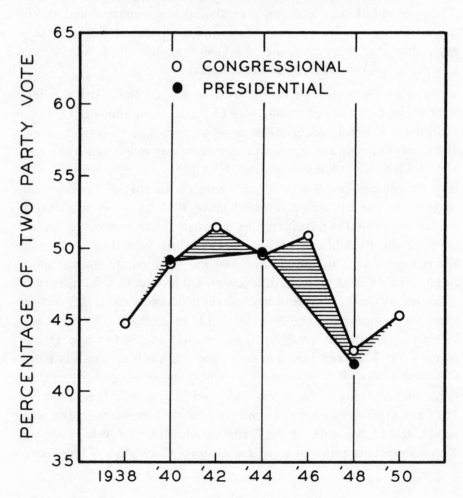

didates run parallel, but that both tap almost identical percentages of the two-party vote. In the latter respect, the near-identity of the presidential - congressional vote taken percentagewise, Missouri's eighth district is something of a rarity in American politics.

Significant in our examples, which are generally characteristic of all our national elections, are two notable points. First, within the same party there is little difference in the percentage of the vote cast for both the presidential and congressional candidates. Second, both candidates will be found to move up or down together when the final count has been tallied. These two points are the core of what has been termed the close parallelism of congressional-presidential voting behavior.

There are, of course, exceptional cases where the percentage-point differences between the presidential and congressional candidates are such that one loses while the other wins. Thus in Ohio's eighteenth district and Minnesota's fourth there have been wide enough discrepancies between the presidential and congressional vote for one candidate to win and his running mate to lose. Yet such a mixed result appears infrequently when we look at the total picture. In the 1948 election, which was unusually close, there were just forty-four cases where the presidential and congressional candidates of the two major parties failed to win or lose together. Stated otherwise, only forty-four out of 435 districts, or slightly over ten percent, demonstrated this type of mixed result in the 1948 elections.

Among the multiple considerations to be borne in mind when evaluating presidential-congressional voting behavior, certainly the personal factor should not be overlooked. Significantly, personality may have a strong bearing on the outcome of a given election. The fact, for example, that in practically every poll that has been taken to measure candidate preferences of men and women in the last twelve years Thomas E. Dewey proved to be less popular with women than men may well have cost him the 58,584 votes that, properly spread, could have put him in the White House in 1948.

Violent shifts in a given election from the usual voting patterns, of course, are not infrequently induced by very special circumstances. Thus the discovery in 1946 that the candidate who won the Democratic nomination from Representative John Costello in California's

old eighteenth district, was a Klansman, was probably responsible
for his complete rout in the general election. Similarly in Milwaukee, the Democratic Committee's disavowal of their Congressional candidate in 1946 for alleged Communist party membership
must have been a central factor in the loss of this normally Democratic seat to the GOP in the general election.[1] In both cases we would
ordinarily expect the GOP presidential candidate to run behind the
local Republican congressional candidate, which indeed was exactly
what happened.

Keeping in mind that there are occasionally sharp exceptions in
the voting behavior of the three representative types of congressional
constituencies we have placed under analysis in this chapter, we may
now attempt to compact the experience of all districts and spread
our results on a larger canvas.

TABLE X

COMPARATIVE SHOWING PRESIDENTIAL-CONGRESSIONAL CANDIDATES 1940-1950

| | Republican | | Democratic | |
	President Ahead	Congressman Ahead	President Ahead	Congressman Ahead
1940	78	128	128	78
1944	63	162	162	63
1948	116	111	111	116

Explanatory note:
1. To show the number of times the presidential or congressional candidates ran ahead in the three elections depicted above, the major parties'
   presidential and congressional vote were compared district by district.
   For example, since the Democratic congressional percentage of the
   two-party vote in New Jersey's fourth district in 1940 was 44.1 and the
   Democratic presidential percentage was 56.8, this was listed as an instance where the Democratic presidential candidate led his party's
   congressional nominee.
2. Since approximately 120 congressional districts have no opposition
   or very limited opposition, and in light of the fact that in the majority
   of metropolitan areas the presidential vote is given either by county or
   by citywide totals, no comparison can be made. Therefore, the totals
   do not add up to 435.

---

[1]The Democratic candidate won 60.9 percent of the two-party vote in
1950; 58.6 in 1948, but in 1946 it was only 47.5.

PRESIDENTIAL-CONGRESSIONAL VOTING: THE NATIONAL PICTURE

Reviewing first the three types of congressional constituencies outlined in this chapter, we find that approximately 120 are strictly one-party districts, located, of course, primarily in the South. About 200 of the nation's 435 constituencies are predominantly one-party districts, and in this group most of the city districts are Democratic while the rural ones are usually Republican. One fourth—105—may be classified as marginal with forty-odd districts falling into the critical marginal category. A comparison showing the number of times the presidential or congressional candidate ran ahead in three national elections is given in Table X.

For the nation as a unit, the close parallelism of congressional-presidential voting can be simply demonstrated. Our graph (see Figure 12) covering the period from 1916 to 1948 reveals a close proximity between the party percentages won by the congressional and presidential tickets. The graph for the Republican party discloses that up to 1928 the GOP presidential nominee ran ahead of his congressional tickets. It also shows a large disparity between the President and his congressional ticket in 1924, when Coolidge ran far ahead of his congressional slate owing to the candidacy of La Follette, who chopped down the Democratic presidential vote.

From 1932 through 1948 GOP presidential nominees have tagged after their congressional tickets in three elections—1932, 1936, and 1944; while twice—Willkie in 1940 and Dewey in 1948—they have run ahead. Quite clearly the Roosevelt avalanche in the balloting of 1936 was responsible for the sharp difference between the Republican presidential and congressional vote.

For the Democratic party the exact converse behavior holds true through 1928—congressional candidates loping consistently ahead of presidential nominees. The widest gap in the Democratic presidential and congressional vote occurred in 1924 when La Follette siphoned off heavy Democratic support by polling four million votes as the Progressive party presidential nominee. In 1932, 1936, and 1944 Roosevelt led his congressional ticket, stumbling only in the Willkie tussle of 1940 when his percentage of the two-party vote

dropped slightly beneath that of the Democratic congressional ticket.[2]
That Truman, though winning the election, should run behind his
congressional ticket in 1948, even in terms of the absolute vote, should
hardly evoke surprise.

FIGURE 12

Presidential—Congressional Voting: A Comparison of National Tickets
1916-1948

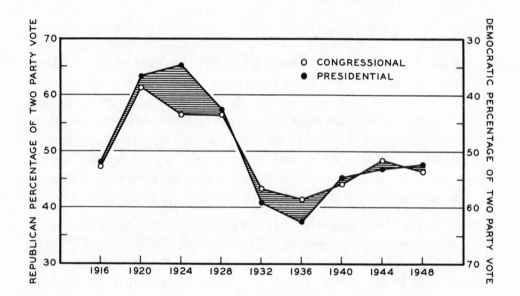

[2]This comparison is between the Democratic percentage of the two-party
presidential vote and the Democratic percentage of the two-party congressional
vote.

Readily apparent as we take in the full sweep of elections from 1916 to 1948 is the way a party's presidential and congressional tickets win and lose in the same way. Each ticket—presidential and congressional—grabs approximately the same percentage of the two-party vote. Thus percentagewise we find a close parallelism in presidential-congressional voting behavior with notable exceptions for each party such as 1924 and 1936.

Marginal districts, of course, where a party may win or lose the Congress, presidency, or both, seem to behave more dynamically as they bobble above and below the 50 percent marker. But even the marginal constituencies ride the election course over a percentage line that parallels the dips and climbs of the presidential vote. Finally both the strictly one-party and predominantly one-party districts, as we observed earlier, follow their own peculiar type of parallelism in their political behavior.

COATTAIL CAPERS

Coattail riding, as we have now had ample opportunity to observe, often involves a reversal of mount and rider. For precisely this reason we need to be chary in overemphasizing the power of either the presidential or congressional coattail. Quite apart from the general lift in interest that the excitement, presidential personality, and financing, bring to a quadrennial election, voters frequently discriminate between presidential and congressional nominees of the same party—a matter we shall examine in detail in the succeeding chapter. There are, moreover, certain congressional stalwarts who must be reckoned with, and many of these "old gladiators" make sweeping generalizations about coattailing all the more hazardous. "Neither the ebb and flow of party fortunes nor the ever-changing complexion of national and state issues seemed to have any effect upon his popularity with people," wrote Lawrence Chamberlain of the late Senator William E. Borah. "Idaho was proud to accept him on his own terms."[3]

---

[3]Lawrence Chamberlain: "Idaho, State of Sectional Schisms," in *Rocky Mountain Politics* (Albuquerque: University of New Mexico Press, 1940) p. 182.

Perhaps the striking example of Borah has fewer counterparts today than in an earlier era of American politics, but the disposition of the electorate to regard presidential and congressional elections as two unconnected events carries on in many constituencies. In New York's 21st district, Representative Javits is able to persuade his constituents to stand by him even though they forsake his party's presidential followers in droves. Equally impressive is the example of Massachusetts' voters in 1948, a state, incidentally, where the tradition to vote a straight party ticket is strong. That year voters of the Bay State gave the Democratic gubernatorial candidate 59.3 percent of the vote, Truman 55.0, and the Democratic senatorial nominee only 46.7, thus returning Republican Leverett Saltonstall to the Senate amidst what otherwise was a Democratic landslide. Obviously in this setting there is little evidence to suggest that the congressional coattail aids the presidential nominee. The really crucial factor in all conjecture about the muzzle velocity of either the presidential or congressional coattail is the relative degree of familiarity that the constituency has with the candidates at both levels. Where the information on a congressional candidate is minimal, the coattail influence of the presidential candidate may set off an important forward impulse. This is very likely to be true of the congressional candidates who are seeking their first term in office.

On the average, seventy-five new members are brought in by each congressional election. Since little is known of many of these new arrivals who fill the back rows of the House, or of how they will behave, more than a few of these congressmen may well trade on the credentials of the presidential coattails. Now where the presidential coattail credentials have broad popular endorsement, the presidential nominee may have an important bearing on the election of quite a number of relatively unknown congressional candidates. Such very likely was the case in the presidential election of 1936 when Franklin Roosevelt seems to have swept in a sizeable group of congressional novitiates.

In the national campaign setting the presidential candidate has certain obvious advantages. The centrality of his position helps to tattoo his name in every memory, for however brief a time, and for whatever the measure of acceptance or rejection. No comparable familiarity attaches to the congressional candidate seeking his first term. Thus the presidential nominee, even though running for his first term, is strategically well-located to sweep some of his party's congressional candidates into office, particularly those nominees who have not yet served their first term in the House. But if the presidential nominee's coattail is to pull any congressional candidates over the hump he must be able to appeal to voters on a meaningful level.

Conceivably Eisenhower in 1952, conducting a campaign of lofty uncertitude such as Dewey's in 1948, might have a more powerful coattail than if he spells out his policies on highly controversial questions in too specific detail. For Dewey obviously—as for most presidential candidates—the 1948 technique was a poor choice. How ill-advised it was may be quickly recognized by looking back at one of his Middlewestern appearances.

In September of 1948, Dewey and Truman were both invited to attend the National Plowing Contest in Dexter, Iowa. Governor Dewey declined—he was leading the polls in Iowa with 55 percent; but Truman went to Dexter. There, in a speech made famous after the election, he pledged to the farmers that the Democratic party would be firm in its maintenance of price supports. (The speech later prompted H. L. Mencken to remark that the "Missouri Wonder was roving and ravaging the land, pouring out hope and promise in a wholesale manner . . . and pledging to the farmer a continuance of the outrageous prices that are reducing the rest of us to eating only once a day.") But while Truman reminded midwestern farmers of his faith in price supports and that "the reactionary Republican answer is to let prices crash to the bottom," Dewey responded at Des Moines two days later with a speech of political abstractions. His national goal, he said, was the unity of all interests. Clearly Dewey's failure to communicate an intent to keep up price supports in language free of spongy phrases was a critical element in the midwestern defection that led not a few pollsters to seek refuge in the nearest corncrib after the 1948 election.

While Dewey was thus censured for not being strictly accountable as he sought to dispel popular distrust of the Republican party, the electorate seemed disposed to grant a generous margin of uncertainty in General Eisenhower's political posture in the early stages of the 1952 campaign. In the national mind Eisenhower appeared to conjure a picture of a leader who stood ready to repudiate the insincerities of modern politics. Having lived apart from politics, moreover, he escaped many liabilities of the traditional presidential candidate whose career moves largely in the convoy of one major party or the other and is accordingly influenced by the mistakes of that party. Yet the luster of his candidacy could be quickly dissipated were his public utterances to strike an unresponsive chord.

Whenever we speak of coattail chasing, experience teaches us that the effect of a particular type of candidacy on the congressional caravan depends upon the information in the electorate's possession. In the absence of familiarity with the candidate the coattail of the presidential nominee is relatively inoperative. Thus the real example of Franklin Roosevelt's coattail influence was provided not in 1932 when his notions of statecraft were as yet little known to the voter, but in 1936 when his widespread identification with particular policies enabled him to carry in a Congress that left just 89 Republicans in the House and a diminutive 17 to rally opposition in the Senate.

Governor Stevenson, on the other hand, stepped into the presidential campaign without the advantage of a name that had been brightened by a decade of intensive publicity. Known locally in his native state of Illinois, Stevenson's strength as head of the Democratic ticket depended on his ability to associate himself with the voters and their interests, and to present critical and complicated issues in the most forceful and understandable terms.

Of course it might be said that one should be enjoined from arguing that presidential coattail influence is operative only when the voter is really familiar with the candidate, particularly so since little precise knowledge was available on Eisenhower's views during the 1952 pre-convention debate, yet his popular esteem was indisputably high. But there is a difference here in the matter of leadership acceptance that needs to be noted. Popularly conceptualized, the embodiment of sincerity, courage, and realism may at a particular point in the passing political parade take on a firmer quality for some voter than the most specific spelling out of ways to dehydrate the budget or solve the complexities of labor-management relations. In place of the uncertainties over issues in the latter case, a judgment is substituted based upon character and past performance. Significantly, however, a meaningful assessment of the candidate is made and a working familiarity is established. Whatever the type of presidential candidate we are dealing with, then, his coattail influence will be effective only where the electorate is actively familiar with him. And by way of a postscript it should assuredly be acknowledged that as campaigns wear on between presidential nominees, coattails worn by a candidate about whom too many uncertainties and contradictions continue, can become frayed no matter how high his earlier popular esteem.

Since we observed that coattailing often involved a reversal of mount and rider, it should be made clear that the same conditions of familiarity apply where the congressional candidates' coattails help the presidential nominee. In the districts where the congressional candidate polls a larger slice of the two-party vote than the presidential nominee, the amount of help that he can furnish the presidential candidate again depends upon the electorate's familiarity with their congressman. Thus Dewey's slim win of 1944 in Colorado's third district was aided by the third successful race of Representative Chenoweth who won 56 percent of the vote. A congressional candidate, of course, no more than a presidential candidate, does not simply emerge from the interstellar spaces. More often than not he has served an apprenticeship in local or state office as state legislator, mayor, public prosecutor, or councilman, and his own following gradually multiplies in strength. By his record and by means of assiduous cultivation within his own bailiwick, a congressman, instead of being a coattail clutcher, may have a coattail rider in tow—a presidential nominee. Occasionally the congressman starts with certain advantages over his party's presidential candidate simply because of the homogeneous character of his constituency. Necessarily if a party wishes to win the presidency it must bid for the support of divergent interest groups—farmers, laborers, white collar workers, and businessmen. Thus the presidential nominee is frequently constrained to temper his appeals where there is reason to believe that to go all out on some commitments would prove offensive to groups with contradictory interests.

In a sense "the party as a whole—as personified in the presidential candidate—must in its campaiging take into account the entire
income and occupational spectrum."[4]   In particular congressional
constituencies, however, a candidate for the House need have no
fear of reprisal if he thumps for the demands of one group.

The homogeneity of certain districts frees the congressional
candidate from the necessity of seeking votes from people belonging
to different occupations and interest groups.   This type of constituency is well-exemplified in urban as well as rural areas.   Moreover,
in this context—the homogeneity of congressional district and its
relation to campaigning—we must be mindful of cultural as well as
occupational similarities.   Constituencies showing a high degree of
uniformity in the national origins of their citizenry whether they be
Irish, Italian, Polish, or of another national extraction, relieve congressional candidates of the task of soliciting votes from people of
all sorts of foreign backgrounds.   And such districts, as Professor
Turner's admirable study on *Party and Constituency* convincingly
demonstrates, have a way of returning representatives who heed their
wishes.[5]

And so it is that congressmen often have presidential nominees
as coattail chasers rather than the reverse setting long familiarized
by the cartoonist where the congressman grasps at the flapping coattail of the presidential candidate.   But cardinal to either situation
in coattail influence is the familiarity of the electorate with one or
the other—presidential or congressional—of the candidates.   Too
often those who enthusiastically uphold the power of the presidential
coattail center their attention only on the national picture and fail
to look at what is actually happening district by district.   As Arthur
Krock wisely pointed out after the 1948 election, simply to compare
the district voting percentage of the congressional candidate with
the state or national voting percentage of the presidential candidate
distorts the true picture of presidential-congressional voting rela-

---

[4]See S. P. Huntington: "A Revised Theory of American Politics," *American Political Science Review,* 44 (1950), pp. 669-677.

[5]See Julius Turner: *Party and Constituency: Pressures on Congress* (Baltimore: Johns Hopkins Press, 1951), pp. 98-127.

tionships. The most meaningful comparisons, therefore, are done district by district.[6] Given the contradictory current of so many of our congressional districts and the complexities of modern political life, there is no greater challenge for the student of political behavior than the study of how this familiarity is achieved—a matter that now compels our attention.

Another factor of great significance in judging the importance or non-importance of coattail influence is the losing ticket. When the winning presidential candidate leads his ticket, this means that the converse must be true of the leading presidential candidate—that he trails his congressional ticket. But does this circumstance warrant the conclusion that he is dragging his feet—that he failed to wield coattail influence to help his congressional ticket and therefore was a poor candidate? Hardly so. If, for example, Governor Stevenson should lose the presidential race in 1952 and trailed his congressional ticket, this would certainly not mean that he lacked coattail pulling power, and therefore was an unfortunate choice as candidate. But the fact is, of course, that it has become the normal thing for a winning presidential candidate to run fairly well ahead of his congressional ticket—a circumstance that applies to the candidates of either party, and may well be connected with a greater vote interest in national rather than local affairs.

In a very tight election, obviously, the influence of a presidential candidate in some of the marginal districts might well be a decisive factor in deciding congressional races. Under such conditions, coattail influence could have a bearing on the outcome. The fact remains, however, that close elections are not usual in national contests.

Thus the critical factor in national elections is not coattail influence but rather the individual strength of the presidential or congressional candidates, and the real battle turns on their ability to acquaint the voter with their views.

While the reputation in American political history of candidates who win by walking on egg shells is legendary, it would be doing disservice to the facts to slight the number of successes of those who won by pitching their appeals on their issues and their record of

----

[6]*The New York Times*, March 15, 1949.

achievement.   Conspicuously Senator Herbert Lehman of New York
in winning seven out of eight campaigns concentrated on the issues
rather than personalities in all but one instance.[7]   Elsewhere examples are not wanting in either party where congressional candidates have won approval by skillfully hanging their campaign appeals on the issues.   Beset by the varying conditions peculiar to each
of our 435 congressional casings, few problems of political leadership
have greater paramountcy than that of how to get a congressional
candidacy off the ground—and not only to get it off the ground, but
having once got it aloft, to make it soar.

---

[7]See the excellent chapter on three case histories of congressional elections
in Stephen K. Bailey and Howard D. Samuel: *Congress at Work* (New York:
Holt, 1952) , pp. 11-65.

CHAPTER 5

The Politics of Electoral
Leadership

"A man only moderately versed in statesmanship, and with only a small degree of sportsmanship, is bound to admit, that in a free Republic, in a government such as ours, it is the undoubted right of the people to change their servants, and to remove one and displace him with another at any time they choose, for a good reason, for a bad reason, or for no reason at all." With these words Senator Henry Fountain Ashurst said goodby to his colleagues in the United States Senate following his defeat by Judge Ernest W. McFarland after twenty-nine years' service in the "greatest deliberative body in the world."[1]

Noteworthy in Senator Ashurst's noble valedictory, despite his wistful references—"The first hour you believe that the earth has slipped from beneath your feet, that the stars above your head have

---

[1] *Congressional Record,* 86 (1940), p. 11902.

119

paled and faded"—is his acknowledgement of the fact that defeat sometimes appears to a Senator or a congressman "for no reason at all." Clearly in his own case this seemed to be no disservice to the facts, for it was generally agreed that Senator Ashurst was held in high esteem by his constituents in Arizona, and that by and large his voting record coincided with their wishes.

Now we know that for the most part, year in and year out, congressmen are returned to Washington on the basis of their voting records. True, running errands for constituents and keeping on the good side of the local party directorate are mighty important ingredients in the re-election formula. A prime determinant of re-election is still one's voting record. Yet since Senator Ashurst's case would seem to indicate that the electorate had little to quarrel with over his voting record, it serves as a reminder of the ever-present uncertainties and occasional contradictions of the ballot box. Quite possibly if one could bore deep enough reasons could be exhumed explaining the outcome of any election, not the least of which might be a popular fatigue with oldtime campaign faces.[2] Without the refinement of technique to measure the causes for defeat or victory in some elections, however, we are bound to concede or at least to make allowances for the fact that congressmen are sometimes displaced for no apparent reason at all. Thus an awareness that overturns do occur, as in the case of Senator Ashurst, is an important matter when one attempts to record the reasons behind the decisive impulses in ballot behavior.

In the overwhelming number of cases, however, the fact is that there are reasons for a congressman's defeat. Our primary concern here, therefore, after a note of caution that the unpredictable may happen in the removal of a veteran for no apparent cause, is not with a congressman or president who has served a long tour of duty, but with the one who is making perhaps his first, second, or third attempt at election or re-election. The compelling problem, obvious-

---

[2] A case in point that might be cited is that of a Congressman from one of the border states whose defeat in a party primary came as a shock after his several terms of service. His upset, however, was apparently explained by the fact that he had become a serious drinker—knowledge of which gradually leaked around to his constituents.

ly, is to get started—"to get a congressional or presidential candidacy off the ground, and then to make it soar" as we concluded in our last chapter. Where the presidential and congressional candidates are making their first run, we have already seen that the presidential nominee—unless the congressional nominee happens to have had an unusually formidable background—has a somewhat better opportunity of becoming known. This accounts for the fact, as we have reviewed earlier, that the successful and even unsuccessful presidential nominees usually run ahead of their congressional tickets. It also accounts for the fact that in the predominantly one-party districts the minority party congressional candidates usually show gains in presidential election years when their percentage of the two-party vote is compared with midterm elections. But the amount of help, by way of coattail influence, that the congressional candidate can receive from his presidential nominee depends upon how well the views of the presidential candidate become known, and in turn on whether these views strike a responsive chord. At present, the presidential nominee is and may be increasingly in a better position to exercise a coattail influence. The accretion of many advantages—the growing stature of presidential office, decline in prestige of Congress, stronger financing of presidential candidates, and the increasing tendency to regard him as the spokesman of all the people—gives the presidential nominee the edge where he and his congressional candidates are making their first bids for their respective offices. But while the match is not equal, both because of the centrality of his position and by reason of his greater resources of finance, the problems of communication—the business of making meaningful appeals and becoming known to the electorate—are common to both. And, however upsetting it may be to the theory that champions the effectiveness of coattail influence, it must be said that by and large the success or failure of congressional candidates is not dependent upon the coattail pull of a presidential candidate.

COATTAIL BEHAVIOR—FACT AND MYTH

Essentially, the major share of what is called coattail charm comes down to depend upon the working knowledge the voter has of a presidential or congressional candidate. Much of the loose talk

about coattail effectiveness, therefore, tends toward exaggeration as
a review of the political behavior of presidential-congressional elections should demonstrate.

Too often in attempting to demonstrate the effectiveness of
presidential coattails, only one side of the picture has been emphasized
—the winning ticket. It is important, however, that the losing ticket
not be neglected. When the winning party's presidential candidate
leads his congressional candidate, the converse must be true for the
losing ticket—that is to say on the losing side the congressional candidate leads his party's presidential nominee. And if the results are
reversed on the winning ticket, with the congressional candidate
leading his party's presidential nominee, the losing party's presidential nominee will run ahead of his congressional teammate. Graph
I of Figure 13 will serve to illustrate this point.

Thus if we take a hypothetical district as illustrated in Graph I
of Figure 13, where one party's presidential and congressional candidates are both above the 50 percent mark with the congressional
candidate leading the presidential nominee, then the other party's
candidates must be below the 50 percent mark of the two-party vote
with the presidential candidate ahead of the congressional nominee.
(See Figure 13, Graphs I and II.)

FIGURE 13

A HYPOTHETICAL CASE IN TWO CONGRESSIONAL DISTRICTS

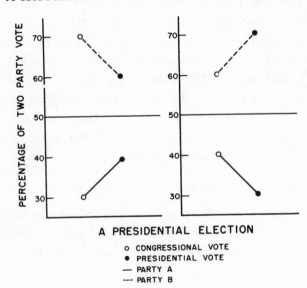

A PRESIDENTIAL ELECTION

o CONGRESSIONAL VOTE
• PRESIDENTIAL VOTE
— PARTY A
--- PARTY B

Judged from the perspective of the winning ticket in Figure 13, the congressional candidate who leads the presidential nominee appears to be wearing the magic coattails, while from the viewpoint of the losing party it might look as if the coattails of the presidential nominee were helping to lift up the candidacy of the congressional candidate. Figure 14, Graphs III and IV, illustrates that the same result will hold when either the presidential or congressional candidate runs ahead on the winning ticket, while the other party loses.

FIGURE 14

ANOTHER HYPOTHETICAL CASE IN TWO CONGRESSIONAL DISTRICTS

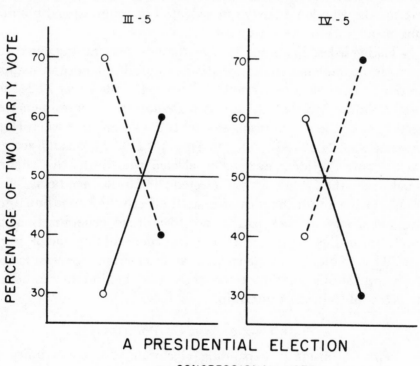

PERCENTAGE OF TWO PARTY VOTE

A PRESIDENTIAL ELECTION

o CONGRESSIONAL VOTE
● PRESIDENTIAL VOTE
— PARTY A
--- PARTY B

No matter what district we take, then, it would appear that someone on either the winning or losing party ticket seems to be wearing the coattails onto which either the congressional or presidential candidate is clutching. Moreover, the fact that presidential nominees who win usually run ahead of the congressional ticket by an average of seven percent, merely signifies that this is the normal result for successful nominees in presidential elections. Thus Graphs II, III, and IV are the typical cases for successful nominees in presidential elections.

To avoid distorting the picture in looking at presidential-congressional voting what we need to do is to cast our eyes about district by district. By this means we may be assured of not losing sight of the peculiarities of districts, personalities, and voting records or views attuned to the needs of the district, that are the crucial factors in determining whether a party's presidential or congressional nominee runs ahead within the constituency.

Taking a last look, one further thought may be suggested that bears on the tendency to exaggerate the coattail influence in national elections. In 1940, a year Franklin Roosevelt polled over 27,243,000 votes (Willkie had 22,304,755), 267 Democratic congressmen were elected, while the Republicans elected 162. Yet in 1948 when Harry Truman won 24,105,812 votes to Dewey's 21,970,065, and actually was the only President ever to be elected who trailed his congressional ticket, the Democrats still elected 263 House members. Surely in light of this result the idea of coattail effectiveness needs qualification and brings us back to the fact that broad generalizations are simply unjustified. And since the true determining factor is not coattail power alone, but the result of an interaction of several factors, it is helpful at this point to explore the reasons behind the candidacies of successful political leadership.

THE 'GROUP BASIS OF POLITICS

With a constantly expanding electorate, the opportunity for primary contacts—that is to say face to face relationships—with the great mass of voters is quite impossible. At the organizational level congressmen and presidents alike are still able to maintain direct primary contact with many party functionaries. Increasingly, however, they seek to accomplish this end by meeting with the leaders of innumerable groups—the Farm Bureau Federation, the National Grange, the American Federation of Labor, and the Congress of

Industrial Organizations, the National Association for Advancement of Colored People, and many other groups. Modern speed in transportation has greatly facilitated the possibilities for such direct communication, and it is notable that many congressmen make weekly, and occasionally even daily flights to their constituencies for the purpose of meeting with group leaders.

By and large, party affiliation is still the strongest determinant in influencing the voter, just as it is in determining the way a representative will vote when he gets to Congress. And today we say that the United States has been transformed during the past twenty years from a nation with a traditional Republican majority to one with a normal Democratic majority. Thus, according to the best estimates approximately 21 million voters are Democrats, 18 million are Republicans, and about 15 million are Independents. Each party, then, would appear to have a bedrock of voting support and a sizeable number of voters who never scratched a ticket.

Even partisans, of course, are basically affected by group influences in our society. But among the independents, it is not difficult to perceive that group influences of a non-partisan character might be expected to have greater effect than political parties. Independent voters, for example, might be more disposed to be guided on the issues by studies prepared by the League of Women Voters, rather than those submitted by political parties. But groups also have a definite influence upon those who consider themselves as regular party affiliates. The extent of group influence on political judgments is indicated by a recent study of Elmo Roper's on this very matter. Taking a group of organizations not affiliated directly with any political party, Roper set out to find out whether voters felt that any of these particular groups could be expected to have sound ideas on candidates running for office. On the basis of this study Mr. Roper calculated that a decided majority of the voters in this country—59 percent—"have respect for the political judgment of nominally non-partisan or non-political organizations."[3] Since the ten organizations

_____

[3] *New York Herald Tribune*, May 10, 1952. Presenting a cross section of the people in the United States with the following list of groups and organizations that he described as not being directly connected with a political party, Roper asked respondents to name any of the groups whose ideas they would

listed by Roper by no means was inclusive of the large number of
groupings in the United States, it is probably safe to conclude that
the number of persons who seek guidance in politics from professedly
non-partisan organizations is probably considerably higher than 59
percent. Outside of the American Federation of Labor and the CIO
of the above group, none of the organizations endorses particular political candidates for congressional or presidential office. But even
so their identification with particular issues inevitably suggests approval or disapproval of certain candidates.[4] The degree of influence of course varies. Almost one-half of the Negroes who were
interviewed by Roper indicated that they had respect for what the
National Association for the Advancement of Colored People might
have to say about candidates. Other groups might not register as
high an appeal, but the significant factor is that a great many voters
show more than a superficial preference for the views of particular
groups, and this involvement with group views undoubtedly plays
a definite role in influencing the decisions that such voters make at
the polls. Obviously, of course, people sometimes say they are inclined to follow the lead of a group and then vote differently. And

---

expect "to be good on candidates running for office." The response was as
follows:

	Total percent*
The American Legion	23
Officials of your church	22
League of Women Voters	17
A.F.L. and C.I.O.	16
Farm Bureau Federation and National Grange	15
National Association for Advancement of Colored People	8
National Association of Manufacturers	6
Prominent Southern Leaders Supporting States' Rights	5
None on the list	41

   *Percentages add to more than 100 percent because some respondents
named more than one group.

---

   [4]Said Philip Murray, president of the CIO, at his Labor Day speech September 1, 1952, in which he mentioned no presidential candidate's name:
"There is no labor vote. But there is a citizen's vote and in every election it
has been cast in the great majority for the principles of the Roosevelt New Deal
and the Truman Fair Deal."—*Baltimore Sun*, September 2, 1952.

in recognition of this tendency Samuel Gompers used to say: "I had not the power to deliver the vote of any man. The only vote which I controlled was my own." Yet the fact remains that group influences do guide and counsel large numbers of voters in political campaigns.

At the outset of a campaign, then, the congressional like the presidential candidate who is making his first bid, finds the political environment conditioned by two major elements. First the party element presents a situation where a voter identification varies from a flickering allegiance for one party to a strong bond of association with a party—"a feeling of group-belonging, and a high degree of involvement with party activities."[5] Thus the general contours of political allegiance follow party lines, and depending upon the area, party lines pretty consistently determine the outcome of an election. In the second major element of political behavior, however—the multifarious groups that are spread throughout the country—we have an increasingly important influence on elections.

The persistence of group influence in elections—"people are inclined to believe in company"—can be convincingly demonstrated wherever we make a test boring. Taft as presidential contender carried counties such as Hutchinson, with a heavy Mennonite concentration, by a better than three-to-one majority in the 1952 South Dakota presidential primary, largely because of local opposition to universal military training. Taft as senatorial contender in Ohio's 1950 general election lost but four counties—all, significantly, soft-coal mining areas where the Taft-Hartley Act stirred little enthusiasm among the precincts.

Confronted with voter involvement in both parties and groups, then, the congressional or presidential candidate, whether he be neophyte or veteran, faces the common problem of relating specific proposals of policies to the objectives and aspirations of particular organizations. Where a congressional district has a somewhat homogeneous composition this task is not as formidable as it might be elsewhere. But homogeneity is not characteristic of most of our con-

---

[5]See George Belknap and Angus Campbell "Political Party Identification and Attitudes Toward Foreign Policy," *Public Opinion Quarterly*, 15 (1951-52) p. 622.

gressional districts, or states, and certainly not of the nation. Even within a single precinct it is not unusual to find a number of distinguishable groups that uphold different points of view. They differ in terms of economic status, occupation or profession, religion and class, or because of other factors such as ethnic characteristics, and they form sundry allegiances that lead to varying degrees of group involvement and identification. And depending upon the degree of involvement, of course, such persons become tightly or loosely associated with the generally accepted attitudes of such groups on candidates and issues. To gain a better perspective on the problem that faces a congressional candidate who must first become known and be able to communicate with his constituents if he is to be elected, in a district that contains an inter-mixture of many groups, let us consider the example of Representative Jacob K. Javits from the twenty-first congressional district of New York City.

Moreover, since Mr. Javits dealt with this problem specifically in an address at the Johns Hopkins University in the Spring of 1952 —"The Congressman and His Constituents"—let him give a profile of this district in his own words:

> Now my district represents a real challenge in respect to this subject, because I come from what has been traditionally a Tammany Hall stronghold, that is a Democratic party stronghold in New York [Representative Javits is a Republican]. The enrolled voters in my district who express their party designation are in the ratio of some three to one against Republicans. There are about 55,000 enrolled Democrats in my district, and some 22,000 enrolled Republicans, and this has been the case ever since I began to run for Congress. That is to say in 1946, 1948, and 1950. The Republican enrollment has improved somewhat through a switch by a few thousand people who felt a certain devotion to me personally and felt that they could best show this by enrolling as Republicans. As a matter of fact the Liberal party enrollment (I run on both tickets) has shown some improvement the same way.
>
> Now that I have told you about the figures in my district politically, I would like to tell you about the composition of my district because it is a typically American district. It is divided almost equally among the three great faiths, one-third Catholic, one-third Jewish, and one-third Protestant. Ten per-

cent of the district is composed of Negroes, which gives it an addition that is not unusual in American life. The average earnings of the heads of families runs about $4,000 per year per family, so that it is very much a middle class district. The men and women who live in it are workers and people who work in offices, and work in warehouses, and who own their own retail stores. My district is quite an interesting place in the latter regard, as a great many people are in business for themselves in a small way—accountants and lawyers, for example. Not the rich ones, not people who are overly or rather remarkably successful in financial terms. In addition I have in my district probably the greatest concentration of cultural institutions within any congressional district of the United States. I have Columbia, Barnard, The City College of New York, Yeshiva University, the Union Theological Seminary, the Jewish Theological Seminary, the Julliard School of Music, and the Medical Center, the College of Physicians and Surgeons. Now this is quite a galaxy of stellar attractions in terms of the cultural world, and so I have a fair population of college professors and people who are concerned with university life, though they by no means dominate my district.

I have also certain groupings in my district of a national origin character; and these, I might add, are very important for a congressman to know. A fair number of people in my district are of Greek extraction, a considerable number have come from Puerto Rico, and a small element is composed of people of Armenian background. The very large part of the Catholic population in my district is Irish or of Irish extraction. The Jewish people in my district, who represent about 30 percent of the population, are very interested in Israel, and so they have in a sense a particular foreign affairs interest. Negroes constitute 35,000 of the district's population—probably about 10,000 families—and I have some Japanese and Chinese who live in the area around Columbia University.

While Mr. Javits' statement that the twenty-first congressional district of New York City is a "typically American district" is misleading in the sense that it is probably not representative of the typical composition of a congressional district, it can be said that this district is quite characteristic of many large city constituencies. Thus the heterogeneity of New York's twenty-first district has its counterpart in congested metropolitan areas scattered throughout the country.

No doubt the ethnic groups may be different in other cities, but the principle of diversity remains the same. Not all voters have the same interests, jobs, income, religion, or party affiliation. And just as diversity or heterogeneity may be true of many metropolitan congressional districts, so we may find in some suburban areas important differences in group composition within constituencies, though they are usually not likely to be as strikingly apparent. But whatever the locale, the matter of getting known to the voters is the prime responsibility of any new congressional candidate, and the problems he faces in accomplishing these tasks are essentially the same. Again for purposes of illustration Mr. Javits' experience serves our purpose well.

In 1946 when Javits ran for Congress for the first time, Elmo Roper conducted a poll for him in the twenty-first district to ascertain the major issues in which the people of the constituency were interested. Included among the questions which were asked in this poll was one designed to determine how many people knew the name of their congressman. At that time 8 percent of the adult people (the total vote in this district ranges from approximately 100,000 to 130,-000) knew the name of the congressman, but not the correct one. Two years later—1948—Javits had another Roper poll conducted, and at this time 30 percent of the adult people in the district knew the name of their congressman and, added Mr. Javits parenthetically, "they knew the right name." Since this district had gone to the Democratic candidate by a vote of two and a half to one in 1944, Mr. Javits' feat of capturing the district in 1946 with 52 percent of the total vote, winning re-election in 1948—a bad year for the Republicans generally—and carrying his district by almost a two to one margin in 1950, the theme of his first campaign slogan in 1946 "know your district, know your congressman" is one that bears careful examination as to the techniques it entailed.

What was behind this 275 percent increase in the number of adult people who knew their congressman—the jump from 8 to 30 percent within two years—is best told in Mr. Javits' own words:

> What I have sought to do, and this is not idealizing it, is to build greater democracy, to tie the people closer to the operations of their government through me, and make them really feel

that I am their voice, their agent, their servant, and that I am not doing them a big favor, but this is my duty, and that I like it. Now, that's the cardinal philosophical basis on which I have proceeded.

Emphasizing that a congressman must have some conception of the needs of his district, he reported the interests of his own constituency, which he felt were fairly typical, as centering around five major questions that arise in Congress. These were the issues of war and peace, civil rights, price and wage control, health, education, and housing. Typical of the "direct relations" by which Congressman Javits sought to become known to his constituents as he serves their interests, were those he maintained in the field of rent, one of the five areas in which he believed a majority of his constituents had a major interest. "I run," he said, "what are called congressional rent clinics in my district, of which there are three located in different areas. They are staffed by volunteers—young lawyers in the Republican or Liberal parties to whom this is a ladder to political advancement—and these clinics give free advice on the State rent law." Supplementing such activities, Javits of course familiarized himself and his views to his constituents by weekly, and many times by two or three visits a week to New York City. To undertake such a program obviously involves not only strenuous physical effort, but it also taxes one's financial resources. And not without significance is the fact that Representative Javits reported that he spent from $7,000 to $10,000 in excess of his congressional salary and allowance to fulfill what he conceived to be the duties and responsibilities of a first-rate representative.

PROBLEMS OF COMMUNICATION

In our brief profile sketch of the experiences of Representative Javits, certain of the communicative problems of political leadership are suggested whose mastery has a great deal to do with the ultimate answer to our major question, how influential are presidential elections on congressional elections? Quite apart from simply making the physical effort to come before constituents or to work through one's political emissaries, is the matter of gaining support by relating issues and proposals to the needs of his constituents in terms of the widest comprehension. Stated briskly by Professor Key, "the idea of 'pump priming' can be more widely understood than Mr. Keynes' treatises on economics." Essentially, the maintenance of popular support, in effect the retention of the power of leadership, is facilitated by the possession of the faculty of explaining simply yet persuasively what is being done and why. Particularly important is the explanation of the "why" and not simply the exposition of a particular state of affairs, no matter how skillfully or dramatically presented. For example, an illustration drawn from the colorful tour of duty of H. L. Mencken as editor of the *Baltimore Evening Sun* serves our purpose well at this point.

Annoyed at the expanding number of federal job holders back in 1938, and equally disturbed by the inability of the average person to conjure a meaningful concept of the number of persons on the federal payroll, Mencken devised the following pictorial gimmick. Thus the grid reproduced below (Figure 15) represents a small section taken from the editorial of the *Evening Sun* on February 10, 1938. Six of the seven columns of the paper that day were filled with

FIGURE 15

dots such as those pictured above, each dot depicting a federal job holder. As anyone can quickly discover by counting them, our sample contains 3,500 dots to the square inch. At this density, as the editors commented, the *Evening Sun* contained 1,000,725 dots. By ten o'clock on the morning of February 10, 1938, when the paper first went to press, there were exactly 990,264 federal employees on the payroll. But since the number of federal job holders was increasing at the rate of 100 per hour, the number of dots reproduced was adjudged sufficiently close. On this basis it was thought that at approximately 45 seconds past midnight the number of printed dots would have corresponded exactly with the roster of federal employees.

No doubt a device such as the one above serves the useful purpose as far as it goes of reminding the voter, in an admittedly unusual way, of an obese federal payroll, the inference being that such a state of affairs is dangerous for the Republic. Thus it does serve the purpose of translating misty conjecture over the question "How many is a million?" into a perceptual image. But in the absence of equally effective communicated reasons as to why conditions would be bettered if the federal payroll were immediately slashed, perhaps a majority of voters remained undisturbed by the size of the federal bureaucracy, or at least remained unconvinced that its immediate contraction was a sound alternative.

To do the complete job effectively, to maximize comprehension of the issues and to interlock his policies with needs and interests as the voters conceive them is no small task. Yet it is done convincingly by a great number of our congressmen. But where it is done successfully it is accomplished through a skillful handling of political appeals—appeals that show a keen awareness of the attitudes and objectives of particular groups and use them as a framework within which ideas and policies can readily be fitted and adjusted.

Bringing together the reasons that lie behind successful congressional or presidential candidacies, they may be subsumed under two headings, the urgency of the voters' own interests, and the skill of candidates in sifting out the dominant interests and identifying himself effectively with them.

Throughout the nation the "tenderness of interest" as the candidates vie with each other can be easily demonstrated. In Plymouth County, Iowa, for example, where the income from livestock jumped by $10,000,000 between 1944 and 1948, and the Republican vote fell about a thousand while the Democrats gained roughly thirteen hundred—the net shift of exactly 2,452 in favor of the Democratic presidential candidate appears to have had no small connection with a "tenderness of interest." Thus whether we take Plymouth County or Loving County, Texas, the dominant interest of the community has a strong influence on the outcome of a given election.

Turning to an assessment of candidates' skills in waging campaigns the identification of critical elements is more difficult. Far too frequently in assaying the "why" of successful candidacy we incline to the notion that the peerless paragons of leadership combine some galaxy of special traits that sets them apart from their fellow citizens—charisma as some psychologists speak of it. On such a faith, no doubt, the idea of a sweeping coattail pull for the presidential candidate gains inflated stature. But more probably—as the 1952 campaign may very well demonstrate—these special qualities with which the charismaticists insist *all leaders* are endowed—do not actually become apparent except in a given situation. Though Mencken may be correct in saying that leadership is usually resolved by people jolly well getting what they deserve, the fact is that who they get depends upon an "interactional" and "associational" process. The greatest single factor in Roosevelt's effectiveness as a speaker, writes his long time adviser and speechwriter, Judge Samuel Roseman, "was his ability to associate himself closely with his listeners. He could give the impression that they were all sitting down together, discussing common problems, common successes, and common failures." And as he showed in his fireside chats, "he was a master at presenting the most complicated matters in the most understandable terms."[6] Thus in principle the matter of effective communication in campaigning is not unlike the truth of Chancellor Carmichael's remark that in good teaching knowledge is "caught not taught."

Presidents and congressmen alike, then, rise as successful leaders in accordance with their knowledge of these groups and their needs, and their mastery of communicating with them effectively in a given social situation. Thus Governor Stevenson's preliminary remark to the American Legion Convention that he was mightily pleased that his listeners had forsaken the pleasures of visiting New York's museums and art galleries in order to hear him, may have been a small joke, as Stewart Alsop reported, but it went over with a wallop.

------

[6]Samuel I. Roseman: *Working with Roosevelt* (New York: Harper, 1952) pp. 490-91, 39.

Again we have an instance of the exercise of skill—in this case a reminder of remembered experience—in a given social situation. What the social situation is, of course, how to filter out the needs of particular communities of interest, and most urgent of all, how to communicate by appearing to associate himself with the group or groups, constitute the really compelling problems of congressional and presidential candidacy.

CHAPTER **6**

Congressional Elections
and the Politics
of Tomorrow

WHATEVER their respective skills in appealing to the electorate, the relations of the presidential and congressional candidates obviously have a bearing on party policy.   And while the coattail influence of the presidential candidate has been demonstrated to be of minor significance, the fact that successful presidential candidates normally run ahead of their congressional tickets suggests that a party's national ticket has become increasingly important.

In a sense the party as a whole is personified in the presidential candidate.   Yet listening to campaign claptrap and some of the parliamentary pyrotechnics of the congressional forum makes it evident that there are times when neither of the presidential candidates appears to be the leader of his party.   Ideologically, then, the presidential candidates and their congressional teammates do not always show close conformity on matters of policy.   Thus, though the steady climb of the presidency in the matter of public policy leadership is one of the patent political truths of this century, this rise has not been accompanied by a corresponding expansion of presidential authority as a party leader. The lack of commensurate authority in the presidential candidate to bring about party responsibility has, therefore, disturbed many students of our party system and has led them to urge reforms that will give presidential candidates a tighter control over party leadership.

Another worry of many critics of our party system is concerned with the adequacy of our representational system as it is now operating. To a very large extent the geographical arrangements of our congressional districts contributes to a somewhat artificial political structure in so far as the representation of particular groups is concerned. Thus in many areas a single group with the same interests or several groups with common interests that might be brought together in a common representational area are kept from joining forces effectively by the geographical boundaries of congressional districts. The long-familiar monstrosities that result from reckless legislative liberties with the gerrymander, moreover, accentuate the difficulties of groups in joining hands to make common cause politically. This circumstance, combined with the fact that the traditional differences between our major parties have been slight, has been endlessly despaired. Our purpose in this chapter will be to look at both the criticisms and assets of the party system, as it concerns congressional elections, and weigh it in the balance to see if it is found wanting.

MODERN CRITICISM OF OUR PARTY SYSTEM

Essentially the impatience with the current functioning of our political system is cradled in two basic considerations. First, the paramountcy of national issues is imperilled by the inordinate attention Congress gives to local affairs. In this view, Congress in the "scuffle of local interests," as Herbert Agar has described it, is simply incapable of coping with the challenge of events and will doubtless continue this way unless the party system is drastically overhauled.

The second element of major discontent with the political system that has led many students to urge re-examination of party responsibility is the existence of what one writer has called "principleless politics."[1] Because our parties are coalitions or loose alliances, the political life of the nation is one of contradictions—so runs the argument. Within each of the major parties are groups that frequently seem to be working at cross-purposes in driving toward their interests and objectives. Most common of the inconsistencies are those usually cited for the Democratic party—Dixiecrat or Southern Bourbon teamed with Americans for Democratic Action, for example, if we wish to contrast groups, or Pat McCarran and Hubert Humphrey if we incline to a comparison of individuals. But the Republican party likewise has a generous range of political gradation. Not unknown by any means in the Republican fold are those crustacean characters of the party who in company with the elderly New England lady believe that if only dear Mr. Coolidge could return from lunch, the most stubbornly resistant problems of the Republic would quickly respond to his taciturn touch.

Of critical argument against the shortcomings of poor discipline within our parties there is no dearth. And much of it is compelling. Among the more ominous objections is one expressed in several quarters that the lack of clearly defined choices in the alternatives offered to the voter is leading us down the steep slopes into a one-party system. So pressing and complex are the problems of our industrial society—so it is claimed—that quarrels among the citizenry involving labor and management, or other groups, cannot continue to be left to the casual temporization that our two-party system has given us in the past. Thus we are nearing the junction of the two parties, and with this confluence we shall take on many of the characteristics of a one-party state. So runs one argument.

Elsewhere E. E. Schattschneider, while conceding the possible merit in an earlier era of a system operated by two similar parties, one largely playing the devil's advocate or obstructionist, believes our altered circumstances now require a party realignment. Again the urgent need for vigorous action marching to the tune of well-defined policies is cited to support the plea for altering party structure. High priority in the task of reconstruction that Professor

[1]The phrase is V. O. Key's.

Schattschneider envisages are two basic changes. One is the amendment of our method of nominating presidential candidates so that the nominees who are selected will be individuals who have clearly established themselves as national leaders of the party.[2] The second, and perhaps more important, step is to redesign the system of making congressional nominations in such a way that the influence of the presidential nominee over these nominations is commensurate with the broad responsibility with which Schattschneider would like to invest him for national party leadership.

From another perspective, a distinguished student of public policy nails his comments on the shortcomings of our undisciplined party structure on the fact that the operations of government and our private economy have become so intimately interrelated. In the interest of continuity and avoidance of incidents that will cause dislocations and disruptions in our economy, Professor Fainsod sees the homogeneous and disciplined political party as a necessary ally of our governmental system.[3] Thus in his view, which is in concert with many others, the real question is not the desirability of disciplined, homogeneous parties, for this is accepted, but rather the discovery of how central party leadership can be institutionalized.

In all conjecture about the future course of American politics the prime concern of those who wish to reshape party organization and reshuffle the voting elements between the major parties, is what consequences are likely to result from inaction. Critical social and economic problems have been stockpiling during the past dozen years and in the eyes of the critics it is the inadequacies of our party system that have brought about a condition of political stalemate. In this situation we have had no effective majority in Congress, and in the absence of a program that will lead to stricter groupings of like-minded voters within one party or the other, no effective majority can be realized that will break the legislative deadlock. Too long a postponement in the reorientation of our party system can therefore

[2] *The Struggle for Party Government* (College Park, Maryland: University of Maryland, 1948).

[3] Merle Fainsod: "Consolidating Party Control," *American Political Science Review*, 42 (1948), pp. 316-326.

result in a fracture of the "social bonds of consensus." [4] Taking an overall look at what it deems the likely prospects of inaction and failure to carry out reform of the party system, the American Political Science Association's Committee on Political Parties singles out four danger marks for special emphasis:

First, it believes that the inadequacy of the party system in providing coherent, positive programs and bringing about broad public support for them will lead to an "explosive era." Second, it is fearful that because of the present deficiencies in our parties the American people may be inclined to compensate for such shortcomings by shifting "excessive responsibility to the President," a course that would imperil constitutional government. Third, it suggests the danger, commented on earlier, that the ineffectiveness and indecision of the party system will hasten the disintegration of our two major parties and perhaps leave us with a one-party system. Finally, it expresses an alarm that the ineptitude of the two parties for translating well-structured programs into national policy will discontent voters to the point that they will be more susceptible to the appeals of extremist parties.[5]

THE ADAPTABILITY OF THE PARTY SYSTEM

Admittedly the arguments urging modification of our traditional and casual two-party arrangement for handling problems of public policy are persuasive. Moreover, the relevance of some of them to needed improvements demands they be given a serious hearing. Yet in the contradictions and imperfections of our party system we may well find some of the mainsprings of constitutional stability. Thus the slight differences between the two parties and the seemingly incompatible configuration of forces within them need not be lamented. Under the traditional system neither party has pressed its advantage after winning a national election to a point that the losing party has refused to tolerate. And in the give and take of our political life the programs and policies of both parties have been shaped by common forces and both have shown remarkable powers

---

[4]Key: *Politics, Parties, and Pressure Groups, op. cit.,* p. 242.
[5]*Toward a More Responsible Two-Party System* (New York: Rinehart, 1950), pp. 92-96.

of adaptation. For a striking example let us dust off the names of the Republicans who represented the New England states and those who came from the Middle West a generation or two ago.

Typical of the New England contingent was George H. Moses, who rose before the New England Manufacturers' Association on November 7, 1929 and said: "Mournfully I prophesy that the program of these *sons of the wild jackass* who now control the Senate will probably go forward to complete consummation." [6]

What Senator Moses was referring to, of course, with his barbed phrase "sons of the wild jackass," was the unreconstructed GOP band of bedouins out in the Middle West who were roving the land pouring out ideas and programs, whose orthodoxy was unacceptable to conservative Republican leadership. Looking at the roster of names serving either a few years earlier or at the time Senator Moses dropped his blockbuster—which promptly inspired an insurgent attempt to unseat him as Chairman of the Republican Senatorial Campaign Committee—the following turn up for New England: from Rhode Island, Jesse H. Metcalf and Le Baron B. Colt; from Massachusetts, W. Murray Crane, Henry Cabot Lodge, and John W. Weeks; and from Connecticut, Frank P. Brandegee, Frederic C. Walcott, and Hiram Bingham; and from New Hampshire, George H. Moses and Henry J. Keyes. That the foregoing, to which further names might be appended, were strong minded in their conservatism hardly requires comment.

Yet out in the Midwest the tincture of progressivism was as strong as the conservatism of the New England senatorial contingent: Beveridge of Indiana, Bristow and Capper of Kansas, Cummins, Brookhart and Dolliver of Iowa, La Follette and Blaine of Wisconsin, Norris of Nebraska, Norbeck of South Dakota, Gronna, Ladd and Frazier of North Dakota and Couzens of Michigan. Taking a leap of thirty years, however, it is clearly seen that the configuration of sentiment among senators of the New England and Middle-western regions is just reversed.

In 1952 the names we find in the New England delegation are Margaret Chase Smith, Charles W. Tobey, Ralph Flanders, George

---

[6]Quoted in George Stimpson: *A Book About American Politics* (New York, 1952), p. 283.

D. Aiken, Leverett Saltonstall, and Henry Cabot Lodge, Jr., while
in the Middlewest the roll call includes Homer Capehart, Everett
Dirksen, William Jenner, Joe McCarthy, Homer Ferguson, Robert
Taft, John Bricker, Hugh Butler, and James Kem. What are the
reasons behind this regional shift where the primacy of liberal leadership of the Republican party passed from the Middle West to New
England? Certainly they are complex and no single explanation will
suffice. Nor should one build too much significance into this regional change in the philosophical stance of the GOP. Yet a few
clues do exist that ought to be pursued.

One clue as to why progressive Republican leadership slipped
away from the Middle West and frontier regions back to the Northeast is very likely to be found in New England's economic geography.
A leader for many years in the nation's economic growth, New
England has lost ground over the last generation.

"From 8.2 percent of the nation's total flow of income to individuals in 1929, New England's share was reduced to 6.7 percent,"
during the ensuing twenty years.[7] Again while the national average
increase of income in the United States was 139 percent for the
period 1929 to 1949, New England's income went up 95 percent.
And taking per capita income, the growth for the region was 67
percent as compared with the 96 percent for the entire nation during
the same twenty year period. The per capita income of New England residents, it should be noted, was still above the national average, in 1949. But while it was 124 percent of the national average
in 1929, the per capita income for New England in 1949 was down
to 105 percent. Finally, among other factors it should be noted that
employment in New England's factories in 1949 was below the peak
reached in 1919.

Beset by a slower rate of growth than the national average and
exposed to the familiar hardships that the entire country experienced
during the depression and recession era, New England more than
elsewhere might be expected to reflect some of the uneasiness of her
economy in her political behavior. Forty-three percent of her popu-

[7]Bureau of Foreign and Domestic Commerce: *Regional Trends in the
United States Economy* (United States Department of Commerce, Washington,
D. C., 1951), p. 15.

lation was in the labor force in 1940, as compared with forty percent for the nation as a whole. And notably in a few areas of the region where factories were moved to other sections of the country some New England residents were living within at least the marginal shadows of a depression since the early 1920's.

All factors considered—not the least of which was the great industrialization of the area and consequent dependence of labor for employment—is it to be wondered that a region bounded in part by a strong traditionalism for Republican loyalty sought to keep that loyalty and yet register a dissent against traditional GOP policy in the primaries? Is it not significant that in June, 1952, the one remaining unbending conservative, Owen Brewster, was defeated in Maine's senatorial primary by Governor Frederick G. Payne, whose election in September made New England's Republican representation in the Senate solid in its progressive orientation?

And so the primary candidates who have been trying to retread the party with progressive ideas are winning in New England primaries. Interestingly one might ask why has the same disposition to elect progressive senators not been reflected in as broad a way in House elections. The answer in large part would seem to be that to win on a state-wide basis, a candidate has had to compromise with forces who have been affected by the very conditions of the economy that we have discussed, while in the House elections he has only had to satisfy the elements of a single district.

SOCIAL STRUCTURE AND THE PARTY SYSTEM

Since parties do adapt themselves to the changing needs of the nation, it follows that the lines of adaptation they take will be largely determined by the group structure of our society. And here again the question of what form of party adjustment should emerge from the shifting patterns and countless antagonisms within our society is the subject of acrimonious debate.

Over a generation ago Professor Holcombe noted that the strong leanings toward geographic sectionalism in American politics were beginning to be modified by a rising urbanism. And in place of the combinations of sectional strength upon which the parties depended

for their power, he predicted that the growth of cities would intro-
duce new interests into politics—a development that would ultimately lead to cleavages along class lines.[8]

That Holcombe's thesis on the shift of power to the cities is
being borne out, seems to be confirmed by the evidence. Thus in
1950 he concluded that congressional districts as they existed at that
time could be classified as follows: 130 urban, 125 mixed urban-
rural, and 180 rural; while in 1952 Gallup lists 94 Northern big
city congressional districts and 134 Northern mixed urban-rural districts—a combined total of 328 or approximately 76 percent of the
House seats. And as Farrelly and Hinderaker point out in their
study of 1950 congressional reapportionment and political power,
although it is difficult to predict the urban rural distribution of seats
until state legislatures have reapportioned on the basis of the 1950
census (Missouri, for example, will have a referendum on the results
of legislative redistricting in November, 1952), the trend toward
more urban and mixed urban districts is unmistakable. In this
respect—reflecting population shifts from farm to city areas—California is probably typical. "In sum," report Farrelly and Hinde-
racker, seven new districts "have been drawn to follow the population in its outward movement from the old urban centers to the
new and suburban areas." [9]

With the growing importance of cities as centers of political
power economic and social interests have also developed whose tendency is to integrate particular groups on a national rather than specifically sectional lines. And it is in this fashion—as particular groups
or interests located in and throughout most urban centers discover
integrating lines of policy—that political alliances are born that
transcend sectional sentiments.

How far the cleavages of metropolitanism have developed that
seem to run along class lines, as Holcombe prophecied, is still inde-

---

[8]A. N. Holcombe: *The New Party Politics* (New York, 1933), pp. 11,
31-34; and see also by the same author: *The Middle Classes in American Politics* (Cambridge: Harvard University Press, 1940), pp. 65-123.

[9]David G. Farrelly and Ivan Hinderaker: "Congressional Reapportionment and National Political Power," *Law and Contemporary Problems,* 17
(1952), p. 357.

terminate. Several test borings by Roper and some by Lubell in analysis of particular wards show marked tendencies for particular groups and classes within given areas to hold common partisan attachments, examples of which we shall refer to later. But the real question which compels our attention now is this: in light of growing urbanization and some definite indications that metropolitanism is conducive to political cleavages along class lines, are the traditional arrangements of our party system inadequate to meet the challenge?

In the eyes of the critics a true integration of labor's political resources has long been frustrated by a party system originally erected upon rural and agrarian interests—a party system now grown obsolete. Recently, moreover, some critics, noting the startling increase of the so-called "new middle classes" again emphasize the fact that an integration of the new interests which this group holds in common remains an unfulfilled hope because of the inadequacies of our party system.

Before tying into these criticisms, certain considerations seem relevant to raise at the outset. First, while much has been said of the partisan faiths of different groups in American politics, and while on the surface certain party preferences seem plain enough, we know that overlapping loyalties are quite common even in groups with strong political leanings. With this in mind it is not improper to ask as we go along whether such independent tendencies within organized groups do not serve rather than hinder a democratic political system. Secondly—and particularly important as we look ahead—we need to be aware of the changing contours of society that our party system is going to serve. Certainly we should recognize the changes that are taking place in the occupational structure of our society if we are to make careful judgments on the case for and against a remodelled party system. For example, it is commonly supposed in many quarters that labor, already well-poised to fight its political battles, may very likely move ahead in political strength, its eventual command well-assured. But sociologists have told us for some time, though perhaps few have listened, of a "dark horse" on the American political scene, a dark horse with a white collar— thirteen million strong as a matter of fact. It is because of the spectacular growth of the new middle classes and the implications that growth has for the future, that consideration of this group serves our purpose well in weighing the merits of the controversy which now bubbles about the status of our party system.

The "New Middle Classes." In this scuffle many writers see the so-called "new middle classes" serving as the spear carriers for a remodelled party system—a system that will lead to a stricter configuration of various group interests and voting forces. Thus Lubell argues that in the interest of bringing about an effective majority no issue has greater paramountcy than the reshuffling of our disparate voting elements. And the power to bring about this realignment—to "nationalize" American politics—he urges, lies with the new middle classes. It is this group that has pulled out of poverty and has within its grasp the means "through which a dramatic reintegration of American life will be accomplished." [10]

If the term "new middle classes" is to be used advisedly when we attempt to assess the political role of this group a note of elaboration is in order. Much of the notion of what constitutes the middle class in the United States rests upon a psychological identification. Not surprising, therefore, is the result of the American Institute of Public Opinion showing that 65 percent of the American people believe they belong to the middle class.[11]

More definitively, however, the new middle class embraces several million white collar employees who work for salaries instead of wages, though again such a distinction is not satisfactory as a rigid criterion for defining the middle class. Historically, the old middle class in the United States was distinguished by the fact that it had a property status in the occupational stratum of society, that is to say practically all persons in the middle class were self-employed enterprisers of one sort or another. But the great bulk of the middle class today are salaried employees with no enterpreneurial property. From three quarters of a million—which was the number of middle class employees in 1870—the ranks of the groups grew to twelve and a

---

[10] *The Future of American Politics, op. cit.,* p. 257.

[11] See Hadley Cantril: *Public Opinion: 1935-1946* (Princeton, 1951), p. 116. Using a measurement device where thirteen possible classifications were suggested, Elmo Roper found that 40 percent of the American people described themselves as belonging to the middle class.

half million by 1940. And "of the three broad strata composing modern society," reports C. Wright Mills, "only the middle class has steadily grown in proportion to the whole." [12] In the period between 1870 and 1940 the old middle class increased 135 percent; wage workers, 255 percent; and the new middle classes, 1600 percent.

Preeminently employees of the lower middle income brackets, the new middle classes are tiered from top to bottom just as we would find members of any of the three broad groups of our society. Not strung out on a single level, the new middle classes fall into a pyramidal structure within society at large, with the managerial element comprising 10 percent, salaried professionals—school teachers, technicians, etc.—accounting for 25 percent, sales personnel 25, and office workers 40 percent.

Clearly those who feel that the steady upthrust of the new middle classes presages the emergence of a powerful juggernaut capable of functioning as the pivotal political force in modern society lean heavily on certain presuppositions. Prominent among these is the notion that since we may infer commonly held hopes and aspirations among the new middle classes, an integration of their interests will develop an independent political policy for this group. In recognition of this possibility it comes as no surprise that the AFL and CIO have announced their intention of spending more than $2,000,000 to try to organize 13,000,000 white collar workers in the United States.[13]

In truth there is much persuasiveness in Lubell's argument that in the recency of the new middle classes climb out of poverty and in the fact that they spring from a different historical era are elements of homogeneity. Thus the new middle class elements, having a heritage of rougher times during the depression and having upgraded their status in a period of expanding governmental authority, "are not as hostile to 'Big Government' as the older middle class elements."[14] In this circumstance the new middle class has acquired

---

[12]See C. Wright Mills: *White Collar* (New York: Oxford University Press, 1951), pp. 63-65.

[13]*Baltimore Evening Sun*, August 15, 1952.

[14]*The Future of American Politics, op. cit.*, pp. 60-61.

the necessary cohesiveness to become politically independent, and
functioning in this role it could well be the social harmonizer in our
society between management and labor.

Certainly the new middle class has experienced a dramatic
numerical growth. Moreover, looking at the long strides taken
by this group, there is much to confirm Lubell's thesis that as
developed over the past two decades the new middle class appears to
be as "Democratic by custom as the older middle class elements are
Republican." [15] Yet the idea that the new middle class has evolved a
common concourse for its political policy is far from being substan-
tiated by the evidence. In so far as an occupational ideology is concerned, Mills says, the middle classes are politically "passive." And
contrary to expectations "these middle groups show no signs of devel-
oping a policy of their own." [16]

Opinion divides sharply, of course, over whether there really
are discernible patterns in the political tendencies of the middle
classes. It ranges from holding that the new middle class will become the ruling group in modern society to the view that this broad
group of our society forms the crucible for the onslaught of fascism,
or that its identity will melt into that of the proletariat.[17] Taking a
sober look at what we know of the political behavior of the new
middle class at the moment, however, a homogeneity in which some
writers profess to see the prayerful hope of the future for American
politics is simply not an established fact. Nor does the emergence
of a homogeneous new middle class organized about a single dominant interest appear to be a likelihood in the foreseeable future. Nor
is it altogether desirable that the new middle class move forward
toward a sternly stratified group outlook and political objective.

---

[15]*Ibid.*, p. 59.

[16]C. Wright Mills: "The Middle Classes in Middle-Sized Cities," *American
Sociological Review*, 11 (Oct., 1946), p. 528.

[17]The idea that fascist movements are of middle class origin probably
needs critical re-examination. While "superficially plausible" as one writer
suggests, generalizations about its broad applicability are questionable and
there are many implications that ought to be studied separately. See Reinhard
Bendix, "Social Stratification and Political Power," *American Political Science
Review*, 46 (1952), pp. 367-375.

Despite its imperfections, a vigorously pluralistic society is a safe roadbed for the many experimental journeys in public policy that need to be taken in the course of constitutional government. It is arguable, of course, that once a unified occupational ideology could be engineered to solidify the new middle class, its growing numerical importance would make this group the true intermediary of our political system. In this setting, then, we would look to the new middle class to induce an equilibrium of interests that would curb social tensions and make possible a progressive system of responsible enterprise. But this is a frail promise. And in the conjecture on both its possibilities of achievement as well as its effects, if attainable, we should not be unmindful of the hazards.

Within the sentiments of the old middle class, it has often been remarked that we sometimes discover the humus for fascist or authoritarian ideologies. Yet we also know that segments of the middle class have allied themselves from time to time with labor or business in quest of political action whose democratic legitimacy is not suspect. Perhaps the political passivity of the middle class which some attribute to the absence of an occupational ideology is responsible for the spastic political tendencies of certain segments within the middle class. And where the alliances are with extremist political groups this is a matter for concern. Yet need we despair of these shifting alignments when we examine them in their totality? If what Mills calls the high white collar class workers of the middle class are 40 percent more Republican than their lower white collar colleagues in a certain city, we are also reminded that the broad gains of the new middle classes of which Lubell speaks have made this group Democratically inclined. And so it goes for any of the broad groups of our society, and underscores the fact that the middle class does "not make up one single compact stratum."

Diversity Within the Middle Classes. No doubt events of the past two decades in American politics have had some amalgamating effect on the middle classes. To cite an example we might take Lubell's reference to the "class feelings stirred by Franklin D. Roosevelt," which he correctly contends "have served as a crucible in which older sectional and cultural antagonisms are being melted down." The incentive to override regional or cultural differences, of course, was an economic one and it was the propelling factor for the working classes as well as the middle classes. But when we begin to look for a middle class solidarity that transcends not only divergent interests within this group but differences of outlook among different segments of it as well, we find wide variations.

Quite apart from divergences that stem from middle class occupations themselves—the schoolteachers and retail salespeople or manager and office worker—are the mixed attitudes of daily life that characterize different groups within the middle class. Comparative studies of family budgets, for example, reveal that although the income is the same it may be spent in quite a different way. Thus some persons spend more for housing and clothes and less for food in the interest of keeping up a certain position, while others may do the reverse. There are also differences of intellectual interests or tastes to which the middle class is subject as we might well expect of any class of society. While any of these factors singly or collectively is probably not strong enough to override a horizontal economic community of interests, they still induce a measure of independence within the sub-group structure of the middle class. And it may be submitted that to have these different groups within the middle class assert an independence that upends a horizontal stratum of interests from time to time, is a wholesome condition for our political system. Well-expressed by David Truman, in a healthy and vigorous political system "there is a connection between some minimum recognition of the claims of organized groups and the vitality of widespread unorganized interests."[18]

The Political Potential of the New Middle Class. Until recently the pivotal possibilities of the new middle classes as a major political force in our society have been scantily weighed. Actually if they could find the common interest to pull in harness politically, their potential voting power might prove the strongest of any group in our society. To get some notion of the striking power of the new middle class it is helpful to examine some of the broad changes that have altered the occupational profile of our economy.

At the outset one of the significant shifts in the occupational

---

[18]*The Governmental Process, op. cit.,* p. 524.

census of the United States that should be remarked is the drop in unskilled workers.   In 1940, out of a total of 51,000,000 persons actively employed, there were fewer than 9,000,000 unskilled workers, that is to say workers without any technical or professional training. This included 3,350,000 agricultural workers, 1,193,000 of whom belonged to the families of farm owners or tenants.   Considering this point, Raymond Aron, editor and political writer of the French daily, *Figaro*, observes that the number of what he calls "absolute proletarians" was down to 18 percent in 1940, while in 1910 it had exceeded 25 percent.[19]   And by 1950 the number of unskilled workers constituted approximately 14 percent of the total labor force in the United States.[20]

Significant as the reduction of our unskilled labor forces may be, however, the noteworthy change in our employment structure lies elsewhere.   In his illuminating study, *Conditions of Economic Progress* the Australian economist, Colin Clark, reminds us of the three basic sectors in the occupational structure of a modern society: (1) primary activities—agricultural production and raw material extraction industries; (2) secondary activities—manufacturing or processing industries; and (3) tertiary activities—public services, transport, trade, commerce, and administration.   Customarily in modern societies we find an initial phase during which secondary activities, that is to say the manufacturing industries, overtake the primary activities, and subsequently an expansion of tertiary activities in turn at the expense of the secondary.   Thus in the United States, Clark estimates that the proportion of primary producers fell steadily from 72.3 percent in 1820 to 23.2 percent in 1929.[21]

Looking at the present division of workers in the United States the further interesting fact is that more than half the working population is working in tertiary activities and approximately 35 percent in secondary activities.   Reflecting on this occupational differen-

---

[19]"Social Structure and the Ruling Class," *British Journal of Sociology*, 1 (March, 1950), p. 6.

[20]Bureau of the Census: *Annual Report on the Labor Force* (Washington, D. C., 1950), Series P50, No. 31, p. 4.

[21]*The Condition of Economic Progress* (London: Macmillan, 1940), p. 185.

tiation in the United States, Raymond Aron sees two clear indications. First, the "Marxist type of industrial worker will not represent the bulk of society for the future, but a decreasing fraction of
the population." Second, the tendency is now self-evident, "we are
moving towards a civilization that will be largely composed of clerical
rather than manual workers." In this setting "planning, organization, administration, and distribution are becoming increasingly
complicated and absorbing an increasing number of men. We are
living," he tells us, "in the administrative age no less than in the
machine age."[22]

What will be the impact of these occupational tendencies on
our party system? Will the reduction in the number of manual
workers and increase in administrative and clerical workers lead
to a greater differentiation and spread of party supporters and political alliances? Or is this trend more likely to produce "new
embracing wholes" in our society with more rigidly cast configurations for political activity? Clearly these are matters that cannot be
accurately foretold at the moment. But beset by the arguments of
those who would hasten the appearance of a new constellation of
forces within our political system, capable of wielding the balance
of power, there are some sober reflections that ought to be set down.

That the voting behavior of many groups whose interests would
appear to coincide because of economic or occupational status is
indeterminate has been demonstrated countless times in American
elections. Talk of the complete solidarity of labor, agriculture, or
business, and threats of a deliverable vote are brandished in every national campaign. Yet when the ballots are tallied there seem to be
quite a few breaches. Broad tendencies in voting among groups
of similar occupational or income bracket there are, of course.[23] But
the strictly disciplined vote, the vote that brings all persons within
an economic group into one political camp, has failed to materialize

[22]"Social Structure and the Ruling Classes," *British Journal of Sociology,*
loc. cit., pp. 6-7.

[23]For example, Elmo Roper's ward analysis of the metropolitan vote in
Boston, arranged according to rental level, revealed that the poor and lower
middle income groups were decidedly less Republican in 1948 than in 1944.

	1944 % Republican	1948 % Republican
Prosperous	57.4	61.6
Upper-middle income	50.4	45.4
Lower-middle income	35.4	27.3
Poor	32.2	17.3

New York Herald Tribune, June 19, 1949.

in American politics and the loyalties or dispositions of the voters falling between the two poles of our income scale are markedly fluid. Economic solidarity, therefore, has not yet brought about a unity of interest that brings about an absolute polarization of American voting habits. Moreover, since there are differences in interests and mixed attitudes in tastes among groups within the same economic stratum that play a part in preventing absolute polarization in the voting behavior of these groups, can we anticipate that these distinctions will gradually disappear? Does it seem likely that in the society of the future which promises an ever-decreasing supply of manual workers, the new middle classes will have their attitudes, interests, and cultural or intellectual tastes homogenized? And will not the middle class intermediary groups of the future society feel the same impulses for independence of political judgment or be driven by the same desires for diversity that are commonly attributed to them today?

The middle classes after all, are composed of many elements—the members of professions, physicians as well as teachers, the small shopkeeper as well as the small businessman. No doubt what Colin Clark describes as "the tendency for the relative number of administrative and clerical workers to increase, till in many spheres they actually outnumber the manual workers" may induce a degree of conformity in political outlook.[24] And such conformity might well have a major bearing on the political consciousness of the middle class. But whatever the strength of the forces for conformity of opinion among the middle classes there are certain to be competing desires and interests that will induce some fractionalization of political outlook. Admittedly the middle class has great dependence upon large properties for its occupational or job security. Income of the new middle class is preeminently from salaries and, like the work-

[24]Clark: *The Conditions of Economic Progress, op. cit.,* p. 220.

ing classes who are paid wages, its dependency on large properties is most formidable. This dependency, moreover, is in turn closely linked with the politics of government, for certain it is that the operations of government and our private economy have become intimately interrelated. Thus it is arguable that the dependence will furnish an incentive for unilateral political action by the middle class and that the discovery of a community of interest by this group will unite it in common political endeavor. Yet inevitably in the course of the group process that may lead to the development of integrating lines of policy for the middle class, some diffusion of interest will occur.

That the middle class will fail to develop communities of interest which will influence variation in political outlook is difficult to conceive. Not only will differences in the nature of the professions or occupations contribute to some pluralistic tendencies in the politics of the middle class. Additional elements of differentiation will affect the political outlook of this broad group of society. Within the middle class it would be unlikely for prestige factors not to attach to different types of work. Nor is it likely that the several outlooks of the multiple groups within the middle class will always coincide. A community of practical interest, a group within one occupation, may compete with another group on occasion. Similarly, they may embrace different outlooks—outlooks that would sometimes take them into disparate paths of political policy. Thus, despite tendencies which the middle class might appear to hold in common such as broadly similar incomes and in the case of a large segment of this group—the clerical and administrative workers of the new middle classes—a similar type of occupation, divergent interests will make themselves felt.

Social differentiation, though perhaps watered down, will also have a bearing on the outlook and attitudes of different groups within the middle class. Stratification of social groups may be significantly eased and the mobility of individuals within the social structure of our society will probably be enhanced. Nonetheless, the continued existence of some social groups is likely, and the presumption is strong that they in turn will intrude elements of diversity into the various components of the middle class.

Of what interest and of what relation to our party system of congressional elections is all such discussion of occupational trends in our society and the political interests of the middle class? Assuredly great and intimate. For in the course of events—in the future of American politics where some of the operable conditions are indistinct and where the configuration of interests for different groups of society are indeterminate—one may yet envisage the loose-limbed American party system upholding constitutional government, awkwardly at times, yet safely. And then as now it may well be that in the very imperfections of our party system are cradled its strength. Indeed, as Key sums up the arguments for and against the casually indifferent techniques of our traditional party system, "perhaps in its very amorphousness and nondoctrinaire quality will be found the resilience to permit adjustment and growth to meet exigencies as they emerge."[25]

Party Politics—Free Style: Malediction or Blessing?

Unquestionably much of the amorphousness is directly attributable to the long-continued arrangements in our congressional elections for each congressional candidate to campaign in terms of his own constituency rather than be governed by the strict dictates of his own thinking or in terms of the distinctive characteristics of his national party policy. And it is essentially because of this habit, that permits congressional candidates to drift away from a rigorously held national party policy and any semblance of unified campaigning, that the present day critics insist that the two-party system will be increasingly put to an unbearable strain in seeking to contend with public problems.

The Party System and Voter Turnout. In assessing the party system it is perhaps as easy to overstate its shortcomings as it is to overlook its defects. And it is also possible to misconstrue the significance of certain well known facts of political behavior. For example, take the diminutive size of the vote that has been endlessly bemoaned by practically every observer of American politics. Such criticism has been particularly directed at the poor record in con-

---

[25]*Politics, Parties, and Pressure Groups, op. cit.,* p. 243.

gressional voting. Thus in 1942 the congressional vote fell off from a total of 47,000,000 in 1940 by nearly 19,000,000; in 1946 the total country-wide vote for members of the House of Representatives dropped away 11,000,000 from the 1944 total; and in 1950 the House vote declined 5,500,000 from the 1948 mark—the latter year yielding an unusually low turnout for a presidential election. Armed with incontrovertible evidence of a relatively low voting turnout in both presidential and congressional elections, it has become commonplace for speakers to bray with alarm that the slimness of our vote foretells disaster. But how much of a story do our moderately filled ballot boxes tell us? Does an 88 percent turnout necessarily mean a more contented constitutionalism, free from the perils of sharpening political conflict that easily leads to authoritarianism, while a 50 to 60 percent vote is a portent of danger ahead? On this point the evidence is far from conclusive. Moreover, it is conceivable, as one student of the subject, Reinhard Bendix, has recently remarked, that "under certain conditions the survival of democratic institutions does not depend upon a more widespread participation in politics, as it is commonly assumed." Rather it may, he continues, depend "on a persistent residue of political apathy which enables the nonparticipants to acquiesce in the democratic process and to ignore its many imperfections."[26] Supporting this conclusion also is the Swedish political scientist, Herbert Tingsten, who holds that "an exceptionally high voting frequency may indicate an intensification of political controversy which may involve a danger to the democratic system."[27] This was particularly true of Austria and Germany in the late twenties and early thirties, reports Tingsten, where the enormous participation figures "were symptomatic of a political tension heightened in the extreme, and foreshadowed the fall of democratic regimes."

Of course a voting turnout that can boast of only a 50 to 60 percent participation record should stir us to greater efforts in crowding the precinct polling places. For the response in national elec-

---

[26]"Social Stratification and Political Power," *American Political Science Review*," 46 (1952), pp. 372-373.

[27]*Political Behavior* (London: P. S. King & Son, 1937), pp. 225-226.

tions is admittedly and inexcusably lame. Yet the inference is still unwarranted that this casual indifference reflects increasing disillusionment and impatience with the imperfections of our party system and suggests its probable demise. And so it is that many arguments —well-intentioned and not without some merit—are overstated and begin to circulate as shibboleths. So also it is that the battle for strong party centralization is urged onward under many banners. Moreover, even when the possibility of party centralization is conceded to be remote, some serious and able writers insist that we make a clean break with the past and place our faith in "a plenitude of presidential power. Perhaps "presidential government operating through a nationalizing bureaucracy with Congress reduced to the role of critic may be far from the ideal party government we might desire," concludes Professor Norton Long. Yet "it still may be our only chance of successfully utilizing the expert knowledge and planning necessary to chart our way in the foul weather ahead."[28]

Against those who would gather at the bier of our party system as it operates under the traditional arrangement is the calm counsel of its defenders. That it has been improperly assailed as nonadjustable has already been remarked in noting the reversal of positions between New England and Middle Western Senate delegations within the span of a generation. Elsewhere we need not search for long to locate other reasoned rejoinders to the mounting tide of discontent with our party system.

Foreign Policy and the Party System. Among the challenges of public policy today, none is more transcendent than that of foreign policy. Maintenance of America's responsibilities in the community of nations together with its own defense takes precedence over any issue facing the Republic. But how often have hands been stretched across the aisle in an unpartisan way in both House and Senate to contain politics "at the water's edge" when crucial matters of foreign policy were at stake? In the past six years eight Republican senators have voted "internationalist" 83 to 95 percent of the time and seven

---

[28]"Party Government and the United States," *Journal of Politics,* **13** (1951), p. 214.

voted "internationalist" 55 to 73 percent of the time.[29] And how often have the patient efforts of a Vandenberg or a Wadsworth prevented critical policies affecting our external affairs from being jettisoned? The list would be long and impressive if compiled.

Yet if the GOP minority in either House had been bound by the policy strictures of the majority, nonpartisan cooperation on foreign policy would have foundered at the outset. Probably no more than a third of the minority members in either chamber during recent years were disposed to take a sufficiently broad view of the scope of American foreign policy to support actively a nonpartisan approach to foreign policy at least on some of its more important aspects.

That a growing sense of responsibility which has characterized both parties in foreign affairs "is the unmistakable verdict of the last decade," is set forth convincingly by a man who should be in a position to know—Ernest Griffith, Director of the Legislative Reference Service of the Library of Congress since 1940. "Both the House Foreign Affairs and Senate Foreign Relations Committees," he tells us, "have operated in a bipartisan and nonpartisan fashion." Furthermore, he reports:

> The Senate Foreign Relations Committee in particular has developed a deeply felt pride in recent years in presenting a unanimous report in all its major recommendations. This practice has survived serious strain— temptations to make partisan capital; slights, especially in the form of failures on the part of the executive to consult in advance before making important moves; issues deeply felt and controversial.[30]

No doubt present arrangements that lead to voting in bipartisan blocs rather than along strict party lines leave something to be desired. Yet how disquieting the thought if congressional voting on foreign policy must divide perfunctorily in accordance with the doctrinaire lines of party policy. Conceivably such an arrangement could be catastrophic for the handling of our external affairs.

The Independent and Party Policy. Disenchantment expressed

---

[29]See George D. Blackwood: "Let's Look at the Record," *The Reporter*, 7 (July 22, 1952), p. 16.

[30]*Congress: Its Contemporary Role* (New York, 1951), p. 98.

with bipartisan or unpartisan tactics in the area of foreign policy, as the late Arthur Vandenberg liked to term it, reminds us that some critics of the party system challenge independence itself and take a dim view of the way we have tended to lionize the independent as the paragon of virtue in American politics. "In the folklore of politics the greatest virtue of officials is 'independence'" complains E. E. Schattschneider, an effective exponent of greater party discipline. "Supposedly then," he says, "independent candidacies are better than party candidates" and the congressman who declines to pull in harness with the members of his own party is "more moral" than his colleagues who always go along with his party. Thus "we cling to this notion in spite of the demonstrable fact that the greater the number of independents the smaller will be the number of partisans able to control Congress, for independence is a synonym of ineffectiveness in a game in which teamwork produces results."[31]

Admittedly Professor Schattschneider's charge that the independent has been overly glamorized and romanticized (particularly in the college classroom) carries some freight. Party programs and party organization with a will to energize party policies are essential ingredients of representative government. And perhaps there are too many times when party discipline is altogether too loose. Yet the overall picture of congressional voting is hardly the likeness of a scrambled egg. Party lines cross to be sure—indecently at times, unpredictably at others, but often in the public interest and compellingly so. Yet the demonstrable fact is that there are discernible differences between the major parties though the nature and constancy of these differences is not always easy to recognize.

One factor which misleads us to believe that there are no significant differences between the parties as they operate, with the consequence that no real choice is offered to the voter, is the fact that possession of the presidency tends to bring about some reversal in party attitude or at least some degree of shift in party policy. Republicans, for example, dutifully supported executive power in the 1920's, while they censured it with all the odiums they could command when a Democratic president was in the cockpit from 1933

---

[31]*The Struggle for Party Government, op. cit.,* p. 39.

through 1952. Notable also as an example of a party shift in and out of power are reversals in attitudes toward foreign policy.

In the framing of foreign policy the only real possibility of an integrated program of policy and action lies with the chief executive. Beset by conflicting viewpoints and personalities, and lacking the positional advantages of a unified command that favors the President in lining up party support behind his program, the minority party inevitably drifts into negativistic habits of opposition. This was true of the Democratic minority during the twenties when even the non-vigorous leadership of Warren Harding was able to win the necessary two-thirds vote of the Senate to ratify several international compacts. It is precisely because the minority party is incapable of uniting behind a positive program under our present party system that it may follow policies not radically dissimilar to the majority party when it comes to power. Thus since we have but two parties, says Professor Grassmuck, with only one integrated foreign policy actually possible—the one that can be developed and directed by the President—"the policy may well be advocated by both parties."[32] Strange as it must appear to those who judge the vagaries of our system from afar, the minority party nonetheless is capable of making facile sideslips upon attaining majority status. Not at all unlikely, therefore, is the prospect of Joe Martin, certainly far from an internationalist in personal sympathies, laboring faithfully to pump Eisenhower's foreign policy measures through the House in the event of a GOP victory in 1952.

The persistence of similarities in policy when the minority party trades positions with the majority party, however, in no way negates the fact that both parties do have channel markers. These channel markers may seem indistinct at times, and both parties occasionally veer wide of the course, but over time they can be observed and identified.

Professor Binkley, for example, discerns two distinct patterns in the matter of executive leadership. In the presidential-congressional scrimmages since the time of Jackson, he sees the Republican

---

[32]*Sectional Biases in Congress on Foreign Policy* (Baltimore: Johns Hopkins Press, 1951), p. 173.

party as the party of congressional supremacy; the Democratic party as the traditional supporter of executive power. "As a matter of record," he asserts, Republican congresses have been almost if not altogether as severe in denouncing the 'usurpations' of Abraham Lincoln and Theodore Roosevelt as they were in decrying Grover Cleveland, Woodrow Wilson, and Franklin Roosevelt, indeed any chief executive who essays vigorous leadership."[33]

Well documented though it is, Dr. Binkley's thesis must be reconciled with the fact that Democrats have been able to muster more enthusiasm for executive power when their own spokesman is in the White House.[34] Granting such allowances, however, comparison of party attitudes on executive power does suggest that this is one area where the parties do differ in degree in any case.

Elsewhere it is possible to distinguish differences in party attitudes by systematic examination of roll calls—a task that has been skillfully undertaken by Julius Turner. Looking at eight modern sessions of Congress, stretching from 1921 through 1948, Turner was able to distinguish specific party behavior on 407 of 455 roll calls in the House. No minor issues, the subjects embraced by these roll calls covered tariffs, monopoly regulations, foreign relations, taxes, business regulations, civil rights, crop controls, relief policies, states' rights, and the extension of executive authority.

When we review the voting behavior of all congressmen within each major party, then, we do find distinguishable differences. True, while national lines of demarcation are detectable, the mixed voting habits of certain congressmen sometimes make it incredibly difficult for the voter to determine the true color of his political banner—a criticism of our party system that cannot be dismissed lightly. Yet such cases are the exception and actually affect few constituencies. Of 4,658 House members covering eleven recent sessions "only 181, or less than four percent (about sixteen congressmen each year),

---

[33]*President and Congress* (New York: A. A. Knopf, 1947).

[34]Turner, for example, demonstrates that Republicans voted for the extension of executive power on five issues in 1921, compared with four supported by the Democrats. See *Party and Constituency: Pressures on Congress, op. cit.,* p. 40.

voted with the opposing party" more frequently than their own.[35]
In the Senate, where greater independent tendencies are traditional,
a study of nine sessions shows only 7.3 per cent—about seven a year—
who left their parties on a majority of the votes. Thus party truancy,
while it leaves a trail of bewilderment in some precincts, is small scale,
relatively speaking. Moreover, most of the party bolting that is done,
at least in the northern states, is inspired by the composition peculiarities of a particular district, an example of which would be Representative Javits' twenty-first district in New York (see Chapter 5).

Unmistakably then, and clearly supported by the evidence,
policy differences do emerge between the parties that present alternatives to the voter. Two conditions, however, appear to mask
the apparentness of these differences. One, the difficulty of party identification of some congressmen within particular districts, has already
been mentioned. But it might be added in passing that despite the
small amount of party irregularity that actually results, the vigor
with which party dissenters conduct themselves often makes their
actions or voting potential appear unduly exaggerated. The second
factor that seems to eclipse some of the actual differences between the
parties is the tendency to simulate each other's policies upon attaining power. When in the opposition, the minority assumes a perverse
posture that does not actually bespeak its true position. In a sense
the minority party, whether Democratic or Republican, seems to
follow a strategy that might be likened to the reply of New Orleans'
famed jazz trumpeter, Willie (Bunk) Johnson, when crowded to compare his horn tooting with Louis Armstrong's. "When he does up,"
said Willie, "I does down!"

And so with the impression that we sometimes acquire from our
major parties as one or the other steps up or down from power. Neg-
ativism sets in when one party shifts over to the opposition and the
minority party sometimes appears to take up wherever its predecessor
left off, just as the newly created majority seems to follow some of the
policy ruts already cut by the party it displaced. It was, after all,
the much-assailed 80th Congress that passed the Marshall Plan just

[35]"Responsible Parties: A Dissent from the Floor," *American Political
Science Review*, 45 (1951), pp. 143-152.

as it was the same Congress that enacted the Hope-Aiken bill which provided a continuation of generous price subsidies for farm products. Crucial in this regard is the well-taken observation of Arthur Macmahon. "Principles," he reminds us, "once enacted are seldom repealed; steps firmly taken are seldom retraced." Thus political campaigns are "concerned with the tempo rather than the trend" and major steps in public policy receive periodic confirmation in a majority electoral verdict that is accepted by both parties.[36]

While principles are infrequently repealed, parties do leave tell-tale imprints in policy distinctions. But we must look for these over a longer period of time. As Professors Stedman and Sonthoff show us, the quality output in congressional legislation varies considerably *over a period of time* with such congresses as those of the Wilsonian and New Deal eras passing numerous large-scale regulatory acts, while during the early twenties the enactment of similar measures was reduced to a trickle.[37]

Periodic fluctuation in Party Policy. Wonderously at times, despite the different hallmarks that characterize the parties over the long pull, one party appears to execute an abrupt policy maneuver and jump out of the sluggish currents of its mainstream. Such was the case of the Republican party under the supercharged stewardship of Theodore Roosevelt.

Far from the beacon that beckoned to the little group of disgruntled Free Soilers, Whigs, anti-slavery Democrats, and others, who foregathered at Ripon, Wisconsin to form the Republican party in 1854, the GOP had sideslipped badly between Lincoln and the Square Deal. Though it regained some prestige under McKinley, the real rescue of the Republican party from its retreat from Lincolnism must be credited to the driving leadership of Theodore Roosevelt, who believed the function of a President should be to exercise a vigorous veto on behalf of the people. But unhappily, as Herbert Agar remarks, "instead of standing by the Square Deal and moving to new

---

[36]"Conflict, Consensus, Confirmed Trends, and Open Choices," *American Political Science Review*, 42 (1948), pp. 1-15.

[37]"Party Responsibility—A critical Inquiry: *Western Political Quarterly*, 4 (1951), pp. 463-465. (Italics added.)

strength in a new world, the party under Warren Harding allowed
a few thieves to revert to the old policy." And this started voters
thinking that the "GOP might be a little out of date; so when Herbert
Hoover spoke of rugged individualism, they showed their discourage-
ment by turning to the Democrats." And while the Republicans had
held a long lease on power (56 out of 72 previous years), "partly by
giving the public domain to homesteaders, railway and mining pro-
moters, cattlemen, sheepherders, and lumber barons," writes Agar,
"the Democrats in 1933 found something to give away even more appealing than the public domain; namely the federal taxes." Con-
tinuing he observes:

> As these poured out—to the farmers . . . to the unemployed for build-
> ing roads, bridges . . . housing projects . . . for preserving forests and farm
> land; to the South for the Tennessee Valley Authority with its attendant
> cheap power . . . the old Jackson party arose from the grave, the farmer-
> labor alliance of Southern and Western agrarians with Eastern industrial
> workers.[38]

In dusting off earlier party traditions and moving forward once
again, both parties have turned to architects of "group diplomacy."
Thus in 1933 the whole vast distribution of income—which was desirable, says Agar, "was directed by one of the great opportunists and
political strategists ever to reach the White House." Under these
circumstances he finds even Landon's vote, which trailed Roosevelt's
by ten million, impressive and Willkie's 22,300,000 ballots in 1940
"a triumph for the man, the party system, and the instinct of the
American people not to divide on class lines." For Agar the real
vibrancy and strength of the American party system is that the controls
can be reversed with much the same results, "the next time fate gives
the Republicans a master of 'group diplomacy,' a Lincoln, McKinley,
or Roosevelt." The sudden coming of the New Deal "with its largesse
for the poor instead of the rich . . . ," he argues, "would never have
happened in the first place if Theodore Roosevelt had stayed with the
party in 1912, or if he had lived to fight for the nomination in 1920."
Had he done so, concludes Agar, "he would have picked up where

---

[38] *The Price of Union* (Boston: Houghton Mifflin, 1950), p. 683.

Woodrow Wilson stopped—insisting, of course, that he was reversing the New Freedom while in fact he completed it and anticipated the New Deal by more than a decade.[39]

So it is that a party driven by a forceful President may bound back in the popular favor. And so it is that within the same party are teamed such odd teammates as Taft and Morse, Taber and Javits, or McCarran and Humphrey, Cox and Celler. Thus even today the European, who, as Lord Bryce reported, is always asking what the difference between a Republican and a Democrat is because he never gets an answer, continues to put the same question seventy-five years later. And nowhere—if pressed for a doctrinaire definition of a Democrat or a Republican—are we more strongly reminded of the truth in Ortega y Gasset's dictum that the true meaning of a word lies not in the dictionary: "it is in the instant."

The Gradualist Course of "Principleless Politics." Whatever the frailties of our party system the people have elected to follow the gradualist course. Within each of the major parties, the hard core of its supporters think and respond pretty much alike, and happily so.[40] Not too zealous for "distinctive principles," "tenets," or hard doctrine, as Lord Bryce would have wished, the parties have labored to compromise differences between regions, classes, and our multiple interest groups. Actually a major party is "intended to bring men and women of all beliefs, occupations, sections, racial backgrounds, into a combination for the pursuit of power."[41] But because of the diversity of this combination and the tendency of the many groups of our society to have overlapping memberships, the broad basis of its convictions cannot be too unyielding. In consequence favors are accorded to each "noisy group" and there is a disposition to identify them as party policies.

By so doing parties do soft-pedal issues that rouse deep feelings, yet they also strengthen our federal union, observes Mr. Agar. For when an issue is too passionately felt, "and discussed in terms of morals, each party may divide within itself, against itself." Our experience

---

[39]*Ibid.*

[40]See Malcolm Moos and Bertram Koslin: "Prestige Suggestion and Political Leadership," *Public Opinion Quarterly,* 16 (1952), pp. 77-93.

[41]*The Price of Union, op. cit.,* p. 689.

between 1850 and 1860 attests to this fact, and the strain that racked the federal structure in 1896 is a case in point. "We men, therefore," concludes Agar, "may seek to dodge such problems as long as possible. And the easiest way to dodge such problems is for both parties to take both sides"—a perfectly normal practice in American politics, one might add.

For the critics of the gradualist course, faith in a party system that runs to a course of deft dodges—a "principleless politics"—is a misguided confidence because such a system wins the battles of reform too slowly. "It is reasonable to suppose," says Schattschneider, "that the internal difficulties of government will, sooner or later, if we do not overcome them, involve all of us in disaster." Yet Agar's defense of the traditional arrangements in which both parties have been swept along by common influences adapting themselves to national needs, does not pale in face of assault. His judgment, moreover, that the campaign of 1896 which produced the sharpest fracture over principle since the Civil War and luckily missed bringing about a catastrophe only by the silver issue resolving itself, has an interesting relation to our earlier discussion of voting apathy as an indication of disaffection with the party system. Interestingly the election of 1896 produced the largest turnout (89.5 percent) of any national election. Thus the election that Agar adjudged as one coming closest to impairing the unity of the nation since the Civil War also brought out the largest vote—suggesting, by way of implication at least, that a huge turnout is not necessarily a reason for rejoicing while a small vote is a cause for alarm.

We pay a price, of course, for the "illogicality" of our party system—too great a price in the eyes of many. Yet when weighed in the balance it is small compared with what we stand to lose by speeding the arrival of a deep cleft between the parties.

Disciplined Parties and Competition in Congressional Elections. An additional problem thus far unmentioned in our census of the probable effects of strictly disciplined parties is what would happen to two-party competition in many congressional districts if we abandoned our present relaxed system. That a shift to sharply disciplined parties will lead to an increase in the number of one-party districts seems most probable. Without some leeway to bolt an unyielding party discipline on an occasional congressional roll call there are many districts where House candidates would have no chance of competing in an election. So futile would be minority party congressional candidacies in such districts that it would be very difficult to induce anyone to file. True, forcing stricter party discipline would do away with the congressmen who operate under party banners that seem ill-matched to their temperments and voting habits. And few would deny that the elimination of certain figures who trade on party labels that seem quite out of character in some particular cases would be a desirable end. But the loss of other congressmen who impart the wholesome sparks of independence to our political system would also be not inconsiderable. Equally depressing, if not more so, however, is the prospect of having no competitors filed in districts where such is the dominance of one party that the only hope of minority party candidacy is to permit its candidate to play truant in voting on certain issues.

Already about one-half of our congressional districts are so-called "safe districts" where the dominant party's candidate normally polls 60 percent of the two-party vote. In the 1950 elections 94, or 40 percent, of the 220 odd safe constituencies were districts with only one party in the race. No Republican candidate ran in 87 of these districts, predominantly in the South, while in 7 there was no Democratic opposition.[42]

Perhaps even a more accurate picture of party competition can be had by looking at the primaries along with the general elections. Out of 965 primary elections in safe districts between 1944 and 1950, Turner found that only 483, or 50.1 percent were contested by two

---

[42]Five of the districts where the GOP had no entry, and six where the Democrats had no candidate were located in California, where cross-filing permits a candidate to win the primary nomination of both parties. In 1948 there were 63 districts where no Republican was entered, and 16 where no Democratic opposition was filed, illustrating the tendency of the GOP to make a greater effort in presidential election years. The increase in the number of seats uncontested by the Democrats in 1948 suggests, perhaps, a general feeling that Truman was not likely to help the general ticket (See Map 1).

or more candidates.[43] Thus in primaries as well as general elections
the question of competition—the business of affording a choice to the
voter is already a matter that calls for serious reflection.

It would be completely unfounded, of course, to suggest either (1)
that because so many congressmen are elected without opposition
the tenets of representative government are not being upheld; or (2)
that the appearance of competition either in a general or primary election necessarily gives the voter a real choice. Many times we simply
have futile candidacies. Furthermore, a representative who has served
with distinction and appears before the voters with a creditable record
as well as worthwhile legislative experience, very likely is to be pre-
ferred with or without competition. But the likelihood is that with
such a large number of House seats going uncontested in the primaries and general elections, an adequate choice is not being offered
to the voters. And while the entrance of a competitor at either the
primary or general election level in no way guarantees opposition of
formidable stature, it helps, at least in some degree, to enliven an
interest in the issues and personalities involved.

Beset, therefore, by conditions that produce one-party areas in
effect, not only in the South but in all sections of the country, the
risk of increasing the number of such areas is certainly not a prospect
to be welcomed. Yet should we shift over to a system in which parties would require strict adherence to a nationally declared policy, it
is almost a certainty that the effect would be to discourage minority
party candidacies in still more congressional districts.

FREE STYLE PARTIES AND OUR UNSYSTEMATIC AMERICAN SYSTEM

Landing on American soil July 4, 1920, to take over the post of
consul general in Philadelphia, Sir Gerald Campbell, one of the
wittiest and wisest British diplomats ever to serve in this country,
endeared himself at once as a man of parts with his first word of
greeting "It was nice," quipped Sir Gerald," to see everyone enjoying
taxation with representation."

---

[43]Primary Elections as the Alternative to Party Competition in 'Safe'
Districts." Unpublished manuscript. This research has been aided by a
grant from the Social Science Research Council.

Within this well-turned blandishment is an ever-worthwhile reminder that the area of virtual agreement and satisfaction with the party system is very wide. Early in this century the reform movement which touched off ripples of revolt certainly did not propose "to scrap the nation's economic and political machine and build another, but rather by a series of adjustments and improvements to make it run better without skipping a beat."[44] And even "when the machine broke down badly in the depression," writes Frederick Lewis Allen with discriminating insight, "the same basic principle of unrevolutionary, and unsystematic and experimental change prevailed." Thus it may well be, he observes, that the strength of our system as a whole—"a system characterized by a large and powerful government and an extraordinary wide and proliferating assortment of voluntary institutions and associations, and societies which contribute to the public good—"is very likely related to the fact that it has developed in such a pragmatic, diverse, and even haphazard way."[45]

In this system the acrimonious exchange of campaigns and testy debate over specific congressional bills tends to deceive us in one very remarkable respect: that despite the turgid language which is generously tossed about, "very few Americans seriously propose any *really wholesale* change in our evolving American system." Even within Congress, notwithstanding the public jousting on the floor of the House or Senate, once congressmen settle down to the serious work of the committee level a surprisingly large measure of agreement is forthcoming from the most bristling partisans. Actually, therefore, such differences as are held by the electorate and reflected in the attitudes of our two parties, are more in degree than in direction, more in tempo than in trend. This broad agreement, moreover, while breached in varying degrees during recent years in the area of foreign policy, has few rents in the domestic field. Thus the vast majority of the citizenry agrees that while government should continue its monitory role of accepting "an overall responsibility for the satisfactory operation of the economy . . . it should keep its inter-

---

[44]"The Unsystematic American System," *Harper's*, 204 (1952), p. 22.

[45]*Ibid.*

vention limited and should let the great bulk of business remain under private management."

If, as Editor Allen argues (and correctly, we think), that the basis of seething political debate today is primarily over "how much of this and how much of that we need" in the way of government intervention and that in our own unsystematic way of patchwork revisions we are evolving not *toward* socialism, but *past* socialism, why forsake our flexible and adaptable party system in favor of a strictly disciplined model—a result that can only lead to a hardening of political conflict?[46] If indeed there is "subconscious" acceptance among the overwhelming majority of Americans of what the late Wendell Willkie liked to call "responsible enterprise" rather than "free enterprise" why abandon the patchwork process of tinkering and repairing as we go along?

Were one convinced that the substantial agitation among critics for change in our party system aimed at adjustment and piecemeal improvements rather than radical transformation, the question of how far we are going with party reform would give us little anxiety. For all will agree that the party system has its blemishes and that continuous study of party operations with a view to adjustment and accommodation of national needs is very much to be desired. But examining the paternity of proposals to reform our party system leads one back to the frequent conclusion that although some advocates of reform favor only minor adjustments, others, and particularly the more vigorous advocates of change, are really hoping for the eventual transplantation of the cabinet system to the United States. Of course, admission of such sweeping change is rarely actually acknowledged— a factor which has proved misleading and embarrassing to critics of the party system who support minor change, but are not prepared to go along with radical reform. Nor have the full implications of such drastic reform been searchingly examined by many of the critics of our present system who seem to want to slip over something closely akin to the parliamentary system. In consequence "we find an attempt to reform American government," complains Professor Goodman, "by grafting upon the Presidential system selected char-

----

[46]*Ibid.,* pp. 24-25. *Italics* Mr. Allen's.

acteristics of the parliamentary system without the protections of the latter and by discarding the protective features of the former."[47] Thus in Great Britain, the Parliament holds effective checks on the Prime Minister, but since he rises or falls together with his party, he is not ordinarily buffeted about the way an American President sometimes is treated by his Congress. In the United States, however, the President with a fixed term of tenure can take defeats from his Congress and even a setback at the midterm congressional elections. But any tendency for a prime minister to be irresponsible, as Goodman observes, is corrected by the parliamentary system because a prime minister simply cannot survive a serious setback. The possibility of presidential irresponsibility, however, should we reform our system to give the parties the disciplined character of those under a parliamentary system, is not to be dismissed lightly. While the prime minister "cannot appeal for votes by making vicarious promises that apparently cannot be carried out," a President with a tightly disciplined party under his control and secure in his office for a fixed term, could, under the guise of enforced party responsibility pursue an irresponsible course. The crux of the matter, of course, is that the features of the parliamentary system that correct a tendency toward unchecked executive power—no fixed tenure for the prime minister, for example—are unlikely to be adopted by the United States. To take on simply part of the characteristics of the parliamentary system, therefore—the disciplined parties—leaves us without the safeguards our party system has evolved as a check against executive irresponsibility and saddles us with "a mechanism we are not prepared to operate."[48]

Elsewhere an aspect of the parliamentary system, alien to the American people, and one likely to be viewed with misgivings if fully understood, is the decline in the significance of individual candidates. Members of parliament are not chosen for their personal merits but rather because they willingly work in party harness.

---

[47]T. William Goodman: "How Much Political Party Centralization Do We Want?" *Journal of Politics,* 13 (1951), p. 548.

[48]"How Much Political Party Centralization Do We Want?" *loc. cit.,* p. 548-549.

Appropriately and not without humor, Ivor Jennings, a careful student of English politics, writes: "He possesses his seat only because he wears a party label. Deprived of his label he would, in the great majority of cases, sink into the comparative insignificance that his character probably merits."[49]

Of course the party label, no doubt, carries the American congressman to power in a great many cases, particularly on an initial run if a dramatic shift in political sentiment is sweeping the country. And not unknown in the annals of congressional personnel are the few, who—to borrow a phrase from Senator Ashurst—"are mere ciphers with the rim removed." But the marked diminution in the role of the individual candidate in English parliamentary elections today suggests a circumstance of sharp distinction from our own congressional practice where personalities are strong factors in election contests. More than simply a difference of practice, the decline in importance of the candidate himself also appears to have a deeper meaning.

Within the frame of the English parliamentary system where the kind of a man the candidate is, and "what kind of things he says appear to matter less and less because his label determines his support," a hardening of political lines between the two major parties—Labor and Conservative—has been won not only at the expense of the Liberals—but also "at the expense of the voter previously of no fixed allegiance—the man who does not like to wear a label." Thus weighing Britain's extraordinarily close elections of 1950 and 1951 Oxford's H. G. Nicholas asks whether the voter "who has traditionally been accorded the role of the pendulum in the British constitutional clock is a disappearing species." More trenchantly put, "is the independent voter declining to a point at which electoral struggles of increasing severity will result in party majorities of diminishing adequacy?"[50] Thus the question Nicholas really asks is, will any party be able to govern successfully if its majority is con-

---

[49]W. Ivor Jennings, *Parliament* (Cambridge University Press, 1939), p. 122.

[50]"The British Election of 1951," *American Political Science Review*, 46 (1952), p. 405.

sistently no larger than the "shade of a shadow" margin which we used to describe the close congressional contests in our own marginal districts?

Less academically, a man in his eighty-second year now shelling pecans down in Uvalde, Texas, jabs at the same problem with characteristic color and persuasiveness in rising to the defense of the American party system. Said John Nance Garner on the eve of the celebrated "purge campaign" June 24, 1938, after serving in Congress for almost 40 years:

> This talk about dividing the country into two political camps—one progressive and the other conservative—is all so much stuff. There will always be agitation of this realignment, but in my considered judgment it will never come. If it did you'd find you'd have a radical and a reactionary party and neither of these could serve the nation. Each of the two parties is in a sense a coalition. Any party to serve the country must be a party of all sorts of views, and through a reconciliation and adjustment of these views you get harmony and a program for good legislation and good administration. The country is neither radical nor reactionary. A party has got to strike a balance.
>
> There are around forty-five million voters in this country. You've got a bedrock of around fifteen million in each party who will never scratch the party ticket and they serve a great purpose of stability. You have another fifteen million who swing often or occasionally, or go fishing or stay home on election days, and these fifteen million serve a great purpose too. That is where you get your changes. No one can figure a better system than that—a third Democratic, a third Republican and a third independent. Most American people have the same general ideas and concepts. Both the Republican and Democratic parties are more than eighty years old and are here to stay. No third party has strength for more than one election and this when special conditions have given it a temporary following. The pendulum swings from party to party on personality of candidates or issues, but at heart the country is always progressive and forward looking.[51]

Time has lifted the voting potential of which the former Vice President speaks, yet the force of his argument with its defense of

---

[51]Bascom N. Timmons: *Garner of Texas* (New York: Harper, 1948), p. 236.

diverse intra-party coalitions and the fluidity of the independent voter remains unchanged.

Weighing the party system today few may gainsay the wisdom of Professor Herring's defense of our workable, if casual arrangements, whereby both parties have been carried along by common influences and have evolved practicable means, though by no means the formidable gadgetry of pat proscription, for serving the needs of the nation. Tellingly, he also fixes the further point that:

> We cannot have a radical party standing for revolutionary change and a conservative stand-pat party. Such parties may only exist on the plane of discussion. Revolutionary communism can only be tolerated by democracy as long as it remains an academic question.[52]

Operating in the frame suggested by Herring, it may be said with little apology that our system of congressional elections—conducted though it is astride the contradictions and incongruities of our major parties—has served the nation reasonably well. For after all, such are the multiple components of our society that our representational system cannot be too unyielding to the demands of different organized interests. Lurking always in the background should the system become too inflexible to group demands is the likely consequence of splinter parties, accompanied in all probability by the usual inconveniences and evils of a multiple party system.

In a sense, then, the 435 congressional constituencies are the mountings—social, economic, and cultural—upon which our political machinery operates and upon which we have wisely pinned our hopes. Individual congressmen, of course, like the parties they serve, often have serious shortcomings. But the congressman, "like men everywhere," as Professor Latham's lucid characterization has it, "comes to his position bearing in his head a cargo of ideas, privileges, prejudices, programs, precepts, beliefs, slogans, and preachments."[53] And not for one minute should we forget that the totality of this

---

[52]E. Pendleton Herring: "Politics, Parties, and the Public Interest," in *Essays in Political Science in Honor of W.W. Willoughby* (Baltimore: Johns Hopkins Press, 1937), p. 102.

[53]Earl Latham: "The Group Basis of Politics: Notes For a Theory," *American Political Science Review*, 46 (1952), p. 391.

cargo of ideas, "represent his adjustment to the dominant group combination among his constituents."

In a setting of growing urbanization the development of horizontal interests stratums is beginning to challenge the old paramountcy of local interests on an increasing scale. Fortunately for us, however, whatever the strains and stresses of this transition, we may count on the flexibility of our party system to graduate the conflicts of adjustment.

How well the newer horizontal interest stratums serve the national interest, of course, is a matter that cannot be foretold, though the answer to the question will depend in no small degree upon the continued vitality and adaptability of the party system. That these powerfully organized groups not become completely rapacious in outlook must necessarily be one of the major concerns of this generation.

It may be, as suggested earlier, that the development of "new embracing wholes" in our society will facilitate a discrimination in pressure group activity that favors the national interest—perhaps under the leadership of the new middle class as Lubell contends. But looking ahead our goal should be not to elevate one particular class, but rather to reconcile in equilibrium the status of the different classes. Yet amidst all such uncertainties, possibilities, and the pluralistic tendencies within groups and classes themselves, experience teaches us that upon our congressional elections—tailored to the peculiarities of several hundred districts and subject only to the casual conformity requirements of our unsystematized party system—we have not placed a misguided reliance. Nor are we likely to regret this confidence if we continue to maintain such reliance, tidying up the imperfections of the system as we move along. Rather than reconstitute the parties by a more careful regrouping of the battlelines between interest groups or working classes, therefore, we have everything to gain by avoiding strict configurations of interest groups within one or the other of the major parties.

Critically important to the ultimate success of congressional elections conducted under the auspices of non-doctrinaire parties, is the leadership of the President More than a century has now passed since deTocqueville predicted that "the struggle between the Presi-

dent and the legislature must always be an unequal one, since the
latter is certain of bearing down all resistance by persevering in its
plans." But in that interim several occupants of the presidency—
Lincoln, Cleveland, Wilson, and the two Roosevelts—have certainly
qualified the notion that the match is unequal. And long before
the first "fireside" it was evident that the president was beginning to
be looked upon more and more as a plebiscitary leader of the people
—and that he was expected to be an agent operating in the transcendent public interest. Unplotted by any diabolical cunning, the development of the presidential office as a repository of policy leadership was an adaptation in response to national need, and as such was
a by-product of our haphazard and unsystematic party system as much
as any of the other characteristics indigenous to our political life.
Thus the chief executive is looked upon today as the leading initiator
of public policy and party leadership, ever ready as the guardian
of the public good to exercise vigorous influence within the rims of
any if not all of our congressional constituencies. Part of this increased stature of the presidency is reflected in the popular mind by
the larger vote customarily given to the winning presidential candidate over his congressional ticket. Presidential coattails, apart
from the tides of their parties, do not boost significant numbers of
congressional candidates into office, but in the long pull the skill
with which the president both drives and leads his party has a way of
stockpiling good will and building party fortunes in the public mind.
And it is partly through the aid of such leadership that we change
from a country with a traditional majority for one party into a
nation with a normal majority for another.

In the presence of resourceful executive leadership, then, congressional supremacy—that haunting ogre with its irresponsible habits which some critics charge to the failure of our party system—is
more noisy than obstructionist in its overall effect. And out of the
healthy interaction of presidential leadership and congressional attitudes comes the gradualist tempo of change in public policy that
has served us well. In fact it is through this blending of attitudes
which the diversity of congressional representation and the party
system inspires that we are spared the sharp wrenches over what direction public policy shall take.

Within this setting, no hierarchical centralized gadgetry to control party policy is indicated. National party councils or directorates and other proposals to standardize party policies not only raise serious practical considerations of workability, but beyond the operational sphere they threaten us in other directions.[54] ". . . By pluralizing our power, we purge it of its indigenous poison," writes philosopher T. V. Smith, reminding us again that formally delegating party control to a national hierarchy at the expense of invigorating local currents is not without its hazards.[55]

As in all societies our individual citizens and various groups—organized as well as unorganized—are not uninfluenced by the tenderness of their own interests. And in our diverse society with its cultural differences and vast number of pressure groups ranging from bolt and nut manufacturers to cranberry producers, the party system has been hard-pressed to accommodate the representation of these interests and simultaneously uphold the national interest. Yet by reasonable standards of judgment it has managed with more than chance success, the delicate task of comprising our heterogeneous interest groups with the national interest.

It has managed this compromise so far with something of the political spectrum of America reproduced in each of the major par-

---

[54]One proposal of a committee of the American Political Science Association, for example, suggests the creation of a National Council to "consider and make recommendations to appropriate party organs in respect to congressional candidates; and make recommendations to the National Convention, the National Committee or other appropriate party organs with respect to conspicuous departures from general party decisions by state or local party organizations." The composition of the Council would be as follows: Five members of the national committee, five members from each House, ten members representing state committees, five governors, and twenty members chosen from the national convention, to include among others Young Republicans and Young Democrats. In addition to these fifty, the President, Vice-President, or nominees for these offices, and cabinet members designated by the President would also serve as members of the Council. See A Report of the Committee on Political Parties *Toward a More Responsible Two-Party System* (New York, Rinehart, 1950).

[55]T. V. Smith: "In Praise of the Legislative Way," *The Antioch Review*, 9 (1949), p. 58.

ties.   Neither party can lay claim to a monopoly of eminent leaders and neither party can be charged with a monopoly of the hate hucksters.   Thus the parties move somewhat together in a broad confluent action, the minority not radically dissimilar from the majority, each ever hoping that one more mighty heave will land it in the seat of power, while the followers of both along with the independents, are guided by the happy thought of Senator Ashurst: "That in a free Republic such as ours, it is the undoubted right of the people to change their servants, and to remove one and displace him with another at any time they choose, for a good reason, for a bad reason, or for no reason at all."

APPENDIX 1

The Republican percentage of the two-party vote in the House of Representatives, 1938-1950:

(a) % of the two-party vote for congressional races by districts.

(b) % of the two-party vote for President by congressional districts.

(c) Names of Congressmen listed in their respective districts.

Note: *Italicized names are Democrats.*

APPENDIX. REPUBLICAN % OF TWO-PARTY VOTE, 1938-1950

DIST.	CONG. % Rep. 1938	PRES. % Rep. 1940	CONG. % Rep. 1940	DIFF. PRES. minus CONG. 1940	CONG. % Rep. 1942	PRES. % Rep. 1944	CONG. % Rep. 1944	DIFF. PRES. minus CONG. 1944	CONG. % Rep. 1946	PRES. % Rep. 1948	CONG. % Rep. 1948	DIFF. PRES. minus CONG. 1948	CONG. % Rep. 1950	REF. LINE
ARIZONA														
1st	*Murdock* 19.7	36.2	*Murdock* 28.9	+7.3	*Murdock* 26.9	41.0	*Murdock* 30.1	+10.9	*Murdock* 33.3	47.5	*Murdock* 41.2	+6.3	*Murdock* 39.4	1,2
2nd					*Harless*		*Harless*		*Harless*	42.8	*Patton* 36.0	+6.8	*Patton* 30.9	1
CALIFORNIA														
1st	*Lea* 37.0	46.0	*Lea* 0	+46.0	*Lea* 0	47.6	*Lea* 0	+47.6	*Lea* 0	54.9	*Scudder* 54.6	+0.3	*Scudder* 54.0	3
2nd	*Englebright* 100	34.7	*Englebright* 100	-65.3	*Englebright* 100	41.3	*Engle* 36.1	+5.2	*Engle* 0	44.8	*Engle* 0	+44.8	*Engle* 0	3
3rd	*Buck* 0	37.3	*Buck* 0	+37.3	*Johnson* 54.4	38.3	*Johnson* 100	-61.7	*Johnson* 100	43.2	*Johnson* 100	-56.8	*Johnson* 100	3
4th & 5th (San. Fran. County)	67.3	39.7	76.0	-36.3	100	39.1	71.6	-32.5	71.0	48.8	71.5	-22.7	16.8	4,6
4th	*Havenner* 38.8		*Rolfe* 55.1		*Rolfe* 100		*Havenner* 49.0		*Havenner* 47.1		*Havenner* 48.2		*Havenner* 32.8	5,6
5th	*Welch* 100		*Welch* 100		*Welch* 100		*Welch* 100		*Welch* 100		*Welch* 100		*Shelley* 0	5,6
6th & 7th (Alameda & Contra Costa Co.)	73.0	43.1	72.1	-29.0	58.4	40.8	45.5	-4.7	27.0	47.8	22.6	+25.2	22.7	4
6th	*Carter*		*Carter*		*Carter*		*Miller*		*Miller*		*Miller*		*Miller*	

181

	44.7		43.8		0		42.1		56.2		51.4		54.0		3,6
8th	Anderson 55.0	48.5	Anderson 100	-51.5	Anderson 100	49.0	Anderson 56.5	-7.5	Anderson 100	57.7	Anderson 100	-42.3	Anderson 100		7
9th	Gearhart 100	35.1	Gearhart 100	-64.9	Gearhart 100	39.9	Gearhart 100	-60.1	Gearhart 53.7	42.5	White 47.8	-5.3	Hunter 52.0		7
10th	Elliott 32.7	42.0	Elliott 0	+42.0	Elliott 0	45.0	Elliott 0	+45.0	Elliott 0	44.3	Werdel 100	-55.7	Werdel 53.7		7
11th thru 18th ('38-40) 12th thru 21st ('42)	44.1	41.1	54.3	-13.2	35.6	43.1	42.2	+0.9	51.0	49.8	56.6	-6.8	57.4		8
11th	Hinshaw 53.4		Hinshaw 100		Outland 49.3	45.1	Outland 44.0	+1.1	Bramblatt. 53.1	52.7	Bramblatt 100	-47.3	Bramblatt 52.1		9,6
12th	Voorhis 35.0		Voorhis 35.5		Voorhis 43.2		Voorhis 44.7		Nixon 56.7		Nixon 100		Hillings 60.1		5,6
13th	Kramer 31.8		Kramer 0		Poulson 53.9		Healy 45.0		Poulson 51.8		Poulson 52.6		Poulson 100		5,6
14th	Ford 31.6		Ford 34.2		Ford 33.0		Douglas 48.4		Douglas 45.6		Douglas 33.2		Yorty 42.7		3,6
15th	Costello 38.3		Costello 43.1		Costello 0		McDonough 57.7		McDonough 100		McDonough 100		McDonough 100		3,6
16th	Ford 74.8		Ford 100		Rogers 45.9		Patterson 45.9		Jackson 63.0		Jackson 57.0		Jackson 59.2		5,6
17th	Geyer 32.2		Geyer 30.4		King 0		King 0		King 0		King 0		King 0		5,6

APPENDIX. REPUBLICAN % OF TWO-PARTY VOTE, 1938-1950

DIST.	CONG. % Rep. 1938	PRES. % Rep. 1940	CONG. % Rep. 1940	DIFF. PRES. minus CONG. 1940	CONG. % Rep. 1942	PRES. % Rep. 1944	CONG. % Rep. 1944	DIFF. PRES. minus CONG. 1944	CONG. % Rep. 1946	PRES. % Rep. 1948	CONG. % Rep. 1948	DIFF. PRES. minus CONG. 1948	CONG. % Rep. 1950	REF. LINE
					CALIFORNIA (Continued)									
18th	Johnson 50.2		Johnson 54.9		Johnson 56.8		Doyle 44.3		Bradley 52.8		Doyle 46.7		Doyle 49.5	3, 6
19th	Sheppard 46.7	50.7	Sheppard 47.1	+3.6	Holifield 36.9		Holifield 28.2		Holifield 0		Holifield 28.2		Holifield 0	
20th	Izac 39.6	44.1	Izac 48.6	-4.5	Hinshaw 53.0		Hinshaw 52.7		Hinshaw 59.3		Hinshaw 100		Hinshaw 100	9
21st	21st added after reapportionment, 1942				Sheppard 0		Sheppard 41.5		Sheppard 47.3		Sheppard 43.6		Sheppard 42.6	10, 6
22nd	22nd added after reapportionment, 1942				Phillips 57.6	56.0	Phillips 100	-44.0	Phillips 62.1	60.2	Phillips 100	-39.8	Phillips 100	11
23rd	23rd added after reapportionment, 1942				Izac 49.5		Izac 44.9	+0.8	Fletcher 56.3	50.8	McKinnon 43.6	+7.2	McKinnon 49.0	12
					COLORADO									
1st	Lewis 33.9	47.2	Lewis 35.1	+12.1	Lewis 46.3	49.0	Gillespie 52.0	-3.0	Carroll 47.9	46.0	Carroll 35.2	+10.8	Rogers 49.0	
2nd	Cummings 47.9	56.9	Hill 53.6	+3.3	Hill 68.1	61.1	Hill 62.9	-1.8	Hill 66.7	52.3	Hill 51.9	+0.4	Hill 57.8	
3rd	Martin 42.6	49.0	Chenoweth 52.0	-3.0	Chenoweth 62.7	51.0	Chenoweth 56.3	-5.3	Chenoweth 54.6	40.5	Marsalis 49.3	-8.8	Chenoweth 51.6	
4th	Taylor		Taylor		Rockwell		Rockwell		Rockwell		Aspinall		Aspinall	

CONNECTICUT

District														
1st	*Miller* 51.6	43.5	*Kopplemann* 45.8	-2.3	*Miller* 51.4	42.7	*Kopplemann* 46.0	-3.3	*Miller* 53.1	45.7	*Ribicoff* 44.7	+1.0	*Ribicoff* 41.8	6
2nd	Ball 52.1	46.8	*Fitzgerald* 47.4	-0.6	*McWilliams* 51.4	47.3	*Woodhouse* 48.8	-1.5	Seely-Brown 55.3	46.5	*Woodhouse* 48.3	-1.8	Seely-Brown 50.8	6
3rd	*Shanley* 49.9		*Shanley* 46.4		Compton 51.7		Geelan 48.5		Foote 58.9		*McGuire* 49.7		*McGuire* 47.9	
4th	Austin 58.0	49.2	*Downs* 49.7	-0.5	Luce 52.8	51.1	Luce 50.5	+0.6	Lodge 61.8	56.7	Lodge 56.0	+0.7	Morano 55.8	
5th	*Smith* 49.9		*Smith* 44.8		Talbot 54.0		Talbot 52.3		Patterson 56.6		Patterson 51.9	+0.6	Patterson 53.7	6
Conn. At Large	*Monkiewicz* 52.0	46.4	*Maciora* 47.3	-0.9	*Monkiewicz* 52.3	47.3	*Ryter* 48.4	-1.1	Sadlak 57.1	50.8	Sadlak 50.2	+0.6	Sadlak 50.4	6
3rd & 5th	49.9	46.3	45.7	-0.6	52.6	48.2	50.1	-1.9	57.9	51.3	50.6	+0.7	50.4	6

DELAWARE

District														
Delaware At Large	Williams 56.3	45.2	*Traynor* 48.6		*Willey* 54.7	45.4	*Traynor* 49.5	-3.4	Boggs 55.2	50.6	Boggs 50.8	-4.1	Boggs 56.7	-0.2

IDAHO

District														
1st	*White* 37.2	43.5	*White* 38.0		*White* 45.9	47.0	*White* 43.4	+5.5	Goff 50.6	46.5	*White* 46.9	+3.6	Wood 50.5	-0.4
2nd	*Dworshak* 53.6	47.0	*Dworshak* 53.1		*Dworshak* 54.8	49.2	*Dworshak* 52.3	-6.1	Sanborn 60.7	50.1	Sanborn 51.1	-3.1	Budge 57.1	-1.0

ILLINOIS

District														
Illinois (Chicago Area)	44.5	45.0	47.8		48.0	42.5	43.8	-2.8	52.0	46.0	43.9	-1.3	50.4	+2.1

APPENDIX. REPUBLICAN % OF TWO-PARTY VOTE, 1938-1950

ILLINOIS (Continued)

DIST.	CONG. % Rep. 1938	PRES. % Rep. 1940	CONG. % Rep. 1940	DIFF. PRES. minus CONG. 1940	CONG. % Rep. 1942	PRES. % Rep. 1944	CONG. % Rep. 1944	DIFF. PRES. minus CONG. 1944	CONG. % Rep. 1946	PRES. % Rep. 1948	CONG. % Rep. 1948	DIFF. PRES. minus CONG. 1948	CONG. % Rep. 1950	REF. LINE
1st	Mitchell 46.6	Mitchell 47.0			Dawson 47.2		Dawson 38.0		Dawson 43.2		Dawson 30.4		Dawson 37.6	6
2nd	McKeough 45.6	McKeough 48.6			Rowan 49.2		Rowan 42.7		Vail 51.3		O'Hara 48.2		Vail 53.6	6
3rd	Kelly 44.0	Kelly 48.8			Busbey 51.3		Kelly 48.0		Busbey 57.2		Linehan 47.1		Busbey 54.6	14,6
4th	Beam 23.6	Beam 22.6			Gorski 21.3		Gorski 19.6		Gorski 29.1		Buckley 47.9		McVey 55.8	6
5th	Sabath 25.2	Sabath 29.0			Sabath 27.8		Sabath 23.7		Sabath 28.4		Gorski 27.6		Kluczynski 34.4	15,6
6th	Maciejewski 41.3	Maciejewski 43.8			O'Brien 43.6		O'Brien 39.9		O'Brien 48.0		O'Brien 31.3		O'Brien 35.4	6
7th	Schuetz 45.7	Schuetz 49.1			Schuetz 49.7		Link 45.4		Owens 55.0		Sabath 26.3		Sabath 28.2	6
8th	Kocialkowski 24.7	Kocialkowski 21.9			Gordon 21.2		Gordon 20.8		Gordon 22.7		Gordon 34.9		Gordon 40.7	6
9th	McAndrews 47.3	Dewey 53.3			Dewey 51.3		Resa 47.2		Twyman 51.3		Yates 44.5		Yates 48.2	6
10th	Church 58.1	Paddock 61.5			Church 63.0		Church 55.8		Church 64.6		Hoffman 58.1		Hoffman 66.5	6
11th	Reed	Reed			Reed 71.0	62.9	Reed 66.2	-3.3	Reed 74.9		Chesney 49.2		Sheehan 56.7	

Rank	Name	%	prev	Name	%	Name	%	Δ	prev	Name	%	Name	%	Δ	prev	Name	%	Name	%	Δ	Dist.
12th	Mason	60.7	54.0	Mason	60.6	Mason	71.4	-6.6	58.2	Mason	61.0	Mason	69.1	-2.8		Jonas	52.7	Jonas	56.2		
13th	Allen	65.6	65.8	Allen	67.6	Allen	79.4	-1.8	67.9	Allen	70.0	Allen	77.8	-2.1		Church	68.0	Church	74.1		16
14th	Johnson	51.5	51.7	Johnson	52.3	Johnson	59.3	-0.6	53.7	Johnson	54.3	Johnson	62.1	-0.6	70.4	Reed	68.3	Reed	74.2	+2.1	17
15th	Chiperfield	54.5	54.5	Chiperfield	56.4	Chiperfield	62.1	-1.9	57.0	Chiperfield	59.3	Chiperfield	64.3	-2.3	57.8	Mason	56.4	Mason	63.3	+1.4	18
16th	Dirksen	63.5	48.6	Dirksen	58.1	Dirksen	68.8	-9.5	53.2	Dirksen	59.0	Dirksen	67.5	-5.8	60.0	Allen	58.5	Allen	67.3	+1.5	19
17th	Arends	60.9	58.9	Arends	61.1	Arends	72.4	-2.2	62.4	Arends	66.3	Arends	71.2	-3.9	61.7	Arends	62.6	Arends	66.8	-0.9	5
18th	Sumner	55.3	53.6	Sumner	53.2	Sumner	62.4	+0.4	57.2	Sumner	56.9	Jenison	65.1	+0.3	54.2	Velde	52.1	Velde	61.6	+2.1	20
19th	Wheat	51.5	48.8	Wheat	50.6	Wheat	57.3	-1.8	52.5	McMillan	55.8	McMillan	62.5	-3.3	55.4	Chiperfield	54.0	Chiperfield	59.1	+1.4	21
20th	*Barnes*	44.6	50.5	*Barnes*	48.3	Simpson	51.0	-2.2	53.3	Simpson	55.6	Simpson	58.8	-2.3	52.0	Simpson	53.1	Simpson	59.3	-1.1	22
21st	*Fries*	49.7	50.7	*Howell*	51.6	*Howell*	58.1	-0.9	51.9	*Howell*	55.7	*Howell*	55.1	-3.8	51.1	*Mack, Jr.*	46.9	*Mack, Jr.*	47.2	+4.2	22
22nd	*Shaefer*	47.6	43.1	*Shaefer*	46.2	Johnson	55.7	-3.1	44.0	*Price*	49.2	*Price*	49.3	-5.2	53.3	McMillan	53.2	*Springer*	60.7	+0.1	23
23rd	*Arnold*	46.2	49.9	*Arnold*	49.0	Vursell	52.7	+0.9	53.9	Vursell	54.7	Vursell	54.9	-0.8	53.1	Jenison	51.8	Jenison	55.9	+1.5	24
24th	*Parsons*	48.9	53.7	Heidinger	53.6	Heidinger	58.4	+0.1	58.6	Clippinger	58.2	Clippinger	58.9	+0.4	52.3	Vursell	50.6	Vursell	55.3	+1.7	25
25th	*Keller*	47.7	50.6	Bishop	50.5	Bishop	55.1	+0.1	54.1	Bishop	53.5	Bishop	59.8	+0.6	37.0	*Price*	30.5	*Price*	35.1	+6.5	26

APPENDIX. REPUBLICAN % OF TWO-PARTY VOTE, 1938-1950

DIST.	CONG. % Rep. 1938	PRES. % Rep. 1940	CONG. % Rep. 1940	DIFF. PRES. minus CONG. 1940	CONG. % Rep. 1942	PRES. % Rep. 1944	CONG. % Rep. 1944	DIFF. PRES. minus CONG. 1944	CONG. % Rep. 1946	PRES. % Rep. 1948	CONG. % Rep. 1948	DIFF. PRES. minus CONG. 1948	CONG. % Rep. 1950	REF. LINE
					ILLINOIS (Continued)									
26th										50.3	*Bishop* 51.9	-1.6	*Bishop* 51.2	27
At Large	*Martin, Smith* 48.3	48.8	*Stratton, Day* 51.2	-2.3	*Day* 51.5	48.3	*Douglas* 47.5	+0.8	Stratton 55.3					28
					INDIANA									
1st	*Schultz* 45.0	39.3	*Schultz* 39.1	+0.2	*Madden* 46.4	39.1	*Madden* 38.3	+0.8	*Madden* 47.4	40.0	*Madden* 38.9	+1.1	*Madden* 47.2	29,3
2nd	Halleck 57.8	55.7	Halleck 58.1	-2.4	Halleck 61.2	61.4	Halleck 61.9	-0.5	Halleck 61.9	58.5	Halleck 55.7	+2.8	Halleck 57.6	5
3rd	Grant 50.8	49.5	Grant 51.3	-1.8	Grant 55.2	51.8	Grant 52.1	-0.3	Grant 56.1	49.7	*Crook* 47.7	+2.0	Crumpacker 53.2	5
4th	Gillie 58.1	57.3	Gillie 58.0	-0.7	Gillie 61.0	59.3	Gillie 60.2	-0.9	Gillie 60.1	55.2	*Kruse, Jr.* 48.7	+6.5	Adair 56.6	3
5th	Harness 54.6	52.7	Harness 54.7	-2.0	Harness 55.7	53.5	Harness 54.0	-0.5	Harness 56.5	49.6	*Walsh* 47.4	+2.2	Beamer 54.5	
6th	Johnson 50.6	51.5	Johnson 55.9	-4.4	Johnson 58.1	55.0	Johnson 55.4	-0.4	Johnson 57.9	51.0	Harden 50.2	+0.8	Harden 52.6	
7th	Landis 51.1	51.0	Landis 52.2	-1.2	Landis 56.9	53.5	Landis 54.2	-0.7	Landis 51.5	50.8	*Noland* 45.8	+5.0	Bray 50.3	
8th	*Boehne, Jr.* 43.6	46.1	*Boehne, Jr.* 44.5	+1.6	LaFollette 53.7	48.4	LaFollette 52.2	-3.8	Mitchell 52.3	45.3	*Denton* 44.3	+1.0	*Denton* 48.6	
9th	Crowe 47.9	51.6	Wilson 50.9	+0.7	Wilson		Wilson	0.8	Wilson		Wilson		Wilson	

Springer 53.5	51.7	Springer 53.0	-1.3	Springer 57.4	54.1	Springer 54.9	-0.8	Springer 61.3	56.1	Delancy 53.1	+3.0	Delancy 59.2	30
11th & 12th													
11th	47.4	49.8	Larrabee 47.7	+2.1	Larrabee 49.7	52.3	Ludlow 48.8	+3.5	Ludlow 48.6	51.4	Jacobs 48.9	+2.5	Brownson 56.8	6
12th	Larrabee 48.4	Larrabee 48.3	Ludlow 46.3	Ludlow 47.1									30,6

IOWA

1st	Martin 58.0	57.7	Martin 60.4	+2.7	Martin 62.6	54.4	Martin 56.7	-2.3	Martin 61.5	52.3	Martin 53.8	-1.5	Martin 61.9	31,5
2nd	Jacobsen 49.7	52.2	Jacobsen 47.8	+4.4	Talle 57.4	54.3	Talle 55.9	-1.6	Talle 59.1	49.8	Talle 57.7	-7.9	Talle 58.8	32
3rd	Gwynne 60.2	53.0	Gwynne 59.9	-6.9	Gwynne 60.7	53.2	Gwynne 56.8	-3.6	Gwynne 62.0	48.7	Gross 58.5	-9.8	Gross 64.3	33
4th	Talle 52.2	55.4	Talle 56.4	-1.0	LeCompte 64.5	50.3	LeCompte 54.9	-4.6	LeCompte 58.4	46.9	LeCompte 51.7	-4.8	LeCompte 57.0	34
5th	LeCompte 53.9	50.1	LeCompte 53.3	-3.2	Cunningham 63.2	46.9	Cunningham 54.1	-7.2	Cunningham 59.4	45.5	Cunningham 51.2	-5.7	Cunningham 57.1	35
6th	Dowell 59.1	47.2	Cunningham 52.4	-5.2	Gilchrist 60.3	47.8	Dolliver 58.8	-10.0	Dolliver 63.4	45.4	Dolliver 55.8	-10.4	Dolliver 64.9	36
7th	Jensen 59.1	58.2	Jensen 58.6	-0.4	Jensen 64.2	57.1	Jensen 61.5	-4.4	Jensen 63.0	52.9	Jensen 56.9	-4.0	Jensen 62.2	5
8th	Gilchrist 62.9	46.7	Gilchrist 58.1	-10.4	Hoeven 64.6	53.3	Hoeven 56.2	-2.9	Hoeven 68.6	47.9	Hoeven 55.4	-6.5	Hoeven 64.2	37
9th	Harrington 49.8	52.8	Harrington 49.2	+3.6										38

APPENDIX. REPUBLICAN % OF TWO-PARTY VOTE, 1938-1950

DIST.	CONG. % Rep. 1938	PRES. % Rep. 1940	CONG. % Rep. 1940	DIFF. PRES. minus CONG. 1940	CONG. % Rep. 1942	PRES. % Rep. 1944	CONG. % Rep. 1944	DIFF. PRES. minus CONG. 1944	CONG. % Rep. 1946	PRES. % Rep. 1948	CONG. % Rep. 1948	DIFF. PRES. minus CONG. 1948	CONG. % Rep. 1950	REF. LINE
KANSAS														
1st	Lambertson 60.3	61.8	Lambertson 61.0	+0.8	Lambertson 59.2	65.3	Cole 67.3	-2.0	Cole 64.3	58.6	Cole 60.5	-1.9	Cole 66.5	39, 5
2nd	Geyer 56.4	53.9	Geyer 54.0	-0.1	Geyer 59.1	55.8	Scrivner 59.1	-3.3	Scrivner 58.8	49.4	Scrivner 51.9	-2.5	Scrivner 52.2	3
3rd	Winter 53.4	55.3	Winter 55.2	+0.1	Winter 59.8	59.2	Winter 60.2	-1.0	Meyer 55.3	53.4	Meyer 55.0	-1.6	George 54.7	3
4th	Rees 63.1	63.3	Rees 62.5	+0.8	Rees 55.7	58.4	Rees 58.6	-0.2	Rees 56.2	54.4	Rees 55.6	-1.2	Rees 58.9	40
5th	Houston 49.7	51.0	Houston 47.5	+3.5	Hope 66.6	60.8	Hope 69.0	-8.2	Hope 62.6	54.9	Hope 65.0	-10.1	Hope 61.8	41
6th	Carlson 63.4	59.7	Carlson 60.8	-1.1	Carlson 64.2	66.0	Carlson 66.0	0	Smith 60.5	57.7	Smith 57.6	+0.1	Smith 59.5	3
7th	Hope 65.5	57.3	Hope 63.9	-6.6										41
KENTUCKY														
1st	Gregory 24.0	28.3	Gregory 0	+28.3	Gregory 32.5	31.3	Gregory 30.2	+1.1	Gregory 33.3	24.1	Gregory 0	+24.1	Gregory 0	
2nd	Vincent 36.2	38.8	Vincent 0	+38.8	Vincent 0	42.9	Clements 42.5	+0.4	Clements 43.4	36.5	Whitaker 36.6	-0.1	Whitaker 0	
3rd	O'Neal		O'Neal		O'Neal				Morton		Morton		Morton	

	(1)	(2)	(3)	(4)	(5)	(6)	(7)	(8)	(9)	(10)	(11)	(12)	(13)
	40.8	42.0	41.5	44.3	+0.5	45.6	45.3	+0.3	46.9	41.6	40.6	+1.0	0
5th	*Spence* 31.5	41.6	*Spence* 38.8	*Spence* 39.5	+2.8	42.8	*Spence* 41.9	+0.9	*Spence* 48.8	38.1	*Spence* 33.8	+4.3	*Spence* 36.7
6th	*Chapman* 34.9	40.4	*Chapman* 39.5	*Chapman* 0	+0.9	41.8	*Chapman* 41.1	+0.7	*Chapman* 45.0	39.9	*Underwood* 39.3	+0.6	*Underwood* 0
7th	*May* 46.8	41.8	*May* 43.2	*May* 49.4	-1.4	44.6	*May* 47.5	-2.9	*Meade* 59.1	39.9	*Perkins* 39.5	+0.4	*Perkins* 43.9
8th	*Bates* 41.1	42.6	*Bates* 42.0	*Bates* 44.0	+0.6	44.8	*Bates* 45.7	-0.9	*Bates* 47.4	38.8	*Bates* 39.5	-0.7	*Bates* 39.5
9th	Robison 66.8	61.6	Robison 61.7	Robison 100	-0.1	67.7	Robison 69.0	-1.3	Robison 100	60.7	Golden 100	-39.3	Golden 100

MAINE

	(1)	(2)	(3)	(4)	(5)	(6)	(7)	(8)	(9)	(10)	(11)	(12)	(13)
1st	Oliver 59.0	48.8	Oliver 63.4	Hale 57.0	-14.6	50.3	Hale 68.8	-18.5	Hale 59.6	55.7	Hale 62.5	-6.8	Hale 54.0
2nd	Smith 54.3	49.9	Smith 64.6	Smith 67.6	-14.7	51.3	Smith 67.8	-16.5	Smith 60.7	56.0	Nelson 67.2	-11.2	Nelson 57.7
3rd	Brewster 63.3	56.6	Fellows 66.1	Fellows 100	-9.5	57.4	Fellows 77.9	-20.5	Fellows 72.9	61.7	Fellows 70.9	-9.2	Fellows 62.9

MARYLAND

	(1)	(2)	(3)	(4)	(5)	(6)	(7)	(8)	(9)	(10)	(11)	(12)	(13)
1st	*Ward* 37.2	44.7	*Ward* 46.1	*Ward* 44.1	-1.4	49.9	*Roe* 49.2	+0.7	Miller 50.9	49.8	Miller 52.4	-2.6	Miller 57.0 [6]
2nd, 3rd & 4th	39.8	38.9	37.6	39.5	+1.3	45.0	39.5	+5.5	44.5	48.6	39.4	+9.2	46.7 [6]
2nd	*Cole, Jr.* 32.9		*Cole, Jr.* 34.3	*Baldwin* 37.8			*Baldwin* 43.0		*Meade* 47.6		Bolton 43.5		Devereux 50.8
3rd	*D'Alesandro,Jr.* 43.4		*D'Alesandro,Jr.* 38.5	*D'Alesandro,Jr.* 26.8			*D'Alesandro, Jr.* 30.2		*D'Alesandro, Jr.* 36.1		Garmatz 29.0		Garmatz 34.3

APPENDIX. REPUBLICAN % OF TWO-PARTY VOTE, 1938-1950

MARYLAND (Continued)

DIST.	CONG. % Rep. 1938	PRES. % Rep. 1940	CONG. % Rep. 1940	DIFF. PRES. minus CONG. 1940	CONG. % Rep. 1942	CONG. % Rep. 1944	PRES. % Rep. 1944	DIFF. PRES. minus CONG. 1944	CONG. % Rep. 1946	PRES. % Rep. 1948	CONG. % Rep. 1948	DIFF. PRES. minus CONG. 1948	CONG. % Rep. 1950	REF. LINE
4th	Kennedy 49.8		Meyer 43.4		Ellison 50.9	Fallon 40.8			Fallon 42.8		Fallon 35.4		Fallon 42.1	6
5th	Sasscer 29.6	41.7	Sasscer 29.0	+12.7	Sasscer 33.3	Sasscer 35.2	52.1	+16.9	Sasscer 41.8	52.4	Sasscer 40.3	+12.1	Sasscer 42.5	
6th	Byron,W.D. 49.2	46.5	Byron,K.E. 46.5	0	Beall 59.5	Beall 57.9	54.8	-3.1	Beall 58.2	56.5	Beall 55.3	+1.2	Beall 61.9	

MASSACHUSETTS

DIST.	CONG. % Rep. 1938	PRES. % Rep. 1940	CONG. % Rep. 1940	DIFF. PRES. minus CONG. 1940	CONG. % Rep. 1942	CONG. % Rep. 1944	PRES. % Rep. 1944	DIFF. PRES. minus CONG. 1944	CONG. % Rep. 1946	PRES. % Rep. 1948	CONG. % Rep. 1948	DIFF. PRES. minus CONG. 1948	CONG. % Rep. 1950	REF. LINE
1st	Treadway 58.8		Treadway 57.1		Treadway 58.1	Heselton 50.5			Heselton 59.4		Heselton 57.2		Heselton 68.9	42,43
2nd	Clason 61.9		Clason 58.4		Clason 61.6	Clason 55.6			Clason 51.4		Furcolo 45.1		Furcolo 45.4	
3rd	Casey 48.2		Casey 45.4		Philbin 49.6	Philbin 38.5			Philbin 37.8		Philbin 26.1		Philbin 28.5	
4th	Holmes 54.1		Holmes 53.6		Holmes 57.2	Holmes 55.5			Donohue 49.5		Donohue 40.8		Donohue 42.8	
5th	Rogers 74.8		Rogers 76.2		Rogers 100	Rogers 73.2			Rogers 71.9		Rogers 100		Rogers 76.1	
6th	Bates,G.J. 74.7		Bates,G.J. 71.6		Bates,G.J. 75.3	Bates,G.J. 67.0			Bates,G.J. 70.2		Bates,G.J. 100		Bates,W.H. 73.7	
7th	Connery 36.2		Connery 36.9		Lane 0	Lane 32.1			Lane 38.2		Lane 20.8		Lane 20.9	
8th	Healey		Healey		Goodwin	Goodwin			Goodwin		Goodwin		Goodwin	

							[43]
9th	Luce 50.7	Eliot 47.9	Gifford 58.8	Gifford 58.5	Gifford 61.7	Nicholson 56.7	Nicholson 58.4
10th	Tinkham 64.4	Tinkham 59.1	Herter 51.1	Herter 55.8	Herter 64.0	Herter 69.5	Herter 58.2
11th	*Flaherty* 0	*Flaherty* 16.2	*Curley* 30.7	*Curley* 34.4	*Kennedy* 27.3	*Kennedy* 0	*Kennedy* 17.3
12th	*McCormack* 22.9	*McCormack* 21.9	*McCormack* 21.3	*McCormack* 24.3	*McCormack* 0	*McCormack* 0	*McCormack* 14.0
13th	Wigglesworth 68.4	Wigglesworth 65.6	Wigglesworth 59.3	Wigglesworth 65.8	Wigglesworth 67.5	Wigglesworth 56.6	Wigglesworth 62.5
14th	Martin, Jr. 59.2	Martin, Jr. 54.4	Martin, Jr. 59.4	Martin, Jr. 62.0	Martin, Jr. 63.6	Martin, Jr 61.4	Martin, Jr. 64.6
15th	Gifford 59.0	Gifford 57.8					
Entire State	53.9	46.6 52.5	47.1 53.0	−5.9 53.8	−5.9 53.7	44.1 49.9	−5.8 50.3 [42,43]

MICHIGAN

							[6]
1st, 13th thru 17th (Detroit Area)	44.6	39.5 40.8	38.1 40.8	−1.3 42.1	−2.7 51.7	41.5 38.8	+2.7 42.0
1st	*Tenerowicz* 19.0	*Tenerowicz* 19.7	*Sadowski* 22.0	*Sadowski* 19.1	*Sadowski* 33.7	*Sadowski* 16.1	*Machrowicz* 16.2
2nd	Michener 64.5	63.3 Michener 62.3	62.9 Michener 64.9	+1.0 Michener 63.5	−2.0 Michener 71.8	62.7 Michener 56.5	+7.2 Meader 60.8
3rd	Shafer 66.0	59.7 Shafer 62.3	61.9 Shafer 63.0	−2.6 Shafer 66.8	−1.1 Shafer 69.8	60.7 Shafer 60.5	+0.2 Shafer 62.0

APPENDIX. REPUBLICAN % OF TWO-PARTY VOTE, 1938-1950

MICHIGAN (Continued)

DIST.	CONG. % Rep. 1938	PRES. % Rep. 1940	CONG. % Rep. 1940	DIFF. PRES. minus CONG. 1940	CONG. % Rep. 1942	PRES. % Rep. 1944	CONG. % Rep. 1944	DIFF. PRES. minus CONG. 1944	CONG. % Rep. 1946	PRES. % Rep. 1948	CONG. % Rep. 1948	DIFF. PRES. minus CONG. 1948	CONG. % Rep. 1950	REF. LINE
4th	Hoffman 59.2	63.5	Hoffman 61.9	+1.6	Hoffman 69.1	66.5	Hoffman 64.4	+2.1	Hoffman 73.2	65.0	Hoffman 66.0	-1.0	Hoffman 69.0	
5th	Mapes 59.1	54.5	Jonkman 53.7	+0.8	Jonkman 54.6	57.7	Jonkman 57.7	0	Jonkman 71.6	57.5	Ford, Jr. 61.2	-3.7	Ford, Jr. 67.0	
6th	Blackney 55.0	50.1	Blackney 51.2	-1.1	Blackney 57.1	51.1	Blackney 55.4	-4.3	Blackney 57.7	53.5	Blackney 50.3	+3.2	Blackney 53.3	
7th	Wolcott 69.0	62.9	Wolcott 65.2	-2.3	Wolcott 67.3	62.8	Wolcott 66.3	-3.5	Wolcott 74.8	59.9	Wolcott 59.4	+0.5	Wolcott 63.2	
8th	Crawford 58.7	61.6	Crawford 61.2	+0.4	Crawford 67.6	64.9	Crawford 67.8	-2.9	Crawford 73.2	64.2	Crawford 62.3	-1.9	Crawford 61.0	
9th	Engel 58.2	54.5	Engel 56.9	-2.4	Engel 65.8	56.4	Engel 62.6	-6.2	Engel 72.2	54.5	Engel 59.1	-4.6	Thompson 54.8	
10th	Woodruff 66.4	61.1	Woodruff 62.0	-0.9	Woodruff 60.5	61.9	Woodruff 65.0	-3.1	Woodruff 71.7	60.4	Woodruff 63.9	-3.5	Woodruff 66.2	
11th	Bradley 51.4	32.1	Bradley 51.2	+0.9	Bradley 58.0	54.3	Bradley 59.2	-4.9	Bradley 66.0	55.9	Potter 64.1	-8.2	Potter 66.6	
12th	*Hook* 48.3	42.2	*Hook* 48.5	-6.3	Bennett 53.1	44.1	*Hook* 49.4	-8.3	Bennett 54.6	48.8	Bennett 56.9	-8.1	Bennett 61.7	
13th	McLeod 50.9	45.1	*O'Brien* 45.1		*O'Brien* 48.9		*O'Brien* 41.9		Coffin 53.0		*O'Brien* 37.3		*O'Brien* 38.4	6
14th	*Rabant*		*Rabant*		*Rabant*		*Rabant*		Youngblood		*Rabant*		*Rabant*	

District														No.
	Dingell 45.8		Dingell 37.9	Dingell 35.4			Dingell 36.1	Dingell 47.9			Dingell 34.7	Dingell 35.8		6
16th	Lesinski 44.7		Lesinski 40.9	Lesinski 41.5			Lesinski 38.4	Lesinski 47.6			Lesinski 37.1	Lesinski 38.8		6
17th	Dondero 61.6		Dondero 54.8	Dondero 56.8			Dondero 57.0	Dondero 65.1			Dondero 53.0	Dondero 55.7		6

MINNESOTA

District														No.
1st	Andresen 64.9	58.0	Andresen 76.4	Andresen 66.4	-18.4	57.5	Andresen 61.7	Andresen 68.3	-4.2	47.4	Andresen 61.4	Andresen 67.1	-14.0	44
2nd	Ryan 45.2	61.3	O'Hara 53.6	O'Hara 70.0	+7.7	61.1	O'Hara 75.7	O'Hara 76.0	-14.6	46.0	O'Hara 63.9	O'Hara 59.9	-17.9	
3rd & 5th (Minneapolis Area)	55.8	46.3	58.3	68.5	-12.0	44.5	52.9	55.3	-8.4	43.8	49.4	53.4	-5.6	
3rd	Alexander 51.4		Gale 56.0	Gale 49.0			Gallagher 49.1	Mackinnon 52.1			Weir 45.4	Weir 48.2		
(St. Paul) 4th	Maas 59.8	42.0	Maas 67.6	Maas 65.7	-15.6	40.3	Starkey 48.2	Devitt 52.2	-7.9	35.2	McCarthy 40.6	McCarthy 39.6	-5.4	
5th	Youngdahl 59.8		Youngdahl 60.3	Judd 64.0			Judd 56.6	Judd 57.3			Judd 54.0	Judd 59.4		6
6th	Knutson 68.9	55.3	Knutson 61.5	Knutson 57.3	-6.2	55.5	Knutson 66.2	Knutson 57.4	-10.7	42.8	Marshall 48.3	Marshall 43.8	-5.5	
7th	Andersen 53.7	50.1	Andersen 60.9	Andersen 54.8	-10.8	50.3	Andersen 65.9	Andersen 65.4	-15.6	39.7	Andersen 52.5	Andersen 61.7	-12.8	
8th	Pittenger 55.5	32.1	Pittenger 65.5	Pittenger 59.2	-33.4	30.4	Pittenger 51.9	Blatnik 42.3	-21.5	30.8	Blatnik 33.4	Blatnik 37.1	-2.6	
9th	Buckler 47.8	40.5	Buckler 49.6	Hagen 49.6	-9.1	42.4	Hagen 59.2	Hagen 63.9	-16.8	38.8	Hagen 54.6	Hagen 64.9	-15.8	44

APPENDIX. REPUBLICAN % OF TWO-PARTY VOTE, 1938-1950

MISSOURI

DIST.	CONG. % Rep. 1938	PRES. % Rep. 1940	CONG. % Rep. 1940	DIFF. PRES. minus CONG. 1940	CONG. % Rep. 1942	PRES. % Rep. 1944	CONG. % Rep. 1944	DIFF. PRES. minus CONG. 1944	CONG. % Rep. 1946	PRES. % Rep. 1948	CONG. % Rep. 1948	DIFF. PRES. minus CONG. 1948	CONG. % Rep. 1950	REF. LINE
1st	Romjue 45.3	49.6	Romjue 49.5	+0.1	Arnold 55.5	50.9	Arnold 50.8	+0.1	Arnold 50.3	43.4	Magee 42.4	+1.0	Magee 45.6	
2nd	Nelson 43.0	48.3	Nelson 46.2	+2.1	Schwabe 50.4	50.4	Schwabe 50.1	+0.3	Schwabe 51.1	44.3	Moulder 43.3	+1.0	Moulder 47.0	
3rd	Duncan 44.7	46.8	Duncan 46.7	+0.1	Cole 56.4	49.0	Cole 50.6	-1.6	Cole 52.8	41.0	Welch 41.2	-0.2	Welch 48.9	
4th & 5th (Kansas City Area)	19.3	42.5	43.2	-0.7	42.8	45.6	45.1	-0.5	49.3	38.3	39.8	-1.5	41.9	
4th	Bell 19.6		Bell 40.0		Bell 39.5		Bell 42.8		Bell 44.9		Irving 35.9		Irving 38.4	6
5th	Shannon 19.0		Shannon 45.8		Slaughter 49.0		Slaughter 47.4		Reeves 53.7		Bolling 44.1		Bolling 45.5	6
6th	Wood 49.7	52.0	Bennett 53.7	-1.7	Bennett 54.5	56.1	Bennett 57.0	-0.9	Bennett 58.6	45.3	Christopher 48.6	-3.3	Armstrong 50.7	
7th	Short 56.3	60.0	Short 59.3	+0.7	Short 63.5	64.0	Short 64.0	0	Short 65.4	54.8	Short 54.0	+0.8	Short 58.7	
8th	Williams 44.7	49.1	Williams 48.9	+0.2	Elmer 51.5	49.7	Carnahan 49.5	+0.2	Banta 51.1	41.9	Carnahan 42.8	-0.9	Carnahan 45.3	
9th	Cannon		Cannon		Cannon		Cannon		Cannon		Cannon		Cannon	

(The following data are printed as a single large table rotated 90° on the page. It is reproduced here as three regional sub-tables. Where a cell contains more than one figure, the figures are separated by a slash. The final column gives footnote reference numbers.)

MISSOURI (St. Louis Area)

11th thru 13th (St. Louis Area)	41.1	42.6 / 44.1	43.3 / +1.5	43.3 / 43.7	39.4 / +0.4	Jones 28.4 / 29.9	Jones 0 / +1.5	
11th	Hennings, Jr. 38.1 / 40.6	Sullivan 44.3 / 45.1 / 46.5	Miller 50.4 / −1.4 / 50.7	Sullivan 41.1 / 43.1 / 39.5	Bakewell 50.8 / +3.6 / 53.2	Sullivan 34.3 / 40.2 / 38.5	Sullivan 35.3 / +1.7 / 43.2	6, 45
12th	Anderson 47.8	Ploeser 53.9	Ploeser 57.0	Ploeser 51.8	Ploeser 58.2	Kurst 44.8	Curtis 50.9	6
13th	Cochran 30.9	Cochran 35.4	Cochran 38.7	Cochran ○	Karsten 45.2	Karsten 29.4	Karsten 32.5	6

MONTANA

1st	Thorkelson 54.4	Rankin 54.5 / 40.1	Mansfield 40.1 / −14.4	Mansfield 31.4 / 45.9	Mansfield 42.4 / +14.5	Mansfield 31.8 / 46.1	Mansfield 39.1 / +14.3
2nd	O'Connor 46.2	O'Connor 37.4 / 41.0	O'Connor 47.2 / +3.6	O'Connor 45.7 / 44.8	D'Ewart 54.6 / −0.9	D'Ewart 51.0 / 43.8	D'Ewart 54.7 / −7.2

NEBRASKA

1st	Heinke 50.2	Copeland 55.6 / 58.9	Curtis 68.9 / +3.3	Curtis 69.9 / 61.7	Curtis 66.4 / −8.2	Curtis 57.2 / 55.8	Curtis 54.5 / −1.4	46, 47
2nd	McLaughlin 41.1 / 44.8	McLaughlin 43.4 / 44.8	Buffett 53.2 / +1.4	Buffett 59.5 / 48.0	Buffett 58.3 / −11.5	O'Sullivan 48.6 / 50.1	Buffett 63.5 / +1.5	5, 47
3rd	Stefan 75.3 / 60.2	Stefan 82.5 / 60.2	Stefan 69.4 / −22.3	Stefan 71.1 / 62.8	Stefan 76.0 / −8.3	Stefan 64.8 / 55.3	Stefan 66.9 / −9.5	5
4th	Curtis 58.2 / 61.8	Curtis 69.6 / 61.8	Miller 67.1 / −7.8	Miller 67.9 / 62.2	Miller 71.3 / −5.7	Miller 63.6 / 55.2	Miller 65.8 / −8.4	47
5th	Coffee 35.3 / 61.4	Coffee 42.0 / 61.4	Coffee / +19.4					48

APPENDIX. REPUBLICAN % OF TWO-PARTY VOTE, 1938-1950

DIST.	CONG. % Rep. 1938	PRES. % Rep. 1940	CONG. % Rep. 1940	DIFF. PRES. minus CONG. 1940	CONG. % Rep. 1942	PRES. % Rep. 1944	CONG. % Rep. 1944	DIFF. PRES. minus CONG. 1944	CONG. % Rep. 1946	PRES. % Rep. 1948	CONG. % Rep. 1948	DIFF. PRES. minus CONG. 1948	CONG. % Rep. 1950	REF. LINE
NEVADA														
At Large	Scrugham 33.6	39.9	Scrugham 35.5	+4.4	Sullivan 46.4	45.4	Bunker 36.9	+8.5	Russell 58.8	48.4	Baring 49.4	-1.0	Baring 47.2	
NEW HAMPSHIRE														
1st & 2nd	56.3	46.8	52.0	-5.2	55.1	47.9	52.6	-4.7	62.0	52.9	56.8	-3.9	60.9	
1st	Jenks 53.9		Jenks 51.1		Merrow 52.1		Merrow 50.9		Merrow 59.7		Merrow 55.8		Merrow 57.5	6
2nd	Stearns 59.1		Stearns 53.0		Stearns 58.4		Adams 54.6		Cotton 65.9		Cotton 57.9		Cotton 64.5	6
NEW JERSEY														
1st	Wolverton 62.3	37.1	Wolverton 55.6	-18.5	Wolverton 61.7	37.0	Wolverton 50.6	-13.6	Wolverton 63.5	46.8	Wolverton 53.7	-6.9	Wolverton 56.7	
2nd	Jeffries 50.8	46.8	Wene 47.8	-1.0	Wene 47.0	48.4	Hand 54.4	-6.0	Hand 67.1	56.4	Hand 62.2	-5.8	Hand 54.3	
3rd & 5th	53.1	51.8	52.1	-0.3	59.2	54.7	57.9	-3.2	63.6	58.3	58.8	-0.5	62.2	
3rd	Sutphin 49.5		Sutphin 48.2		Auchinloss 53.4		Auchinloss 57.0		Auchinloss 66.0		Auchinloss 59.4		Auchinloss 62.8	6
4th	Powers 61.5	43.2	Powers 55.9	-12.7	Powers 63.9	42.6	Matthews, Jr. 55.7	-13.1	Matthews, Jr. 52.6	45.6	Howell 38.5	+7.1	Howell 47.8	
	Eaton		Eaton		Eaton		Eaton		Eaton		Eaton		Eaton	

	62.2	53.1	55.5	-2.4	58.9	53.3	56.3	-3.0	66.2	56.7	57.5	-8.0	62.2	
7th thru 9th	61.2	56.9	62.2	-5.3	65.8	59.0	62.9	-3.9	69.7	60.8	56.7	+4.1	65.9	
7th	Thomas 64.3		Thomas 64.9		Thomas 68.8		Thomas 66.1		Thomas 69.0		Thomas 56.5		Widnall 69.6	6
8th	Seger 59.6		Canfield 58.9		Canfield 66.8		Canfield 58.7		Canfield 71.5		Canfield 50.1		Canfield 63.9	6
9th	Osmers, Jr. 59.8		Osmers, Jr. 62.7		Towe 61.7		Towe 63.5		Towe 69.1		Towe 62.2		Towe 63.8	6
10th thru 14th (Essex & Hudson Counties	39.7	44.4	46.2	-1.8	40.5	44.7	44.7	0	48.6	45.1	43.2	+1.9	45.2	
10th	Hartley, Jr. 58.4		Hartley, Jr. 58.0		Hartley, Jr. 54.1		Hartley, Jr. 53.7		Hartley; Jr. 53.4		*Rodino, Jr.* 47.4		*Rodino, Jr.* 39.0	6
11th	Vreeland 52.9		Vreeland 57.2		Sundstrom 60.7		Sundstrom 52.8		Sundstrom 61.7		*Addonizio* 49.2		*Addonizio* 47.9	6
12th	Kean 57.1		Kean 55.9		Kean 62.7		Kean 51.7		Kean 64.7		Kean 51.9		Kean 54.3	6
13th	*Norton* 20.1		*Norton* 29.8		*Norton* 20.4		*Norton* 29.9		*Norton* 34.3		*Norton* 31.9		*Sieminski* 44.4	6
14th	*Hart* 21.2		*Hart* 34.7		*Hart* 21.1		*Hart* 36.8		*Hart* 36.5		*Hart* 37.2		*Hart* 40.8	6
NEW MEXICO														
At Large	*Dempsey* 41.5	43.3	*Anderson* 41.2	-2.1	*Anderson* 42.0	46.5	*Anderson* 44.5	-2.0	*Lusk* 47.6	43.3	*Miles* 41.3	-2.0	*Dempsey* 42.5	49,50
At Large					Fernandez		Fernandez		Fernandez		Fernandez		Fernandez	

APPENDIX. REPUBLICAN % OF TWO-PARTY VOTE, 1938-1950

NEW YORK

DIST.	CONG. % Rep. 1938	PRES. % Rep. 1940	CONG. % Rep. 1940	DIFF. PRES. minus CONG. 1940	CONG. % Rep. 1942	PRES. % Rep. 1944	CONG. % Rep. 1944	DIFF. PRES. minus CONG. 1944	CONG. % Rep. 1946	PRES. % Rep. 1948	CONG. % Rep. 1948	DIFF. PRES. minus CONG. 1948	CONG. % Rep. 1950	REF. LINE
1st & 2nd (Suffolk & Nassau)						67.3	68.6	-1.3	77.9	72.3	69.8	+2.5	60.1	51
1st							Sharp 69.6		Macy 77.3		Macy 67.6		Greenwood 49.9+	6
2nd							Hall 67.9		Hall 78.4		Hall 69.9		Hall 68.2	6
3rd thru 6th (Queens)						55.5	50.1	+4.1	61.0	54.6	50.3	+4.3	49.5	
3rd							Latham 60.6		Latham 75.5		Latham 61.6		Latham 62.6	6
4th							Barry 47.2		McMahon 59.9		Clemente 48.3		Clemente 43.5	6
5th							Roe 45.7		Ross 53.0		Quinn 46.4		Quinn 45.9	6
6th							Delaney 44.8		Nodar, Jr. 53.8		Delaney 42.1		Delaney 40.7	6
7th thru 15th (Brooklyn)						34.2	33.9	+0.3	37.3	36.3	31.3	+5.0	30.1	
7th							Delaney		Delaney		Delaney		Heller	

District					Ref.
	40.5	46.1	29.7	Anjaso 30.5	6, 52
9th	Keough 35.3	Keough 39.8	Keough 30.9	Keough 29.4	6, 52
10th	Somers 31.9	Somers 36.8	Somers 31.7	Kelly 27.6	6, 52
11th	Heffernan 34.2	Heffernan 39.6	Heffernan 35.5	Heffernan 31.8	6, 52
12th	Rooney 45.0	Rooney 46.0	Rooney 34.6	Rooney 34.8	6, 52
13th	O'Toole 39.7	O'Toole 46.5	O'Toole 40.3	O'Toole 39.2	6, 52
14th	Rayfiel 27.5	Rayfiel 25.0	Multer 24.8	Multer 22.2	6, 52
15th	Celler 18.9	Celler 21.2	Celler 18.6	Celler 19.1	6, 52
16th thru 22nd (Manhattan & Richmond)	37.1 / 38.1	-0.1 / 48.5	40.6 / 41.0	44.5	52
16th	Buck 53.5	Buck 61.2	Murphy 47.1	Murphy 46.8	6, 52
17th	Baldwin 57.2	Coudert, Jr. 62.8	Coudert, Jr. 58.9	Coudert, Jr. 56.3	6, 52
18th	Marcantonio see line ref. 53	Marcantonio see line ref. 53	Marcantonio see line ref. 53	Donovan see line ref. 53	6, 52, 53
19th	Dickstein 26.7	Klein 28.6	Klein 21.1	Klein 26.4	6, 52

APPENDIX. REPUBLICAN % OF TWO-PARTY VOTE, 1938-1950

NEW YORK (Continued)

DIST.	CONG. % Rep. 1938	PRES. % Rep. 1940	CONG. % Rep. 1940	DIFF. PRES. minus CONG. 1940	CONG. % Rep. 1942	CONG. % Rep. 1944	PRES. % Rep. 1944	DIFF. PRES. minus CONG. 1944	CONG. % Rep. 1946	PRES. % Rep. 1948	CONG. % Rep. 1948	DIFF. PRES. minus CONG. 1948	CONG. % Rep. 1950	REF. LINE
20th						*Bloom* 29.2			*Bloom* 38.9		*Bloom* 32.0		*Roosevelt, Jr.* 33.8	6, 52
21st						*Torrens* 30.7			*Javits* 53.6		*Javits* 50.7		*Javits* 65.2	6, 52
22nd						*Powell, Jr.* 10.9			*Powell, Jr.* 37.5		*Powell, Jr.* 18.1		*Powell, Jr.* 30.2	6, 52
23rd thru 26th (The Bronx)						28.4	31.9	+3.5	44.7	33.9	11.8	+22.1	32.0	52
23rd						*Lynch* 20.5			*Lynch* 36.7		*Lynch* 0		*Fine* 25.6	6, 52
24th						*Rabin* 15.2			*Rabin* 30.0		*Dollinger* 0		*Dollinger* 17.1	6, 52
25th						*Buckley* 30.6			*Buckley* 49.8		*Buckley* 0		*Buckley* 38.7	6, 52
26th						*Quinn* 43.9			*Potts* 54.2		*McGrath* 38.4		*McGrath* 38.7	6, 52
27th & 28th (Putnam & West-Chester)						63.7	61.9	-1.8	71.8	65.0	59.9	+5.1	66.4	
27th						Gwinn			Gwinn		Gwinn		Gwinn	

Ward								
	Gamble 65.5		Gamble 75.4		Gamble 65.7		Gamble 69.4	
29th	62.2	Bennet 100	St. George 60.2	-37.8	64.6 / St. George 62.2		St. George 62.7	+2.4
30th	61.3	Le Fevre 63.0	Le Fevre 69.5	-1.7	66.5 / Le Fevre 64.8		Wharton 67.3	+0.7
31st	55.1	Kearney 60.0	Kearney 59.2	-4.9	58.0 / Kearney 57.2		Kearney 65.5	+0.8
32nd	46.0	Byrne 42.8	Byrne 44.9	+3.2	44.3 / Byrne 42.5		Byrne 39.9	+1.8
33rd	58.7	Taylor 64.5	Taylor 69.9	-5.8	62.5 / Taylor 65.4		Taylor 70.1	-2.9
34th	58.3	Kilburn 62.9	Kilburn 74.1	-4.6	58.9 / Kilburn 61.8		Kilburn 67.6	-2.9
35th	52.9	Fuller 52.3	Fuller 54.3	+0.6	51.8 / Davies 49.9		Williams 52.8	+1.9
36th	52.3	Hancock 53.2	Riehlman 63.3	-0.9	56.0 / Riehlman 52.2		Riehlman 61.9	+3.8
37th	62.5	Hall 69.2	Hall 71.7	-6.7	60.4 / Hall 65.0		Hall 64.6	-4.6
38th	65.1	Taber 67.5	Taber 72.1	-2.4	64.4 / Taber 58.0		Taber 68.8	+6.4
39th	64.2	Cole 70.9	Cole 72.5	-6.7	66.1 / Cole 65.5		Cole 67.0	+0.6
40th & 41st (Rochester Area)	52.6	54.8	66.5	+2.2	53.6 / 54.8		65.8	-1.2
40th		Rogers 49.6	Keating 60.5		Keating 51.4		Keating 66.4	

APPENDIX. REPUBLICAN % OF TWO-PARTY VOTE, 1938-1950

DIST.	CONG. % Rep. 1938	PRES. % Rep. 1940	CONG. % Rep. 1940	DIFF. PRES. minus CONG. 1940	CONG. % Rep. 1942	PRES. % Rep. 1944	CONG. % Rep. 1944	DIFF. PRES. minus CONG. 1944	CONG. % Rep. 1946	PRES. % Rep. 1948	CONG. % Rep. 1948	DIFF. PRES. minus CONG. 1948	CONG. % Rep. 1950	REF. LINE
					NEW YORK (Continued)									
41st							Wadsworth 63.2		Wadsworth 71.5		Wadsworth 60.1		Ostertag 64.8	6
42nd thru 44th (Buffalo Area)						49.2	52.9	-3.7	58.8	47.7	49.1	-1.4	53.7	
42nd							Andrews 57.2		Andrews 62.5		Pfeiffer 52.3		Miller 58.6	6
43rd							Elsaesser 51.1		Elsaesser 65.3		Tauriello 48.0		Radway 51.4	6
44th							Butler 50.1		Butler 57.5		Gorski 47.2		Butler 51.0	6
45th						63.1	Reed 64.1	-1.0	Reed 72.5	62.4	Reed 62.2	+0.2	Reed 66.6	6
					NORTH DAKOTA									
At Large	Lemke 75.2	55.5	Burdick 67.2	-11.7	Lemke 65.6	55.2	Lemke 65.4	-10.2	Lemke 74.3	54.7	Lemke 69.7	-15.0	Aandahl 70.7	54,50
At Large	Robertson		Robertson		Burdick		Robertson		Robertson		Burdick		Burdick	50
					OHIO									
1st & 2nd (Cincin-	58.6	51.0	57.1	-6.1	62.7	51.8	56.4	-4.6	63.7	52.8	49.4	+3.4	55.8	54

	58.2		58.0		61.5		56.8		64.2		51.6		59.0	6
2nd	Hess 59.0		Hess 56.3		Hess 64.0		Hess 56.0		Hess 63.2		***Wagner*** 47.2		Hess 52.7	6
3rd	Routzohn 55.8	43.0	*Hollrock* 47.4	-4.4	Jeffrey 51.6	44.7	*Gardner* 47.4	-2.7	Burke 52.0	45.2	*Breen* 41.8	+3.4	*Breen* 45.5	
4th	Jones 62.9	57.2	Jones 57.8	-0.6	Jones 63.5	60.5	Jones 61.2	-0.7	Jones 59.2	53.0	McCulloch 55.7	-2.7	McCulloch 66.8	
5th	Clevenger 56.8	67.3	Clevenger 60.7	+6.6	Clevenger 63.6	70.9	Clevenger 68.1	+2.8	Clevenger 60.3	59.3	Clevenger 52.1	+7.2	Clevenger 57.5	
6th	*Polk* 49.5	49.4	*Davis* 47.8	+1.6	McCowen 51.1	52.8	McCowen 51.8	+1.0	McCowen 54.8	49.0	*Polk* 46.9	+2.1	*Polk* 49.2	
7th	Brown 57.6	53.2	Brown 58.3	-5.1	Brown 69.1	58.5	Brown 61.8	-3.3	Brown 68.0	56.3	Brown 100	-43.7	Brown 68.4	
8th	Smith 54.5	58.2	Smith 52.5	+5.7	Smith 59.8	63.0	Smith 59.8	+3.2	Smith 64.0	58.3	Smith 54.5	+3.8	Betts 62.7	
9th	*Hunter* 49.5	49.9	*Hunter* 45.3	+4.6	Ramey 51.8	51.0	Ramey 51.6	-0.6	Ramey 50.1	45.0	*Burke* 46.2	-1.2	*Reams* *Independent* 48.9	55
10th	Jenkins 66.0	54.0	Jenkins 58.9	-4.9	Jenkins 64.2	55.9	Jenkins 64.4	-8.5	Jenkins 66.6	54.0	Jenkins 57.9	-3.9	Jenkins 65.2	
11th	*Claypool* 47.9	49.6	*Claypool* 46.2	+3.4	Brehm 61.3	55.4	Brehm 53.6	+1.8	Brehm 60.6	50.3	Brehm 50.8	-0.5	Brehm 53.1	
12th	Vorys 50.9	48.9	Vorys 51.3	-2.4	Vorys 58.4	52.6	Vorys 54.3	-1.7	Vorys 62.0	53.8	Vorys 52.1	+1.7	Vorys 64.1	
13th	White 69.4	63.6	Baumhart 60.8	+2.8	Weichel 61.6	66.3	Weichel 100	-33.7	Weichel 72.1	57.7	Weichel 59.1	-1.4	Weichel 70.9	
14th	*Harter* 46.7	44.6	*Harter* 47.2	-2.6	Rowe 51.3	45.2	*Huber* 49.7	-4.5	*Huber* 46.8	46.9	*Huber* 42.5	+4.4	Ayres 50.5	

APPENDIX. REPUBLICAN % OF TWO-PARTY VOTE, 1938-1950

OHIO (Continued)

DIST.	CONG. % Rep. 1938	PRES. % Rep. 1940	CONG. % Rep. 1940	DIFF. PRES. minus CONG. 1940	CONG. % Rep. 1942	PRES. % Rep. 1944	CONG. % Rep. 1944	DIFF. PRES. minus CONG. 1944	CONG. % Rep. 1946	PRES. % Rep. 1948	CONG. % Rep. 1948	DIFF. PRES. minus CONG. 1948	CONG. % Rep. 1950	REF. LINE
15th	Secrest 47.7	57.3	Secrest 41.2	+16.1	Griffiths 60.2	59.8	Griffiths 60.0	-0.2	Griffiths 53.2	53.4	Secrest 43.6	+9.8	Secrest 38.4	
16th	Seccomb 50.7	45.7	Thom 43.7	+2.0	Carson 52.7	49.1	Thom 47.0	+2.1	Carson 55.8	51.4	McSweeney 47.7	-3.7	Bow 50.7.	
17th	Ashbrook 47.4	52.6	McGregor 55.1	-2.5	McGregor 62.8	58.3	McGregor 62.9	-4.6	McGregor 65.3	55.6	McGregor 52.8	+2.8	McGregor 64.2	
18th	Lewis 50.3	42.8	Imhoff 45.5	-2.7	Lewis 53.3	45.2	Lewis 51.1	-5.9	Lewis 58.8	43.4	Hays 45.8	-2.4	Hays 49.2	
19th	Kirwan 47.6	39.2	Kirwan 38.1	+1.1	Kirwan 43.6	39.7	Kirwan 36.6	+3.1	Kirwan 40.1	41.0	Kirwan 31.9	+9.1	Kirwan 36.2	
20th thru 22nd (Cleveland Area)	44.5	38.6	44.6	-6.0	47.5	40.6	44.4	-3.8	57.5	46.2	41.0	+5.2	50.5	
20th	Sweeney 29.6	32.3	Sweeney 32.3		Feighan 28.9		Feighan 24.1		Feighan 33.0		Feighan 0		Feighan 25.8	6
21st	Crosser 31.3		Crosser 22.9		Crosser 35.3		Crosser 22.3		Crosser 36.0		Crosser 24.1		Crosser 24.6	6
22nd	Bolton 55.5		Bolton 56.7		Bolton 57.1		Bolton 57.4		Bolton 71.7		Bolton 54.7		Bolton 62.7	6
At Large	Bender		Bender		Bender		Bender		Bender		Young		Bender	

OKLAHOMA

District														
1st	*Disney* 36.5	50.5	*Disney* 37.6	+12.9	*Disney* 45.0	53.4	Schwabe 51.1	+2.3	Schwabe 54.5	47.8	*Gilmer* 46.7	+1.1	Schwabe 52.9	56
2nd	*Nichols* 28.7	45.3	*Nichols* 37.8	+7.5	*Nichols* 49.6	43.8	*Stigler* 42.0	+1.8	*Stigler* 36.9	33.9	*Stigler* 30.1	+3.8	*Stigler* 33.8	
3rd	*Cartwright* 14.6	28.6	*Cartwright* 20.9	+7.7	*Stewart* 21.4	27.9	*Stewart* 23.9	+4.0	*Albert* 15.0	20.4	*Albert* 16.1	+4.3	*Albert* 17.2	
4th	*Boren* 28.4	39.2	*Boren* 28.9	+10.3	*Boren* 43.2	40.7	*Boren* 38.3	+2.4	*Johnson* 35.6	31.8	*Steed* 27.9	+3.9	*Steed* 31.9	
5th	*Monroney* 27.7	40.1	*Monroney* 27.2	+12.9	*Monroney* 30.0	42.3	*Monroney* 37.1	+5.2	*Monroney* 48.0	38.4	*Monroney* 32.6	+5.8	*Jarman* 41.2	
6th	*Johnson* 30.2	40.6	*Johnson* 29.9	+10.7	*Johnson* 42.1	40.6	*Johnson* 40.0	+0.6	*Morris* 34.4	32.2	*Morris* 26.3	+5.9	*Morris* 32.9	
7th	*Massingale* 23.9	35.7	*Massingale* 28.9	+6.8	*Wickersham* 30.0	39.0	*Wickersham* 29.2	+9.8	*Peden* 21.3	26.1	*Wickersham* 20.6	+5.5	*Wickersham* 32.9	
8th	*Ferguson* 49.5	53.8	*Rizley* 54.1	-0.3	*Rizley* 60.7	53.9	*Rizley* 58.0	-4.1	*Rizley* 54.8	51.2	*Wilson* 42.0	+9.2	*Belcher* 53.3	
At Large	*Rogers* 31.0	42.4	*Rogers* 33.9	+8.5										

OREGON

District														
1st	*Mott* 70.7	49.3	*Mott* 69.5	-20.2	*Mott* 64.3	50.5	*Mott* 66.7	-16.2	*Norblad* 72.0	54.1	*Norblad* 66.0	-11.9	*Norblad* 66.5	57, 58
2nd	*Pierce* 42.1	43.1	*Pierce* 42.8	+0.3	*Stockman* 61.4	47.4	*Stockman* 65.7	-18.3	*Stockman* 67.4	49.4	*Stockman* 58.2	-8.8	*Stockman* 64.3	3, 63
3rd	*Angell* 50.9	43.0	*Angell* 51.0	-8.0	*Angell* 51.8	42.6	*Angell* 55.1	-12.5	*Angell* 56.7	48.0	*Angell* 59.9	-11.9	*Angell* 53.8	3, 63

APPENDIX. REPUBLICAN % OF TWO-PARTY VOTE, 1938-1950

DIST.	CONG. % Rep. 1938	PRES. % Rep. 1940	CONG. % Rep. 1940	DIFF. PRES. minus CONG. 1940	CONG. % Rep. 1942	PRES. % Rep. 1944	CONG. % Rep. 1944	DIFF. PRES. minus CONG. 1944	CONG. % Rep. 1946	PRES. % Rep. 1948	CONG. % Rep. 1948	DIFF. PRES. minus CONG. 1948	CONG. % Rep. 1950	REF. LINE
OREGON (Continued)														
4th					Ellsworth 59.9	53.4	Ellsworth 64.0	-10.6	Ellsworth 69.2	56.8	Ellsworth 66.6	-9.8	Ellsworth 59.5	59
PENNSYLVANIA														
1st thru 6th (Philadelphia)	50.5	40.0	41.0	-1.0		41.1	41.8	-0.7	56.7	49.5	49.0	+0.5	46.2	60,61
1st	Sacks 46.5		Sacks 38.1				Barrett 41.6		Gallagher 57.3		Barrett 46.6		Barrett 46.2	6
2nd	McGranery 47.3		McGranery 38.6				Granahan 37.3		McGarvey 51.4		Granahan 45.7		Granahan 43.0	6
3rd	Bradley 49.3		Bradley 36.6				Bradley 41.7		Scott 62.1		Scott 52.0		Scott 50.3	6
4th	Daly 45.9		Sheridan 36.4				Sheridan 33.8		Maloney 53.0		Chudoff 41.7		Chudoff 42.5	6
5th	Gartner 53.1		Smith 43.9				Green, Jr. 45.8		Sarbacher, Jr. 56.9		Green, Jr. 49.2		Green, Jr. 44.5	6
6th	Myers 48.8		Myers 38.3				McGlinchey 49.2		Scott, Jr. 58.5		Scott, Jr. 57.0		Scott, Jr. 50.1	6
7th	Darrow 59.6		Scott, Jr. 51.1			55.1	Wolfender 51.5	+3.6	Chadwick 66.5	62.0	James 61.9	+0.1	James 62.7	6, 60,61
8th	Wolfender		Wolfender				Gerlach		Gerlach		Lichtenwalter		King	

Note: This is a wide, landscape-oriented table (rotated on the page) showing, for each Congressional district (row), a candidate name and percentage for a series of successive ballots/polls, together with change (±) columns. The topmost row (district numbers cut off at the top of the page) carries only numeric values.

District	Ballot 1	Ballot 2 (a)	Ballot 2 (b)	Δ	Ballot 3 (a)	Ballot 3 (b)	Ballot 4	Δ	Ballot 5 (a)	Ballot 5 (b)	Ballot 6	Δ
9th (cont.)	36.8	30.5	32.5	−2.0	60.9	61.3	72.7	−0.4	67.7	67.1	67.2	+0.6
10th	Kinzer 64.3	Kinzer 57.2	Kinzer 57.7	−0.5	Murphy 44.4	Murphy 43.6	Scoblick 51.0	+0.8	O'Neill 41.8	O'Neill 41.5	O'Neill 48.4	+0.3
11th	Boland 47.5	Boland 43.5	Boland 47.4	−3.9	Flood 48.0	Flood 47.9	Jenkins 50.8	−0.1	Flood 53.7	Flood 48.2	Flood 45.6	+5.5
12th	Flannery 48.8	Flannery 44.0	Flannery 42.2	+1.8	Fenton 56.5	Fenton 56.8	Fenton 62.7	−0.3	Fenton 60.3	Fenton 60.6	Fenton 56.8	−0.3
13th	Fenton 53.2	Fenton 47.0	Fenton 50.8	−3.8	Hoch 44.6	Hoch 43.5	Muhlenburg 57.1	+1.1	Rhodes 45.3	Rhodes 48.0	Rhodes 48.8	−2.7
14th	Moser 47.2	Moser 37.6	Moser 39.8	−2.2	Gillette 64.0	Gillette 65.0	Gillette 67.3	−1.0	Gillette 64.0	Gillette 65.2	Carrigg 60.8	−1.2
15th	Rutherford 61.9	Rutherford 56.4	Rutherford 60.6	−4.2	Rich 61.5	Rich 61.0	Rich 68.5	+0.5	Rich 63.4	Rich 61.6	Bush 62.4	+1.8
16th	Rich 61.9	Rich 59.6	Rich 60.5	−0.9	McConnell, Jr. 62.1	McConnell, Jr. 63.7	McConnell, Jr. 74.4	−1.6	McConnell, Jr. 67.5	McConnell, Jr. 66.9	McConnell, Jr. 66.1	−0.6
17th	Ditter 68.7	Ditter 59.7	Ditter 62.2	−2.5	Simpson 63.5	Simpson 64.6	Simpson 66.2	−1.1	Simpson 64.7	Simpson 64.5	Simpson 62.8	+0.2
18th	Simpson 60.5	Simpson 57.8	Simpson 57.6	+0.2	Kunkel 58.8	Kunkel 62.5	Kunkel 69.0	−3.7	Kunkel 66.5	Kunkel 63.7	Mumma 63.7	+2.8
19th	Kunkel 55.0	Kunkel 51.4	Kunkel 54.4	−3.0	Gavin 63.1	Gavin 64.2	Gavin 59.5	−1.1	Gavin 65.8	Gavin 63.7	Gavin 62.8	+2.1
20th	Jarrett 61.9	Jarrett 60.5	Jarrett 58.8	+1.7	Walter 46.5	Walter 42.7	Walter 47.4	+3.8	Walter 47.2	Walter 41.2	Walter 41.7	+6.0
21st	Walter 49.1	Walter 44.3	Walter 43.8	+0.5	Gross 51.3	Gross 52.6	Gross 52.0	−0.7	Lind 53.3	Lind 46.3	Lind 47.8	+7.0
22nd	Gross 50.3	Haines 46.6	Haines 44.9	+1.7	Brumbaugh 55.2	Brumbaugh 57.8	Van Zandt 65.9	−2.6	Van Zandt 58.3	Van Zandt 60.4	Van Zandt 59.5	−2.1

(An additional value "62" appears at the top of the rightmost column, associated with the 9th-district continued row.)

APPENDIX. REPUBLICAN % OF TWO-PARTY VOTE, 1938-1950

PENNSYLVANIA (Continued)

DIST.	CONG. % Rep. 1938	PRES. % Rep. 1940	CONG. % Rep. 1940	DIFF. PRES. minus CONG. 1940	CONG. % Rep. 1942	PRES. % Rep. 1944	CONG. % Rep. 1944	DIFF. PRES. minus CONG. 1944	CONG. % Rep. 1946	PRES. % Rep. 1948	CONG. % Rep. 1948	DIFF. PRES. minus CONG. 1948	CONG. % Rep. 1950	REF. LINE
23rd	Van Zandt 57.3	51.7	Van Zandt 56.3	-4.6		45.6	Snyder 45.4	+1.2	Crow 52.9	44.0	Cavalcante 45.7	-1.7	Sittler, Jr. 51.8	
24th	Snyder 48.7	42.4	Snyder 43.3	-0.9		38.0	Morgan 37.8	+0.2	Morgan 43.2	36.7	Morgan 35.0	+1.7	Morgan 40.9	
25th	Faddis 46.9	37.1	Faddis 39.0	-1.9		49.7	Graham 50.4	-0.7	Graham 58.8	52.7	Graham 52.6	+0.1	Graham 52.4	
26th	Graham 52.8	48.8	Graham 50.9	-2.1		48.8	Tibbott 52.5	-3.7	Tibbott 54.6	46.5	Coffey 44.6	+1.9	Sayler 52.5	62
27th	Tibbott 56.2	48.9	Tibbott 51.9	-3.0		41.4	Kelley 40.3	+1.1	Kelley 47.1	40.3	Kelley 37.8	+2.5	Kelley 42.9	
28th	Allen 45.9	39.8	Kelley 43.1	-3.3		58.0	Rodgers 54.6	+3.4	Kearns 63.9	60.6	Kearns 54.5	+6.1	Kearns 57.0	62
29th	Rodgers 54.1	55.6	Rodgers 54.5	-1.1			Campbell 50.2		McDowell 53.5		Davenport 45.8		Denny, Jr. 52.9	6
29th & 33rd (1940) 30th-34th (1942) (Pittsburgh Area)	48.1	41.7	44.0	-2.3		42.7	43.5	-0.8	51.7	43.7	42.9	+0.8	49.6	
30th	Corbett 51.2	-	Scanlon 49.9				Corbett 51.7		Corbett 60.1		Corbett 50.3		Corbett 56.5	6
31... M De...		Weiss					Fulton		Fulton		Fulton		Fulton	

RHODE ISLAND							
32nd	Eberharter 36.4	Eberharter 31.2		Eberharter 28.4	Eberharter 37.1	Eberharter 27.3	Eberharter 31.3
33rd	McArdle 48.4	McArdle 44.9		Weiss 30.7	Buchanan, F. 42.1	Buchanan, F. 30.8	Buchanan, V. 34.2
34th	Dunn 49.8	Wright 46.2					
1st, 2nd (Whole State)	53.7	43.2 44.4	-1.2 41.8	41.3 40.2	+1.1 45.3	41.8 39.0	+2.8 38.1
1st	Risk 50.3	Forand 42.5	Forand 41.0	Forand 38.1	Forand 42.9	Forand 38.0	Forand 36.8
2nd	Sandager 57.0	Fogarty 46.2	Fogarty 42.6	Fogarty 42.2	Fogarty 47.4	Fogarty 40.0	Fogarty 39.2
SOUTH DAKOTA							
1st	Mundt 54.0	Mundt 57.6 59.6	Mundt -2.0 60.5	Mundt 58.0 64.0	Mundt -6.0 61.5	Lovre 51.7 53.5	Lovre -1.8 60.8
2nd	Case 61.4	Case 56.8 66.1	Case -9.3 71.9	Case 59.6 69.0	Case -9.4 73.7	Case 54.9 65.9	Berry -9.0 60.3
UTAH							
1st	Murdock 40.3	Granger 40.6 43.0	Granger -2.4 49.8	Granger 41.8 42.2	Granger -0.4 49.9	Granger 45.9 41.0	Granger +4.9 48.9
2nd	Robinson 37.7	Robinson 35.3 36.7	Robinson -1.4 44.2	Robinson 37.8 37.7	Dawson +0.1 52.7	Bosone 45.2 42.5	Bosone +2.7 46.6
VERMONT							
At Large	Plumley 64.0	Plumley 54.9 63.8	Plumley -8.9 70.2	Plumley 57.1 62.4	Plumley -5.3 64.3	Plumley 62.5 60.8	Prouty +1.7 74.2

Appendix. Republican % of Two-Party Vote, 1938-1950

DIST.	CONG. % Rep. 1938	PRES. % Rep. 1940	CONG. % Rep. 1940	DIFF. PRES. minus CONG. 1940	CONG. % Rep. 1942	PRES. % Rep. 1944	CONG. % Rep. 1944	DIFF. PRES. minus CONG. 1944	CONG. % Rep. 1946	PRES. % Rep. 1948	CONG. % Rep. 1948	DIFF. PRES. minus CONG. 1948	CONG. % Rep. 1950	REF. LINE
WASHINGTON														
1st, 2nd, 6th (Seattle-Tacoma)	35.3	38.7	39.2	-0.5	36.3	40.3	42.7	-2.4	56.7	45.0	47.3	-2.3	49.0	
1st	Magnuson 28.3		Magnuson 38.4		Magnuson 34.2		De Lacy 46.6		Jones 63.8		Mitchell 48.0		Mitchell 47.9	6
2nd	Wallgren 38.5		Wallgren 42.6		Wallgren 40.1		Jackson 39.6		Jackson 46.1		Jackson 36.6		Jackson 38.4	6
3rd	Smith 39.7	39.5	Smith 44.6	-5.1	Norman 57.1	41.1	Savage 48.0	-6.9	Norman 53.9	42.6	Mack 52.1	-9.5	Mack 53.1	
4th	Hill 47.1	44.0	Hill 47.3	-3.3	Holmes 63.6	45.9	Holmes 60.2	-14.3	Holmes 67.6	43.5	Holmes 53.2	-9.7	Holmes 64.3	
5th	Leavy 42.4	49.5	Leavy 44.5	-5.0	Horan 62.7	52.6	Horan 52.3	-0.3	Horan 62.7	47.6	Horan 65.4	-17.8	Horan 60.2	
6th	Coffee 27.0		Coffee 37.2		Coffee 35.7		Coffee 38.8		Tollefson 53.9		Tollefson 57.4		Tollefson 60.8	6
WEST VIRGINIA														
1st	Schiffler 54.8	43.4	Ramsay 46.8	-3.4	Schiffler 54.7	44.6	Neely 49.6	-5.0	Love 53.1	42.1	Ramsay 42.7	-0.6	Ramsay 48.3	
2nd	Randolph 38.4	42.3	Randolph 42.5	-0.2	Randolph 49.8	49.2	Randolph 45.9	+3.3	Snyder 51.4	40.9	Staggers 45.3	-4.4	Staggers 45.7	
3rd	Edmiston 44.7	45.0	Edmiston 43.4	+1.6	Rohrbough 53.2	45.8	Bailey 47.5	-1.7	Rohrbough 51.5	42.0	Bailey 42.9	-0.9	Bailey 45.6	

(partial row, cut off at top edge)

	41.1	41.9 / 41.3	52.2	50.6	52.2	51.3 / 51.2	52.6	48.4 / 46.9	+1.3 / 48.4

District										
5th	*Kee* 38.7	*Kee* 37.5	*Kee* 42.8	+0.4	*Kee* 35.4	*Kee* 43.1	*Kee* 42.1	*Kee* 34.9	−2.9 / +7.2	*Kee* 34.3
6th	*Smith* 37.7	*Smith* 38.3	*Smith* 48.2	0	*Hedrick* 40.8	*Hedrick* 47.1	*Hedrick* 39.2	*Hedrick* 37.5	−0.9 / +1.7	*Hedrick* 38.4

WISCONSIN

District									
1st	**Bolles** D. 21.4 / R. 55.8 / Pr. 22.8 — 50.1	**Smith** D. 26.6 / R. 73.4 / Pr. --	**Smith** D. -- / R. 75.6 / Pr. 24.4 — 48.2		*Smith* 56.9 — 48.9	*Smith* 52.2	−3.3	*Smith* 57.2	63
2nd	**Sauthoff (Pr.)** D. 13.3 / R. 42.5 / Pr. 44.2 — 48.2	**Sauthoff (Pr.)** D. 9.7 / R. 39.9 / Pr. 50.4	**Henry** D. 26.1 / R. 57.1 / Pr. 16.8 — 55.3	−27.4	*Henry* 63.4 — 48.2	*Henry* 54.1	−5.9	*Henry* 57.7	63
3rd	**Stevenson** D. 10.0 / R. 46.0 / Pr. 44.0 — 57.1	**Stevenson** D. 10.2 / R. 47.0 / Pr. 42.8	**Stevenson** D. 26.7 / R. 73.3 / Pr. -- — 58.0	−15.3	**Stevenson** 100 — 50.7	*Withrow* 69.5	−18.8	*Withrow* 58.9	63
4th & 5th (Milwaukee Area)	D. 29.1 / R. 39.6 / Pr. 31.6 — 38.5	D. 45.8 / R. 34.0 / Pr. 20.2	D. 59.1 / R. 40.9 / Pr. -- — 41.0	−0.1	54.6 — 42.5	43.7	−1.2	45.6	63
4th	**Wasiliewski** D. 35.6 / R. 21.6 / Pr. 32.8	**Wasiliewski** D. 50.1 / R. 31.2 / Pr. 18.7	**Wasiliewski** D. 65.2 / R. 34.8 / Pr. --		**Brophy** 52.5		*Zablocki* 41.4	*Zablocki* 39.1	6,63
5th	**Thill** D. 22.8 / R. 44.4 / Pr. 32.8	**MacMurray** D. 44.7 / R. 38.7 / Pr. 16.6	**Biemiller** D. 52.9 / R. 47.1 / Pr. --		**Kersten** 56.1		*Biemiller* 45.7	*Kersten* 51.6	6,63

APPENDIX. REPUBLICAN % OF TWO-PARTY VOTE, 1938-1950

WISCONSIN (Continued)

DIST.	CONG. % Rep. 1938	PRES. % Rep. 1940	CONG. % Rep. 1940	DIFF. PRES. minus CONG. 1940	CONG. % Rep. 1942	CONG. % Rep. 1944	PRES. % Rep. 1944	DIFF. PRES. minus CONG. 1944	CONG. % Rep. 1946	PRES. % Rep. 1948	CONG. % Rep. 1948	DIFF. PRES. minus CONG. 1948	CONG. % Rep. 1950	REF. LINE
6th		59.0	Keefe D. 25.9 R. 57.4 Pr. 16.7		Keefe D. 20.4 R. 63.3 Pr. 16.3	Keefe D. 32.7 R. 67.3 Pr. --	60.5	-6.8	Keefe 64.9 64.9	54.9	Keefe 55.9 55.9	-1.0	Van Pelt 65.0 65.0	63
7th		55.2	Murray D. 12.7 R. 51.6 Pr. 35.7		Murray D. 28.1 R. 71.9 Pr. --	Murray D. 30.3 R. 69.7 Pr. --	59.3	-10.4	Murray 72.0 72.0	51.9	Murray 63.4 63.4	-11.5	Murray 68.3 68.3	63
8th		54.2	Johns D. -- R. 55.9 Pr. 44.1	-1.7	Johns D. 45.5 R. 54.5 Pr. --	Byrnes D. 45.5 R. 51.1 Pr. 3.4	55.2	+4.1	Byrnes 64.7 64.7	51.6	Byrnes 57.0 57.0	-5.4	Byrnes 62.2 62.2	63
9th		57.9	Hull (Pr.) D. 5.8 R. 41.4 Pr. 52.8		Hull (Pr.) D. 5.6 R. 32.6 Pr. 61.8	Hull (Pr.) D. -- R. -- Pr. 100	59.1	+59.1	Hull 100 100	46.1	Hull 100 100	-53.9	Hull 70.8 70.8	63
10th		40.4	Gehrmann(Pr.) D. 16.4 R. 35.7 Pr. 47.9		O'Konski D. 10.5 R. 48.4 Pr. 41.1	O'Konski D. 31.6 R. 58.2 Pr. 10.2	41.2		O'Konski 55.5 55.5	43.8	O'Konski 56.9 56.9	-13.1	O'Konski 57.0 57.0	63

WYOMING

DIST.	CONG. % Rep. 1938	PRES. % Rep. 1940	CONG. % Rep. 1940	DIFF. PRES. minus CONG. 1940	CONG. % Rep. 1942	CONG. % Rep. 1944	PRES. % Rep. 1944	DIFF. PRES. minus CONG. 1944	CONG. % Rep. 1946	PRES. % Rep. 1948	CONG. % Rep. 1948	DIFF. PRES. minus CONG. 1948	CONG. % Rep. 1950	REF. LINE
At Large	Horton		McIntyre		Barrett	Barrett			Barrett		Barrett		Harrison	

REFERENCES TO APPENDIX 1

1. From 1941 to 1948, Arizona had two congressmen, both of whom were elected at large.
2. From 1938 to 1941, Arizona had one congressman, elected at large.
3. Not redistricted in general redistricting, 1941.
4. The area of the two districts was the same before and after 1941, although each of the districts' boundaries was shifted slightly.
5. Slightly redistricted; substantially unchanged.
6. Indicates sub-total districts, lumped together above for comparison with presidential vote. Line through box marked PRES and % DIFF also indicates district as sub-total.
7. In same general area as old district (same no.) widely redistricted.
8. Los Angeles county alone before 1941; Los Angeles and San Bernardino after 1941.
9. Old 11th substantially became new 20th district. New 11th taken from Dist. 10 is composed of coastal counties north of Los Angeles.
10. San Bernardino and part of Los Angeles county substantially the same as pre-1941 19th.
11. Substantially redistricted.
12. Substantially the same as old 20th district.
13. In 1948, Illinois was very widely redistricted for the first time since 1901. Up to 1948 Chicago area had districts 1 through 10; after 1948, the Chicago area had districts 1 through 13.
14. 1948 redistricting—district is substantially the same.
15. Largely composed after 1948 of old 4th district area.
16. Since 1948 the new 13th is substantially the old 10th.
17. Since 1948 the new 14th district is substantially the old 11th.
18. Since 1948 the new 15th district is substantially the old 12th district.
19. Since 1948, the new 16th district is substantially the old 13th.
20. Since 1948, new 18th district is exactly the same as the old 16th.
21. Since 1948, 19th district composed of parts of old 15th and 14th districts.
22. Since 1948, this district has remained substantially the same.
23. Since 1948, the new 22nd district is exactly the same as the old 19th.
24. Since 1948, the new 23rd district is composed in part of old 18th and 23rd districts.

25. Since 1948, the new 24th district is substantially the old 24th, but is represented by old 23rd's representative, C. W. Vursell.
26. Since 1948, the new 25th district is substantially the old 22nd.
27. The new 26th district was created by redistricting in 1948 and is substantially the old 25th.
28. Illinois had 2 representatives at large, 1938-1941; it had 1 representative at large, 1941-1948, and has had no representatives at large from 1948 on.
29. The state of Indiana was redistricted in 1941.
30. 11th and 12th largely combined when Indiana lost one member in 1941. 12th redistricted out of existence.
31. The state of Iowa was redistricted in 1941.
32. Since 1941 the new Second District composed of old 2nd plus half of old 4th.
33. Since 1941 the new 3rd composed of old 3rd plus half of old 4th.
34. Since 1941 the new 4th is the old 5th with the boundaries unchanged.
35. The new 5th is the old 6th, boundaries unchanged.
36. The new 6th is the old 8th, approximately, since 1941.
37. The new 8th since 1941 is the former 9th.
38. The old 9th redistricted out of existence (became 8th) in 1941.
39. Kansas was redistricted in 1941, losing one member.
40. The new 4th since 1941 includes the old 4th approximately with the addition of all of the old 5th.
41. The new 5th since 1941 is substantially the old 7th.
42. Since the state of Massachusetts' congressional districts do not conform to county boundaries, the vote of the state as a whole for Congress has been taken for comparative purposes with the presidential vote.
43. Massachusetts was redistricted in 1941; there was no 15th district after 1940.
44. The Democratic and Farmer-Labor vote are combined for comparative purposes, 1941.
45. J. J. O'Sullivan, Dem., died, was succeeded by C. I. Bakewell, Rep. elected at special election, 1951.
46. Nebraska was redistricted in 1941, losing one member.
47. Since 1941 the old 1st district was divided among the new 1st, 2nd, and 3rd.
48. Since 1941 the new 4th district is nearly the same as the old 5th district in location and size.
49. New Mexico gained a congressman (at large) in 1941.
50. The vote of two congressmen "at large" is measured by dividing the number of votes cast for each candidate by 2, since the electorate had to vote twice on each ballot for Congress.
51. New York State was radically redistricted by the legislature in 1944, leaving only 4 districts out of 43 to 45 with identical areas before and after redistricting. This redistricting was so extensive as to destroy for all

practical purposes any continuity before and after 1944. Therefore, only data from 1944 on have been used for this state.

52. The four-party situation in New York City is partially carried over into the congressional races. Generally the ALP gets between 10 and 20% of the total vote in the congressional races in Brooklyn, Bronx, and certain parts of Manhattan, and polls almost as well as the Republican congressional ticket in the Bronx. These minor parties are negligible upstate.

53. (18th District). The coalitions arising and dissolving in this district among the four major partes of New York City make comparisons impossible, and its vote has not been shown here.

54. In Ohio, up to 1941, there were two congressmen who were elected at large. From 1941 on only one was so elected. Thus the state was not redistricted even though it lost one seat in Congress.

55. In the 9th (Toledo) District in 1950, a three-way race was held, in which the Independent candidate won over both the Democratic and Republican candidates. The actual three-party percentage was:

	D	R	Ind.
9th Dist.	32.4	31.0	36.6

56. Oklahoma, which had a congressman at large before 1941, lost a seat by reapportionment in that year. There was no redistricting of the state, therefore, but no congressmen at large were elected after 1940.

57. Oregon was redistricted in 1941, and one seat was gained by that state.

58. Since 1941, the new 1st district is composed approximately of the northern half of the old 1st district.

59. The new 4th district, created in 1941, consists approximately of the southern half of the old 1st district.

60. Pennsylvania was redistricted twice during the 1940's; once, in 1941, when the Democrats controlled the legislature, and again in 1943 after the Republicans had recaptured it. The 1941 redistricting was very extensive and applied only to the election of 1942. The 1943 redistricting left a maximum of the pre-1941 districts unchanged, reducing Philadelphia's representation from 7 to 6 and shifting a few boundaries elsewhere. Therefore, 1942's election has been omitted.

61. Nearly all districts (or counties embracing more than one district) remain unchanged after 1943 and are directly comparable except where noted otherwise. Each district number from 8 on is one point lower than it was prior to 1941. Thus, the new district 24 corresponds exactly to old district 25.

62. Slightly redistricted in 1943: the new 19th, 26th, and 28th districts are substantially the same as the old 20th, 27th, and 29th districts.

63. Because the Progressive Party was of such great local importance in Wisconsin until 1946, the three-party percentage for the congressional elections of 1940, 1942, and 1944, is given. Where no comparisons can be made between presidential and congressional races the box labeled "% DIFF." is left blank.

215

APPENDIX 2

The Republican percentage of the two-party vote in the Senate, 1938-1950:

    (a) % of the two-party vote for senatorial races by States.

    (b) % of the two-party vote for President by States.

    (c) Names of Senators listed in their respective States.

Note: *Italicized names are Democrats.*

APPENDIX. REPUBLICAN % OF TWO-PARTY VOTE, 1938-1950

STATE	SEN. % Rep. 1938	PRES. % Rep. 1940	SEN. % Rep. 1940	DIFF. PRES. minus SEN. 1940	SEN. % Rep. 1942	PRES. % Rep. 1944	SEN. % Rep. 1944	DIFF. PRES. minus SEN. 1944	SEN. % Rep. 1946	PRES. % Rep. 1948	SEN. % Rep. 1948	DIFF. PRES. minus SEN. 1948	SEN. % 1950	REF. LINE
Arizona	*Hayden* 23.5	36.2	*McFarland* 28.1	+8.1	No Election	41.0	*Hayden* 30.6	+10.4	*McFarland* 30.3	44.9	No Election		*Hayden* 36.5	
California	*Downey* 45.1	41.9	*Johnson* 100	-58.1	No Election	43.2	*Downey* 47.7	-4.5	Knowland 55.0	49.8	No Election		Nixon 59.1	1
Colorado	*Adams* 40.8	51.3	No Election		*Johnson* 49.5 / *Millikin* 57.1	53.4	Millikin 56.4	-3.0	No Election	47.3	*Johnson* 32.7	+14.6	Millikin 52.7	1
Connecticut	Danaher 51.7	46.4	*Maloney* 46.2	+0.2	No Election	47.3	*McMahon* 47.6	-0.3	Baldwin 57.9	50.8	No Election		*McMahon* 47.4 / *Benton* 49.9	2
Delaware	No Election	45.2	*Tunnell* 48.3	-3.1	Buck 54.7	45.4	No Election		Williams 55.2	50.6	*Frear, Jr.* 48.7	+1.9	No Election	
Idaho	*Clark* 45.1	45.5	Thomas 53.0	-7.5	Thomas 51.6	48.3	*Taylor* 48.9	-0.6	Dworshak 58.6	48.6	*Miller* 49.3	-0.7	Welker 61.3	3
Illinois	*Lucas* 48.5	48.8	Brooks 50.3	-1.5	Brooks 53.4	48.3	*Lucas* 47.2	+1.1	No Election	49.6	*Douglas* 44.7	+4.9	Dirksen 53.9	3
Indiana	*VanNuys* 49.8	50.7	Willis 50.7	0	No Election	52.9	Capehart 50.7	+2.2	Jenner 55.9	50.4	No Election		Capehart 53.3	4

Kansas	Reed 56.2	57.3	No Election		Capper 58.6	60.6	Reed 58.7	+1.9	No Election	53.6	Schoeppel 56.2	-2.6	Carlson 55.6	5
Kentucky	Barkley 38.0	42.4	Chandler 41.7	-0.7	Chandler 44.7	45.4	Barkley 45.0	+0.4	Cooper 53.4	42.2	Chapman 48.5	-6.3	Clements 45.4	
Maine	No Election	51.2	Brewster 58.7	-7.5	White, Jr. 66.7	52.5	No Election		Brewster 63.6	57.3	Smith 71.3	-14.0	No Election	
Maryland	Tydings 30.0	41.2	Radcliffe 34.1	+7.1	No Election	48.1	Tydings 38.3	-9.8	O'Conor 49.8	50.7	No Election		Butler 53.5	
Massachusetts	No Election	46.6	Walsh 43.5	+3.1	Lodge, Jr. 52.9	47.1	Saltonstall 64.8	-17.7	Lodge, Jr. 60.0	44.1	Saltonstall 53.3	-9.2	No Election	6
Michigan	No Election	50.2	Vandenburg 52.8	-2.6	Ferguson 51.2	49.5	No Election		Vandenburg 67.7	50.8	Ferguson 52.0	-1.2	No Election	
Minnesota	No Election	48.1	Shipstead(F.L.) 53.4	-5.3	Ball 54.8	47.2	No Election		Thye 59.7	41.1	Humphrey 40.0	+1.1	No Election	7
Missouri	Clark 39.2	47.6	Truman 48.8	-1.2	No Election	48.5	Donnell 50.1	-1.6	Kem 52.8	41.7	No Election		Hennings, Jr. 46.2	
Montana	No Election	41.6	Wheeler 26.6	+15.0	Murray 49.7	45.3	No Election		Ecton 54.1	44.9	Murray 43.0	+1.9	No Election	
Nebraska	No Election	57.2	Butler 57.9	-0.7	Wherry 69.0	58.6	No Election		Butler 70.8	54.1	Wherry 56.7	-2.6	No Election	
Nevada	McCarran 41.0	39.9	Pittman 39.5	+0.4	Scrugham 41.3	45.4	McCarran 41.6	+3.8	Malone 55.2	48.4	No Election		McCarran 42.0	8
New Hampshire	Tobey 54.2	46.8	No Election		Bridges 54.6	47.9	Tobey 50.9	-3.0	No Election	52.4	Bridges 58.6	-5.7	Tobey 59.4	
New Jersey	Barbour 53.7	48.2	Barbour 55.5	-7.3	Hawkes 53.7	49.3	Smith 50.8	-1.5	Smith 59.3	52.3	Hendrickson 51.9	+0.4	No Election	
New Mexico	No Election	43.3	Chavez 44.1	-0.8	Hatch 40.8	46.5	No Election		Chavez 48.5	43.3	Anderson 42.5	+0.8	No Election	9

APPENDIX. REPUBLICAN % OF TWO-PARTY VOTE, 1938-1950

STATE	SEN. % Rep. 1938	PRES. % Rep. 1940	SEN. % Rep. 1940	DIFF. PRES. minus SEN. 1940	SEN. % Rep. 1942	PRES. % Rep. 1944	SEN. % Rep. 1944	DIFF. PRES. minus SEN. 1944	SEN. % Rep. 1946	PRES. % Rep. 1948	SEN. % Rep. 1948	DIFF. PRES. minus SEN. 1948	SEN. % Rep. 1950	REF. LINE
New York	*Wagner* 45.2 / *Mead* 46.1	48.2	*Mead* 46.7	+1.5	No Election	47.5	*Wagner* 46.8	+0.7	Ives 52.6	50.5	No Election		*Lehman* 47.4	10 / 10
North Dakota	Nye 87.3	55.5	Langer 59.0	-3.5	No Election	54.2	*Moses* 42.2	+12.0	Langer 69.7	54.8	No Election		Young 67.6	11, 12
Ohio	Taft 53.6	47.8	Burton 52.4	-4.6	No Election	50.2	Taft 50.3	-0.1	Bricker 57.4	49.9	No Election		Taft 57.5	
Oklahoma	*Thomas* 34.2	42.4	No Election		Moore 55.1	44.3	*Thomas* 44.2	+0.1	No Election	35.3	*Kerr* 36.1	-0.8	*Monroney* 45.2	
Oregon	Holman 54.8	45.9	No Election		McNary 77.1	47.5	Morse 60.7 / Gordon 57.5	-13.2	No Election	51.8	Gordon 60.0	-8.2	Morse 75.2	13
Pennsylvania	Davis 55.2	46.5	*Guffey* 47.8	-1.3	No Election	48.6	*Myers* 49.8	-1.2	Martin 59.8	52.0	No Election		Duff 51.8	13

Rhode Island	No Election	*Gerry* 44.8	-1.6	*Green* 42.0	41.3	No Election	-1.2	*McGrath* 44.9	41.9	*Green* 40.7	-1.2	*Pastore* 38.3	14
South Dakota	Gurney 52.5	No Election		Bushfield 58.7	58.3	Gurney 63.9	-5.6	No Election	52.4	Mundt 59.3	-7.9	Case 63.9	
Utah	*Thomas* 44.2	*Murdock* 37.2	+0.4	No Election	39.5	*Thomas* 40.1	-0.6	Watkins 51.3	45.5	No Election		Bennett 54.0	
Vermont	Gibson 65.7	Austin 66.4 / Aiken 61.6	-11.5	No Election	57.1	Aiken 65.8	-8.7	Flanders 74.6	62.5	No Election		Aiken 77.8	15
Washington	*Bone* 37.2	*Wallgren* 45.8	-4.7	No Election	42.6	*Magnuson* 44.6	-2.0	Cain 54.6	44.8	No Election	-0.6	*Magnuson* 46.1	15
West Virginia	No Election	*Kilgore* 43.7	-0.8	Revercomb 55.4	45.1	No Election		*Kilgore* 49.7	42.4	*Neely* 43.0		No Election	
Wisconsin	Wiley 64.2	*LaFollette, Jr. (Pr.)* 47.8	+1.3	No Election	50.8	Wiley 54.2	-3.4	McCarthy 62.1	47.7	No Election	+4.9	Wiley 53.4	16
Wyoming	No Election	*O'Mahoney* 41.3	+5.7	Robertson 54.6	51.2	No Election		*O'Mahoney* 43.8	47.8	*Hunt* 42.9		No Election	

REFERENCES TO APPENDIX 2

1. In Colorado in 1942, a short-term election to fill an unexpired term was held in addition to an election for a full term.
2. In Connecticut in 1950, two elections were held, one for a full term (won by Sen. McMahon), the other for the unexpired term of R. E. Baldwin (won by Sen. Benton).
3. In Idaho, two elections—long-term and short-term—were held in 1950 for the Senate. Both were won by Republicans.
4. In 1940, a special senatorial election was held in Illinois to fill a vacancy. It was won by a Republican.
5. Special elections to fill vacancies were held in Kentucky in 1940 and 1946.
6. A special election was held in Massachusetts in 1944 to fill a vacancy caused by the resignation of Sen. Lodge.
7. Until 1943, there were three major parties in Minnesota—Democratic, Republican, and Farmer-Labor. The Republican percentage of the vote for the Senate in 1940 and 1942 as given here is the Republican percentage of the total vote.
8. A special election was held in Nevada in 1942 to fill a vacancy caused by the death of Sen. Pittman.
9. Special elections for the Senate were held in New Jersey in 1938, 1942, and 1944.
10. In 1938, two elections for the Senate—long- and short-term—were held in New York, both being won by the Democrats.
11. Sen. Moses (Dem.) of North Dakota died in 1945, and M. R. Young (Rep.) held that seat from that time on.
12. During several senatorial elections (1938, 1940, 1944, and 1946) in North Dakota, there was a heavy independent vote. The proportion of each party in these elections was as follows:

Senate	Dem.	Rep.	Ind.
1938	7.3	50.1	42.6
1940	26.8	38.1	35.1
1944	45.2	33.0	21.8
1946	23.2	52.3	23.5

13. In 1944, two elections were held in Oregon for the Senate, one being for the unexpired remainder of the term of the late Sen. McNary.

14. In 1950 a special senatorial election was held in Rhode Island to fill the vacancy caused by the resignation of Sen. J. H. McGrath.

15. In addition to the regular election for Senator in Vermont in 1940, a special election was held to fill the vacancy caused by the death of Sen. Gibson.

16. Until 1946, the Progressive Party was an important if not dominating factor in Wisconsin politics. The three-party percentage of the vote for U. S. Senator follows:

Senate	Dem.	Rep.	Ind.
1930	25.0	48.2	26.8
1940	13.2	41.4	45.4
1944	43.2	50.9	5.9
1946	37.9	62.1	......

In the main body of the tables the "two-party" vote is Republican-Progressive or Republican-Democratic from 1938 to 1944, whichever of the opposition parties was stronger.

APPENDIX 3

COMPOSITION OF CONGRESS BY POLITICAL PARTY AFFILIATION, 1937-1951

D—Democrat
R—Republican

Year	President	Congress	House Major Party	House Principal Minor Party	House Other (except Vacancies)	Senate Major Party	Senate Principal Minor Party	Senate Other (except Vacancies)
1937-38	D F. Roosevelt	75th	D-331	R-89	13	D-76	R-16	4
1939-41	D F. Roosevelt	76th	D-261	R-164	4	D-69	R-23	4
1941-42	D F. Roosevelt	77th	D-268	R-162	5	D-66	R-28	2
1943-44	D F. Roosevelt	78th	D-218	R-208	4	D-58	R-37	1
1945-46	D (F. Roosevelt / H. Truman)	79th	D-242	R-190	2	D-56	R-38	1
1947-48	D H. Truman	80th	R-245	D-188	1	R-51	D-45	..
1949-50	D H. Truman	81st	D-263	R-171	1	D-54	R-42	..
1951-	D H. Truman	82nd	D-234	R-199	2	D-48	R-47	1

INDEX TO APPENDIX 1

226   POLITICS, PRESIDENTS AND COATTAILS

Milliken, Eugene D.	Colo.	Taft, Robert A.	Ohio
Monroney, A. S. (Mike)	Okla.	Taylor, Glen H.	Idaho
Moore, Edward H.	Okla.	Thomas, Elbert	Utah
Morse, Wayne L.	Ore.	Thomas, Elmer	Okla.
Moses, John	N. D.	Thomas, John	Idaho
Mundt, Karl E.	S. D.	Thye, Edward J.	Minn.
Murdock, Abe	Utah	Tobey, Charles W.	N. H.
Murray, James E.	Mont.	Truman, Harry S.	Mo.
Myers, Francis J.	Pa.	Tunnell, James M.	Del.
Neely, Matthew M.	W. Va.	Tydings, Millard E.	Md.
Nixon, Richard M.	Cal.	Vandenburg, Arthur H.	Mich.
Nye, Gerald P.	N. D.	Van Nuys, Frederick	Ind.
O'Conor, Herbert R.	Md.	Wagner, Robert F.	N. Y.
O'Mahoney, Joseph C.	Wyo.	Wallgren, Mon C.	Wash.
Pastore, John O.	R. I.	Walsh, David I.	Mass.
Pittman, Key	Nev.	Watkins, Arthur V.	Utah
Radcliffe, George L.	Md.	Welker, Herman	Idaho
Reed, Clyde M.	Kans.	Wheeler, Burton K.	Mont.
Revercomb, W. Chapman	W. Va.	Wherry, Kenneth S.	Neb.
Robertson, Edward V.	Wyo.	White, Wallace H., Jr.	Me.
Saltonstall, Leverett	Mass.	Wiley, Alexander	Wis.
Schoeppel, Andrew F.	Kans.	Williams, John J.	Del.
Scrugham, James G.	Nev.	Willis, Raymond E.	Ind.
Shipstead, Henrik	Minn.	Wilson, George A.	Iowa
Smith, H. Alexander	N. J.	Young, Milton R.	N. D.
Smith, Margaret C.	Me.		

INDEX TO APPENDIX 2

Bunker, Berkeley L.	Nev.	at large
Burdick, Usher L.	N. D.	at large
Burke, Raymond H.	Ohio	3rd
Burke, Thomas H.	Ohio	9th
Burnside, M. G.	W. Va.	4th
Busbey, Fred E.	Ill.	3rd
Bush, Alvin R.	Pa.	15th
Butler, John C.	N. Y.	44th
Byrne, William T.	N. Y.	32nd
Byrnes, John W.	Wis.	8th
Byron, William D.	Md.	6th
Campbell, Howard E.	Pa.	29th
Canfield, Gordon	N. J.	8th
Cannon, Clarence	Mo.	9th
Carlson, Frank	Kans.	6th
Carnahan, Albert S. J	Mo.	8th
Carrigg, Joseph L.	Pa.	14th
Carroll, John A.	Colo.	1st
Carson, Henderson H.	Ohio	16th
Carter, Albert E.	Cal.	6th
Cartwright, Wilburn	Okla.	3rd
Case, Clifford P.	N. J.	6th
Case, Francis	S. D.	2nd
Casey, Joseph E.	Mass.	3rd
Cavalcante, Anthony	Pa.	23rd
Celler, Emmanuel	N. Y.	15th
Chadwick, E. Wallace	Pa.	7th
Chapman, Virgil M.	Ky.	6th
Chelf, Frank L.	Ky.	4th
Chenoweth, J. Edgar	Colo.	3rd
Chesney, Chester A.	Ill.	11th
Chiperfield, Robert B.	Ill.	15th, 19th
Christopher, George H.	Mo.	6th
Chudoff, Earl	Pa.	4th
Church, Marguerite S.	Ill.	13th
Church, Ralph E.	Ill.	10th, 13th
Clason, Charles R.	Mass.	2nd
Claypool, Howard K.	Ohio	11th
Clemente, T. Gary	N. Y.	4th
Clements, Earle C.	Ky.	2nd
Clevenger, Cliff	Ohio	5th
Clippinger, Roy	Ill.	24th
Cochran, John J.	Mo.	13th
Coffee, Harry B.	Neb.	5th
Coffee, John M.	Wash.	6th
Coffey, Robert L., Jr.	Pa.	26th
Coffin, Howard A.	Mich.	13th
Cole, Albert	Kans.	1st
Cole, William C.	Mo.	3rd
Cole, W. Sterling	N. Y.	39th
Cole, William P., Jr.	Md.	2nd
Compton, Ranulf	Conn.	3rd
Connery, Lawrence J.	Mass.	7th
Copeland, Oren S.	Neb.	1st
Corbett, Robert J.	Pa.	30th
Costello, John M.	Cal.	15th
Coudert, Frederic R., Jr.		
	N. Y.	17th

Crawford, Fred L.	Mich.	8th
Creal, Edward W.	Ky.	4th
Crook, Thurman C.	Ind.	3rd
Crosser, Robert	Ohio	21st
Crow, William J.	Pa.	23rd
Crowe, Eugene B.	Ind.	9th
Crumpacker, S. J., Jr.	Ind.	3rd
Cummings, Fred N.	Colo.	2nd
Cunningham, Paul H.	Iowa	5th, 6th
Curley, James M.	Mass.	11th
Curtis, Carl T.	Neb.	1st, 4th
Curtis, Thomas B.	Mo.	12th
D'Alesandro, Thomas, Jr.		
	Md.	3rd
Daly, John B.	Pa.	4th
Darrow, George P.	Pa.	7th
Davenport, Harry I.	Pa.	29th
Davies, John C.	N. Y.	35th
Davis, Jacob E.	Ohio	6th
Dawson, William A.	Utah	2nd
Dawson, William L.	Ill.	1st
Day, Stephen A.	Ill.	at large
De Lacy, Hugh	Wash.	1st
Delaney, James J.	N. Y.	6th
Delaney, John J.	N. Y.	7th
Dempsey, John J.	N. M.	at large
Denny, Harmar D., Jr.	Pa.	29th
Denton, Winfield K.	Ind.	8th
Devereux, James P. S.	Md.	2nd
Devitt, Edward J.	Minn.	4th
D'Ewart, Wesley A.	Mont.	2nd
Dewey, Charles S.	Ill.	9th
Dickstein, Samuel	N. Y.	19th
Dingell, John D.	Mich.	15th
Dirksen, Everett M.	Ill.	16th
Disney, Walter E.	Okla.	1st
Ditter, John W.	Pa.	17th
Dollinger, Isidore	N. Y.	24th
Dolliver, James I.	Iowa	6th
Dondero, George A.	Mich.	17th
Donohue, Harold D.	Mass.	4th
Donovan, James G.	N. Y.	18th
Douglas, Emily T.	Ill.	at large
Douglas, Helen G.	Cal.	14th
Dowell, Cassius C.	Iowa	6th
Downs, LeRoy D.	Conn.	4th
Doyle, Clyde	Cal.	18th
Duncan, Richard M.	Mo.	3rd
Dunn, Matthew	Pa.	34th
Eaton, Charles A.	N. J.	5th
Eberharter, Herman P.	Pa.	32nd
Edmiston, Andrew	W. Va.	3rd
Eliot, Thomas H.	Mass.	9th
Elliott, Alfred J.	Cal.	10th
Ellis, Herbert S.	W. Va.	4th
Ellison, Daniel	Md.	4th
Ellsworth, Harris	Ore.	4th
Elmer, William P.	Mo.	8th

Hull, Merlin	Wis.	9th
Hunter, Allan O.	Cal.	9th
Hunter, John F.	Ohio	9th
Imhoff, Laurence E.	Ohio	18th
Irving, Leonard	Mo.	4th
Izac, Edward V. M.	Cal.	20th, 23rd
Jackson, Donald L.	Cal.	16th
Jackson, Henry M.	Wash.	2nd
Jacobs, Andrew	Ind.	11th
Jacobsen, William S.	Iowa	2nd
James, Benjamin F.	Pa.	7th
Jarman, John	Okla	5th
Jarrett, Benjamin	Pa.	20th
Javits, Jacob K.	N. Y.	21st
Jeffrey, Harry P.	Ohio	3rd
Jeffries, Walter S.	N. J.	2nd
Jenison, Edward H.	Ill.	18th, 23rd
Jenkins, Mitchell	Pa.	11th
Jenkins, Thomas A.	Ohio	10th
Jensen, Ben F.	Iowa	7th
Johns, Joshua L.	Wis.	8th
Johnson, Anton J.	Ill.	14th
Johnson, George W.	W. Va.	4th
Johnson, Jed J.	Okla.	4th
Johnson, Leroy	Cal.	3rd
Johnson, Noble J.	Ind.	6th
Johnson, William R.	Ill.	22nd
Johnson, William W.	Cal.	18th
Jonas, Edgar A.	Ill.	12th
Jones, Homer R.	Wash.	1st
Jones, Paul C.	Mo.	10th
Jones, Robert F.	Ohio	4th
Jonkman, Bartel J.	Mich.	5th
Judd, Walter H.	Minn.	5th
Karst, Raymond W.	Mo.	12th
Karsten, Frank M.	Mo.	13th
Kean, Robert W.	N. J.	12th
Kearney, B. W.	N. Y.	31st
Kearns, Carroll D.	Pa.	28th
Keating, Kenneth B.	N. Y.	40th
Kee, John	W. Va.	5th
Keefe, Frank B.	Wis.	6th
Keller, Kent E.	Ill.	25th
Kelley, Augustine B.	Pa.	27th, 28th
Kelly, Edna F.	N. Y.	10th
Kelly, Edward A.	Ill.	3rd
Kennedy, Ambrose J.	Md.	4th
Kennedy, John F.	Mass.	11th
Keough, Eugene J.	N. Y.	9th
Kersten, Charles J.	Wis.	5th
Kilburn, Clarence E.	N. Y.	34th
King, Cecil R.	Cal.	17th
Kinzer, John R.	Pa.	10th
Kirwan, Michael J.	Ohio	18th
Klein, Arthur G.	N. Y.	19th
Kluczynski, John C.	Ill.	5th
Knutson, Harold	Minn.	6th

Kocialkowski, Leo P.	Ill.	8th
Kopplemann, Herman P.		
	Conn.	1st
Kramer, Charles	Cal.	13th
Kruse, Edward H., Jr.	Ind.	4th
Kunkel, John C.	Pa.	18th, 19th
La Follette, Charles M.	Ind.	8th
Lambertson, William P.		
	Kans.	1st
Landis, Gerald W.	Ind.	7th
Lane, Thomas J.	Mass.	7th
Larrabee, William H.	Ind.	11th
Latham, Henry J.	N. Y.	3rd
Lea, Clarence F.	Cal.	1st
Leavy, Charles H.	Wash.	5th
Le Compte, Karl M.	Iowa	4th, 5th
Le Fevre, Jay	N. Y.	30th
Lemke, William	N. D.	at large
Lesinski, John	Mich.	16th
Lesinski, John, Jr.	Mich.	16th
Lewis, Earl R.	Ohio	18th
Lewis, Laurence	Colo.	1st
Lichtenwalter, F. H.	Pa.	8th
Lind, James F.	Pa.	21st
Linehan, Neil J.	Ill.	3rd
Link, William W.	Ill.	7th
Lodge, John D.	Conn.	4th
Love, Francis J.	W. Va.	1st
Lovre, Harold D.	S. D.	1st
Luce, Clare B.	Conn.	4th
Luce, Robert	Mass.	9th
Ludlow, Louis L.	Ind.	11th
Lusk, George L.	N. M.	at large
Lynch, Walter A.	N. Y.	23rd
MacKinnon, George E.		
	Minn.	3rd
McAndrews, James	Ill.	9th
McArdle, Joseph A.	Pa.	33rd
McCarthy, Eugene J.	Minn.	4th
McConnell, Samuel K.	Pa.	16th
McCormack, John W.	Mass.	12th
McCorven, Edward O.	Ohio	6th
McCulloch, William M.		
	Ohio	4th
McDonough, Gordon L.		
	Cal.	15th
McDowell, John R.	Pa.	29th, 31st
McGarvey, Robert N.	Pa.	2nd
McGlinchey, Robert J.	Pa.	6th
McGranery, James P.	Pa.	2nd
McGrath, Christopher	N. Y.	26th
McGregor, J. Harry	Ohio	17th
McGuire, John A.	Conn.	3rd
McIntyre, John J.	Wyo.	at large
McKeough, Raymond S.		
	Ill.	2nd
McKinnon, Clinton D.	Cal.	23rd

Poulson, Norris   Cal.   13th
Powell, Adam C., Jr.   N. Y.   22nd
Powers, D. Lane   N. J.   4th
Price, Charles M.   Ill.   22nd, 25th
Prouty, Winston L.   Vt. at large

Quinn, Peter A.   N. Y.   26th
Quinn, T. Vincent   N. Y.   5th

Rabaut, Louis C.   Mich.   14th
Rabin, Benjamin J.   N. Y.   24th
Radway, Edmund P.   N. Y.   43rd
Ramey, Homer A.   Ohio   9th
Ramsay, Robert L.   W. Va.   1st
Randolph, Jennings   W. Va.   2nd
Rankin, Jeannette   Mont.   1st
Rayfiel, Leo F.   N. Y.   14th
Reams, Frazier   Ohio   9th
Reed, Chauncey W.   Ill   11th, 14th
Reed, Daniel A.   N. Y.   45th
Rees, Edward H.   Kans.   4th
Reeves, Albert L.   Mo.   5th
Resa, Alexander J.   Ill.   9th
Rhodes, George M.   Pa.   13th
Ribicoff, Abraham A.   Conn.   1st
Rich, Robert F.   Pa.   15th, 16th
Riehlman, R. Walter   N. Y.   36th
Risk, Charles F.   R. I.   1st
Rizley, Ross   Okla.   8th
Robertson, Charles R.   N. D. at large
Robinson, J. W.   Utah   2nd
Robison, John M.   Ky.   9th
Rockwell, Robert F.   Colo.   4th
Rodgers, Robert L.   Pa.   28th, 29th
Rodino, Peter W., Jr.   N. J.   10th
Roe, Dudley G.   Md.   1st
Roe, James A.   N. Y.   5th
Rogers, Byron G.   Colo.   1st
Rogers, Edith Nourse   Mass.   5th
Rogers, George F.   N. Y.   40th
Rogers, Will   Okla. at large
Rogers, Will   Cal.   16th
Rohrbaugh, Edward G.
                         W. Va.   3rd
Rolfe, Thomas   Cal.   4th
Ronjue, Milton A.   Mo.   1st
Rontzohn, Harry N.   Ohio   3rd
Rooney, John J.   N. Y.   12th
Roosevelt, Franklin D., Jr.
                         N. Y.   20th
Ross, Robert T.   N. Y.   5th
Rowan, William A.   Ill.   2nd
Rowe, Ed   Ohio   14th
Russell, Charles H.   Nev. at large
Rutherford, Albert G.   Pa.   15th
Ryan, Elmer J.   Minn.   2nd
Ryter, Joseph F.   Conn. at large
Sabath, Adolph J.   Ill.   5th, 7th
Sacks, Leon   Pa.   1st
Sadlak, Antoni N.   Conn. at large

Sadowski, George G.   Mich.   1st
St. George, Katharine T.
                         N. Y.   29th
Sandager, Harry   R. I.   2nd
Santhoff, Harry   Wis.   2nd
Sarbacher, George W., Jr.
                         Pa.   5th
Sasscer, Lansdale G.   Md.   5th
Savage, Charles R.   Wash.   3rd
Saylor, John P.   Pa.   26th
Scanlon, Thomas E.   Pa.   30th
Schiffler, Andrew C.   W. Va.   1st
Schuetz, Leonard W.   Ill.   7th
Schultz, William T.   Ind.   1st
Schwabe, George B.   Okla.   1st
Schwabe, Max   Mo.   2nd
Scoblick, James P.   Pa.   10th
Scott, Hardie   Pa.   3rd
Scott, Hugh, Jr.   Pa.   6th, 7th
Scrivner, Errett P.   Kans.   2nd
Scrugham, James G.   Nev. at large
Scudder, Hubert R.   Cal.   1st
Seccombe, James   Ohio   16th
Secrest, Robert T.   Ohio   15th
Seeley-Brown, Horace   Conn.   2nd
Seger, George N.   N. J.   8th
Shaefer, Edwin M.   Ill.   22nd
Shafer, Paul W.   Mich.   3rd
Shanley, James A.   Conn.   3rd
Shannon, Joseph B.   Mo.   5th
Sharp, Edgar A.   N. Y.   1st
Sheehan, Timothy P.   Ill.   11th
Shelley, John G.   Cal.   5th
Sheppard, Harry T.   Cal.   19th, 21st
Sheridan, John E.   Pa.   4th
Short, Dewey   Mo.   7th
Sieminski, Alfred D.   N. J.   13th
Simpson, Richard M.   Pa.   17th, 18th
Simpson, Sid   Ill.   20th
Sittler, Edward L., Jr. Pa.   23rd
Slaughter, Roger C.   Mo.   5th
Smith, Clyde H.   Maine   2nd
Smith, Francis R.   Pa.   5th
Smith, Frederick   Ohio   8th
Smith, J. Joseph   Conn.   5th
Smith, Joe L.   W. Va.   6th
Smith, Margaret C.   Maine   2nd
Smith, Martin F.   Wash.   3rd
Smith, Thomas V.   Ill. at large
Smith, Wint   Kans.   6th
Snyder, J. Buell   Pa.   23rd, 24th
Snyder, Melvin C.   W. Va.   2nd
Somers, Andrew L.   N. Y.   10th
Spence, Brent   Ky.   5th
Springer, Raymond S.   Ind.   10th
Springer, William L.   Ill.   22nd
Staggers, Harley O.   W. Va.   2nd
Starkey, Frank T.   Minn.   4th
Steed, Tom   Okla.   4th

INDEX

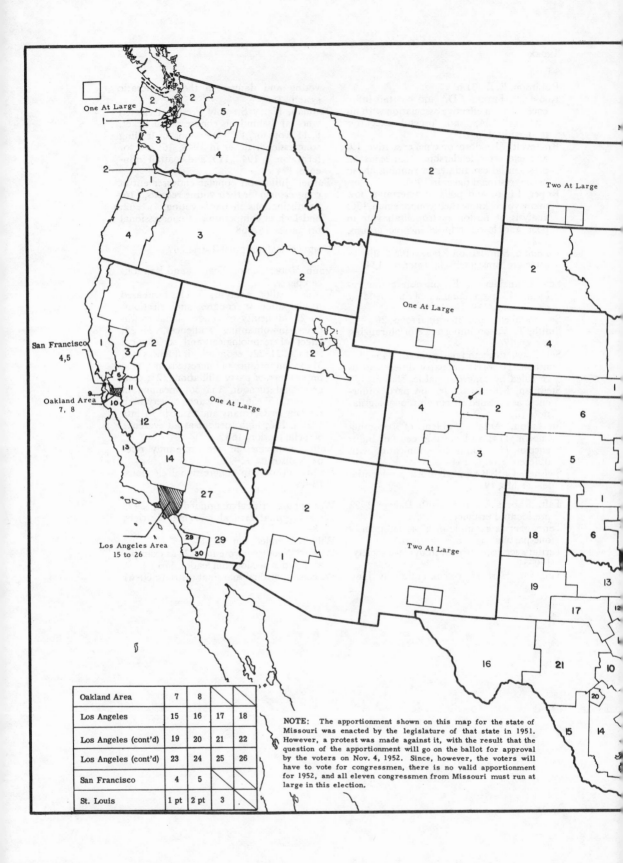

One At Large

San Francisco
4,5

Oakland Area
7, 8

One At Large

Los Angeles Area
15 to 26

Two At Large

One At Large

Two At Large

Oakland Area	7	8		
Los Angeles	15	16	17	18
Los Angeles (cont'd)	19	20	21	22
Los Angeles (cont'd)	23	24	25	26
San Francisco	4	5		
St. Louis	1 pt	2 pt	3	

NOTE: The apportionment shown on this map for the state of Missouri was enacted by the legislature of that state in 1951. However, a protest was made against it, with the result that the question of the apportionment will go on the ballot for approval by the voters on Nov. 4, 1952. Since, however, the voters will have to vote for congressmen, there is no valid apportionment for 1952, and all eleven congressmen from Missouri must run at large in this election.

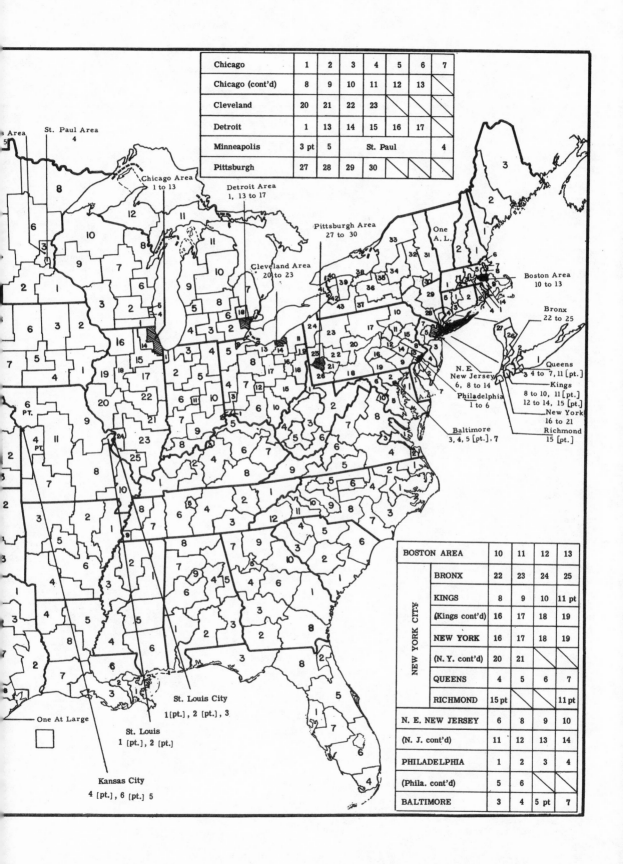

Chicago	1	2	3	4	5	6	7
Chicago (cont'd)	8	9	10	11	12	13	
Cleveland	20	21	22	23			
Detroit	1	13	14	15	16	17	
Minneapolis	3 pt	5	St. Paul				4
Pittsburgh	27	28	29	30			

St. Paul Area
4

Chicago Area
1 to 13

Detroit Area
1, 13 to 17

Pittsburgh Area
27 to 30

Cleveland Area
20 to 23

One
A. L.

Boston Area
10 to 13

Bronx
22 to 25

Queens
3, 4 to 7, 11 [pt.]

Kings
8 to 10, 11 [pt.]
12 to 14, 15 [pt.]

New York
16 to 21

Richmond
15 [pt.]

N. E.
New Jersey
6, 8 to 14

Philadelphia
1 to 6

Baltimore
3, 4, 5 [pt.], 7

St. Louis City
1 [pt.], 2 [pt.], 3

One At Large

St. Louis
1 [pt.], 2 [pt.]

Kansas City
4 [pt.], 6 [pt.] 5

	BOSTON AREA	10	11	12	13
NEW YORK CITY	BRONX	22	23	24	25
	KINGS	8	9	10	11 pt
	(Kings cont'd)	16	17	18	19
	NEW YORK	16	17	18	19
	(N. Y. cont'd)	20	21		
	QUEENS	4	5	6	7
	RICHMOND	15 pt			11 pt
N. E. NEW JERSEY		6	8	9	10
(N. J. cont'd)		11	12	13	14
PHILADELPHIA		1	2	3	4
(Phila. cont'd)		5	6		
BALTIMORE		3	4	5 pt	7